TRUE TO THE LAND

FOODS AND NATIONS is a new series from Reaktion that explores the history – and geography – of food. Books in the series reveal the hidden history behind the food eaten today in different countries and regions of the world, telling the story of how food production and consumption developed, and how they were influenced by the culinary practices of other places and peoples. Each book in the Foods and Nations series offers fascinating insights into the distinct flavours of a country and its culture.

Already published

Al Dente: A History of Food in Italy
FABIO PARASECOLI

Beyond Bratwurst: A History of Food in Germany
URSULA HEINZELMANN

Cabbage and Caviar: A History of Food in Russia
ALISON K. SMITH

Delicioso: A History of Food in Spain
MARÍA JOSÉ SEVILLA

Feasts and Fasts: A History of Food in India
COLLEEN TAYLOR SEN

Gifts of the Gods: A History of Food in Greece
ANDREW AND RACHEL DALBY

Rice and Baguette: A History of Food in Vietnam
VU HONG LIEN

A Rich and Fertile Land: A History of Food in America
BRUCE KRAIG

Savoir-Faire: A History of Food in France
MARYANN TEBBEN

True to the Land: A History of Food in Australia
PAUL VAN REYK

True to the Land

A History of Food in Australia

Paul van Reyk

REAKTION BOOKS

For Amaya

Published by Reaktion Books Ltd
Unit 32, Waterside
44–48 Wharf Road
London N1 7UX, UK
www.reaktionbooks.co.uk

First published 2021

Printed and bound in India by Replika Press Pvt. Ltd

A catalogue record for this book is available from the British Library

ISBN 978 1 78914 406 2

Aboriginal and Torres Strait Islander readers should be aware that this book contains images of people who may be deceased.

CONTENTS

INTRODUCTION 7

ONE
The Wide Brown Land *11*

TWO
Foodways of the First Peoples *18*

THREE
Settlers to Squatters, 1788–1850 *41*

FOUR
Golden Soil and Wealth for Toil, 1851–99 *66*

FIVE
Federation, 1900–1913 *98*

SIX
Between World Wars, 1914–45 *125*

SEVEN
Boundless Plains to Share, 1946–65 *153*

EIGHT
Transformations, 1966–79 *179*

NINE
Foodie Nation, 1980–99 *206*

TEN
Millennium Reckonings, 2000–2020 *229*

References *259*
Bibliography *274*
Acknowledgements *277*
Photo Acknowledgements *278*
Index *279*

INTRODUCTION

This book tells the story of the 60,000-year history of Australian food, from its beginnings with the arrival of the First Peoples and their stewardship of the land, to today, when the production and consumption of food is fraught with anxieties and competing priorities.

A history of food and drink in any country is more than a summary of what food was eaten by whom and when. It encompasses the food, how it is collected or produced, how it is distributed and how it is consumed. These food activities are influenced by geography (including both the landforms and the climate), economic policies, cultural practices, social relationships, global relationships and technologies. The term 'foodways' is used in this book to mean this interrelated set of factors.

Foodways change over time as shifts happen in the weight of influence each of these factors has. The book is generally organized chronologically, with each chapter built around events that significantly impacted foodways in Australia over a particular timespan. There are also themes that weave through the history, moving in and out of focus at times, or showing themselves in new lights.

The book was written during two years of one of the worst droughts on record in Australia. These droughts are cyclical, caused by an interplay between the land – its geology, landforms, oceans, inland waterways – and particular climate systems whose workings have only been relatively recently understood. The challenges this interplay produces for sustainable food practices loom large throughout.

Formerly accepted knowledge about Indigenous Australians has been critically re-evaluated. The impact of its racist underpinnings has been exposed. This history continues that process, looking at the impact of colonization and subsequent policies and practices on Indigenous Australians'

Aboriginal woman fishing from a bark canoe.

foodways, and thus their health and culture. The book also looks at the part Indigenous Australians have played as participants in Australian foodways. Throughout the book, 'Indigenous Australians' is used to include Aboriginal Australians and Torres Strait Islanders. It is important to recognize that the two peoples are not the same. What is known about how each population migrated to Australia is described in Chapter Two. Where a particular Indigenous nation is written about, the name of that nation is given.

Australia boasts of being a model multicultural society. The panoply of cuisines on offer for dining in or out of home is often promoted as evidence of this. But this obscures the past of White Australia and the racially discriminatory legal, economic and social practices that formed it. These practices also affected the opportunities for broadening the Australian foodscape, which for so long was decried as a reproduction of British cuisine unsuited to Australia's climate and resource capacities. This history foregrounds migrants and their part in the development of Australian foodways, acknowledging and celebrating their hard-won place at the Australian table.

Celebrity male chefs dominate the public food imagination in Australia today. This was not the case until the last decades of the twentieth century. Women wrote the cookery pages in women's magazines, authored cookery books and contributed recipes to community-fundraising cookbooks through which knowledge about food came into the Australian home. Their stories are a significant part of this history.

The book closes on a note of caution. The first two decades of the 2000s have brought to attention the adverse consequences of past foodways and calls for urgent remedies. In some areas the remedies are clear but the will to act by government and industry is lacking. In others, the impact of climate change and sustainable water management being the main areas, what is to be done remains contested. The impact of climate change was dramatically and tragically made clear in the catastrophic bushfires that roared across the eastern coast of Australia from August 2019 to February 2020. Some 18 million ha (45 million ac) of land were reduced to ash, more than 2,000 homes were destroyed, 34 people were killed and an estimated 1 billion animals died, most of them iconic native fauna. 'Farmers have fled as fires claim farmlands around the country,' wrote Paula Thomas in January 2020,

> dreading the worst for their animals. Livestock losses will surpass 100,000, according to reports from the Federal Agriculture Minister, affecting the meat and dairy industries. Dairy farmers fear there will be a milk shortage after assessing their losses both in terms of numbers of dairy cows and the availability of grazing land, much of which has now turned to charcoal. The lack of fodder to feed the remaining animals will also have an impact on their future production. Small farmers are in distress. After destroying their crops, the flames burned through infrastructure and farm tools. Even in areas the fires have spared farmland, the heat and intense drought pose a threat to food production.[1]

The impact of these events on food production is yet to be fully assessed, but that recovery will take a long time is clear and much will depend on successive governments' policies and practices to address climate change.

ONE

The Wide Brown Land

Before people arrived, there was the land. So it is with the land that this history also begins.

Around 160 million years ago a mass of land separated off from the southern super-continent Gondwana, comprised of present-day South America, Africa, Arabia, Madagascar, India, Australia and Antarctica. Around 35 million years ago that mass also broke up, forming Antarctica, New Zealand and Sahul, the name given to a landmass encompassing present-day mainland Australia, the island of Tasmania, New Guinea and the Indonesian island of Seram and neighbouring islands. Rising sea levels at the end of the last global glacial period around 12,000 years ago formed Bass Strait, a sea strait separating Tasmania from the southern part of the landmass and the Torres Strait separating New Guinea from the northern part. Mainland Australia currently lies between latitudes 9 degrees and 44 degrees south, and between longitudes 112 degrees and 154 degrees east. It continues to drift north a few centimetres a year.

Australia is the lowest, flattest and oldest continental landmass on Earth. Only 6 per cent of Australia is over 600 m (1,970 ft) high. Its flatness is a result of prolonged erosion by wind and water, with the resulting detritus filling depressions formed by folding or inland drainage of rivers. The only significant relief to this flatness is the Great Dividing Range, thrust up around 95 million years ago, running 3,700 km (2,300 mi.) down the entire length of the eastern coast and across the lower southwestern area. Mount Kosciuszko, its highest point, is just 2,228 m (7,310 ft) above sea level. There are a handful of smaller ranges in the centre, south and west of the country. Some 65 million years ago there was volcanic activity along the length of the area parallel to the Great Dividing Range, which continued until a few thousand years ago. For the most part, however,

Mt Feathertop, Australian Alps, Great Dividing Range, Victoria.

Australia has had a relatively stable geological history without constant weathering of newly thrown up rock. The result of this has been that overall Australia has some of the oldest and poorest soils: nutrients have been drained or blown away without being replaced.

Australia's total land mass is 7.69 million sq. km (2.97 million sq. mi.): 7.66 million sq. km (2.96 million sq. mi.) of mainland and 32,000 sq. km (12,400 sq. mi.) of island area, making it the world's smallest continent but the sixth largest country. Mainland Australia has a total coastline length of 36,000 km (22,000 mi.) and there are an additional 24,000 km (15,000 mi.) of island coastlines. The mainland of Australia is approximately 3,860 km (2,400 mi.) long from its most northerly point at the top of Cape York in Queensland, to its most southerly point at South East Cape in Tasmania and is almost 4,000 km (2,485 mi.) wide, from Cape Byron, in the eastern state of New South Wales, to Steep Point in Western Australia. The Torres Strait Islands extend some 300 km (185 mi.) east to west across the top of Cape York and 150 km north to south across the Strait, with the northernmost island, Boigu, being just 4 km (2½ mi.) from Papua New Guinea.

To its west is the Indian Ocean; to the south the Antarctic Ocean; to its east the Pacific Ocean, with New Zealand separated by the Tasman Sea; and to the north is the Torres Strait separating it from New Guinea, and the Arafura and Timor seas separating it from the Indonesian archipelago.

The Great Barrier Reef, the world's largest coral reef, lies a short distance off the northeast coast and extends for over 2,000 km (1,245 mi.).

In 1908 the nineteen-year-old Australian Dorothea Mackellar, holidaying in London, wrote the poem 'My Country', the second stanza of which succinctly captures the Australian mainland landscape and its erratic climate, two factors that have had a strong influence on the history of food in Australia.

> I love a sunburnt country
> A land of sweeping plains,
> Of ragged mountain ranges,
> Of drought and flooding rains . . .
> The wide brown land for me!

Australia is the second driest continent in the world. It sits in a global belt of high pressure around the southern tropics, which leads to generally dry conditions. Around 80 per cent of Australia has an annual rainfall of less than 600 mm (25 in.). Coastal areas of Australia have the highest average rainfalls. The Great Dividing Range is sufficiently high to cause major rain-bearing winds from the east to release their moisture before reaching the interior of the continent. As a result, the southeastern coastal strip is

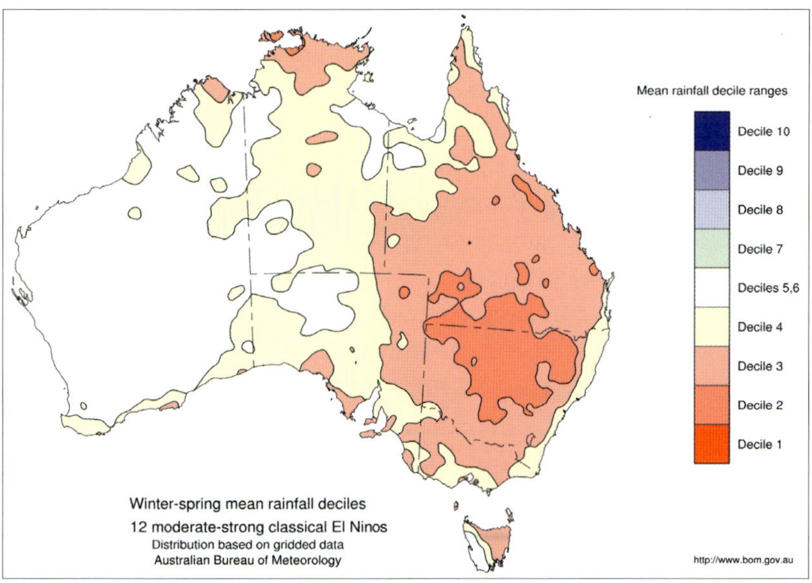

Australian winter/spring mean rainfall deciles for twelve El Niño events.

the only area on the mainland that has reasonably high and reliable rainfall. The wet tropics of north Queensland experience the highest rainfall intensities during the the northwest monsoon season from November to March. It shares with the Tasmanian mountains the record for the highest average annual rainfall on the continent. The average annual rainfall in the Australian desert is low, ranging from 81 to 250 mm (3–10 in.).

Rainfall in Australia is also highly erratic from year to year. The main source of this variability, and of Australian climate variability in general, is the El Niño Southern Oscillation (commonly called simply El Niño), a climate pattern caused by the interaction of ocean and atmosphere in the central and eastern tropical areas of the Pacific Ocean that recurs every three to seven years. It is a two-phase system. The El Niño phase leads to low rainfall and hotter-than-average temperatures on the eastern and southeastern parts of the Australian mainland, which at its worst can lead to severe droughts. The La Niña phase that follows brings heavy rains with extensive flooding at its worst, and severe cyclones in northern Australia. On the western side of the continent there is a similar cycle called the Indian Ocean Dipole event. Two other weather systems contribute to rainfall variability in Australia: the Southern Annular Mode, which disrupts the normal pattern of westerly winds that bring rain to southern Australia, and summer monsoons in northern Australia, including the Torres Strait.

The seasonality and variability of annual rainfall is reflected in Australia's waterways. The permanently flowing rivers are concentrated in the eastern states of New South Wales, Victoria and the island state of Tasmania. Of these, the largest is the Murray–Darling system covering an area of more than 1 million sq. km (386,000 sq. mi.), or about 14 per cent of Australia. Most of the inland rivers flow mainly or only during floods. Even in the tropical north, few of the rivers have permanent flows. Central Australia was subject to repeated incursions over millennia by the Antarctic Ocean, leaving salt lakes that fill in major floods. Lake Eyre in South Australia is the largest of these. None of the rivers that flow into Lake Eyre are permanent. There are also subsurface waters in Australia. The most significant of these is the Great Artesian Basin, the largest and deepest artesian basin in the world, extending for 1,700,000 sq. km (656,375 sq. mi.) under parts of South Australia, the Northern Territory, Queensland and New South Wales. It is the only source of fresh water across a large swathe of inland Australia. Aboriginal Australians were adept at locating natural springs in the basin. Now water is extracted from it by artesian bores and wells.

As the continent dried and warmed, vegetation across much of Australia adapted to suit these changes and the nutrient-poor soil. Vast hummock grasslands spread across the dry inland, dotted with saltbush. Sclerophylls, with their thick, leathery leaves usually with waxy coatings and oil glands to conserve water, became the dominant plants of the forests, both wet and dry. These are the iconic trees of the Australian 'bush', the eucalypts: gums, bloodwoods, ironbarks, stringybarks, peppermints, box, ash and mallee. The presence of sclerophylls in the main contribute to a significant feature of the Australian landscape – bushfires. The volatile oils in their leaves are highly flammable. Lightning strikes and other natural phenomena in these forests can result in fires of great heat and immense intensity when they burn. Dry-forest sclerophylls also produce large amounts of dry litter – leaves, bark, twigs – that provide extra fuel. Many Australian plants have developed specific adaptations that allow them to survive and regenerate after fires. The use Aboriginal Australians made of fire and its regenerative possibilities is discussed in the next chapter.

Charles Weetman, Darling River at Wentworth, *c.* 1954.

The leaves of eucalyptus are leathery and have a waxy coating, typical of sclerophylls.

The sea between ancient Sahul and the Asian mainland acted as a significant barrier that led to the independent development of Australia's fauna. First recognized by Alfred Russel Wallace in 1860, this barrier is now called the Wallace Line. Marsupials – including the emblematic kangaroos, wallabies and koalas – became the characteristic fauna, well adapted to the drier conditions. Sea life, on the other hand, is similar to that found elsewhere in the world.

Aridity and variability of rainfall also have had their impact on human settlement in Australia from the arrival of the First Peoples. While they populated even the harshest desert environments, the majority lived in the same temperate coastal regions that are currently the most heavily populated. In 2019 Australia ranked as one of the most sparsely populated countries in the world, with an average population density of just 3.3 people per sq. km (⅓ sq. mi.). The bulk of its population – more than 90 per cent – live within 100 km (60 mi.) of the coast. Some 67 per cent live in capital cities and another 23 per cent in urban areas, making Australia one of the most highly urbanized countries in the world.

Mackeller's land of droughts and flooding plains has tested the ability of its human inhabitants to wrest a reliable and sustainable supply of food to the present day.

The Commonwealth of Australia

The Commonwealth of Australia comprises the mainland of the Australian continent, the island of Tasmania, the islands in the Torres Strait (lying between the tip of Cape York Peninsula in the north of the mainland and Papua New Guinea), and the territories of Norfolk Island (lying in the Pacific Ocean between the mainland and New Zealand), Christmas Island (in the Indian Ocean northwest of the mainland), the Cocos (Keeling) Islands (also in the Indian Ocean midway between the mainland and India) and the Australian Antarctic Territory. The mainland is comprised of the states of New South Wales, Queensland, South Australia, Western Australia and Victoria, and the Northern Territory and the Australian Capital Territory. Australia's neighbouring countries are Papua New Guinea, Indonesia and East Timor to the North; the Solomon Islands and Vanuatu to the northeast; and New Zealand to the southeast.

Australia on the cusp of federation, from William Balfour Irvine, *British Possessions and Colonies* (1899).

TWO

Foodways of the First Peoples

The history of food in Australia does not begin with the establishment of the first British settlement at Sydney Cove on the east coast in 1788. It begins with the migration of the First Peoples to the Australian mainland and the later migrations to the Torres Strait Islands. What we know of the food practices of the earliest human occupants of Australia is scant. Tim Flannery, author and palaeontologist, wrote in 1994: 'Much [of the Australian archaeological record] is quite literally skeletal, consisting of stone tools and bones . . . Indeed, often the record is barely sufficient to detect the small, incremental changes in diet and technology that reveal ecological co-adaptation.'[1] This chapter details what evidence has been found to date. That material is expanded with descriptions of the foodways of Indigenous Australians at the time of British colonization in 1788 as observed by, or as told to, early colonial diarists. Indigenous Australians responded to the different environments in which they lived with different foodways. This chapter is not meant to be a complete picture of these: it describes examples that show the breadth of the foodways. Later chapters look at how practices have continued or changed since that time and the consequences of these changes.

The earliest known human remains of Aboriginal Australians are found at Lake Mungo in the Willandra Lakes system of southwest New South Wales. Mungo Man and Mungo Lady, as they are called, are dated back to 42,000 years ago. Archaeological evidence in recent years has pushed back the arrival of Aboriginal Australians much further. In July 2017 excavations at Madjedbebe, a sandstone rock shelter in Arnhem Land, in the Northern Territory, brought to light ground-edged hatchet heads, grind stones and charred plant matter from species still found and eaten in the area. The materials were dated to 65,000 years ago.[2] Grindstones of relatively more recent origin, still counted in millennia, have been found at other sites. Remains of wallabies and wombats in southwest Tasmania show a consistent pattern of hunting between 40,000 and 15,000 years ago. Middens – refuse piles – dating back as far as 8,000 years in coastal Tasmania show evidence of fire being used to roast molluscs.

From where and how did Australia's first people arrive? Current thinking among paleoarchaeologists is that modern human people (*Homo sapiens*) in Sundaland (comprising present-day Vietnam, the Malay peninsula and the Indonesian islands as far as Bali and Kalimantan) began to take advantage of fluctuating sea levels to island hop eastwards into Sahul (present-day New Guinea and Australia). Why they did this is still debated: population increases leading to competition for food resources, or small climate changes that also affect the availability of food, can lead to groups of people moving locale.[3] How many times the journey was made, what the exact sequence of island hops was, how many individuals made the journey and whether more than one journey was made also are still to be determined. Recent genetic evidence and significant changes in stone toolmaking suggest there may have been waves of migration at least until 5,000 years ago.[4]

Tjukurrpa: The Dreaming

The Dreaming is the Aboriginal Australian belief system that underpins land and food resource management. The historian Bill Gammage describes the system thus:

> The Dreaming is comprehensive . . . It gives and explains a role to every part of creation, and decrees how each must act . . . Aboriginal landscape awareness is rightly seen as drenched in religious sensibility, but equally the Dreaming is saturated with environment consciousness . . . the cycles of life and season change constantly, and a [person's] duty is to shepherd land and creatures safely through these changes . . . This might require dramatic or spasmodic change (burning forests, culling eels, banning or restricting a food), and it certainly demands active intervention in the landscape. The Dreaming taught why the world must be maintained; the land taught how. One made land care compulsory, the other made it rewarding. One was spiritual and universal, the other practical and local. Songlines

> [routes through the country associated with ancestral beings and along which trade and cultural exchange happened] distribute land spiritually; 'country' distributed it geographically. Everyone had a country: narrowly defined, land, water and their sites and knowledge in the care of a family under its head.[5]

Fire and Water

How did Aboriginal Australians care for the land? The most dramatic active intervention was the controlled use of fire. In his expedition diary of 1831 Major Thomas Mitchell, Surveyor General from 1828 to 1855, wrote: 'we crossed a beautiful plain covered with shining verdure, and ornamented with trees, which, although "dropt in nature's casual haste", gave the country the appearance of an extensive park.'[6]

He was not the only early explorer to comment on this park-like appearance of vast tracts of country. These grasslands were not accidental. They were a deliberate strategy of resource management using controlled burn-offs. Evidence from charcoal particles and pollen cores indicate an increase in firing of the country after the arrival of the First Peoples. Fires deliberately lit by humans are one of the most important environmental shaping agents in Australia.[7] Kangaroos and wallabies are herbivores with grass being a major part of their diet. Creating grasslands ensures that there is plenty for them to graze on and creates a terrain in which hunting is easier. Sporadic bushfires rarely destroy sclerophyll forests. These regenerate from lignotubers (woody swelling of the root crown as a protection against destruction of the plant stem) or through new growth sprouting from sub-bark buds. Firing every two to four years will in time make grassland by retarding growth or ultimately destroying the tree altogether. Firing less often will allow some low scrub to develop and make a more open woodland, giving shelter to prey in which they can replenish numbers. Regular firing also clears the ground of a build-up of highly flammable timber and so reduces the risk of catastrophic fires.

Learning how to control fire meant being able to 'burn with purpose . . . [to] move from limiting fire to shaping country'.[8] In 2018 the New South Wales Rural Fire Service began working with Aboriginal elders in the south-coast Shoalhaven area as part of the Firesticks project to rehabilitate a 1,100-ha (2,700-ac) property that had been extensively logged, farmed and overgrown with lantana weed. Cultural burning, as the practice is called, uses Aboriginal low-intensity fire techniques to reduce fuel build-up in forests and encourage regrowth of native grasses and vegetation as well as the return of native wildlife.[9]

There are examples also of earthworks aimed to capture or divert water. The explorer Ernest Giles in 1889 described three clay wall dams in the Great Victoria Desert of South Australia and Western Australia built in sandhills across impermanent water courses. R. J. and J. M. Rowlands in 1969 described a dam on the Bulloo River Overflow in Northern New South Wales 'a bank which extends for almost 330 ft. [100 m] in a smooth curve . . . broken only by a gap, 40 ft. [12 m] wide at the top, where the watercourse passes through . . . [the top] is about 6 ft [2 m] above the bed of the watercourse'.[10] Among the stones on the top of the bank were many flaked pieces and chips, and a few roughly worked implements. The section of river here is not permanent, only flowing when floodwaters pour down from Queensland into the Bulloo Lake and the Caryapundy Swamp and then into the Overflow. The dam, like others, appears to have been built to capture and hold fresh water, though whether only for drinking or also for watering crops is not known. Rupert Gerritsen, writing in 2008, describes the Iliaura and Wanji of the eastern Northern Territory blocking up small creeks and channels so that they overflowed and flooded the surrounding plains, promoting the growth of grasses such as millet (*Panicum decompositum*).[11]

Food from Plants

Watkin Tench was a lieutenant in the British Marine Corps stationed at the colonial settlement of Port Jackson, at Sydney Cove, in 1788–91. He was a keen observer of the life of the colony and of the Gadigal, the traditional owners of the land around Sydney Cove. Summing up the food production ways of the Gadigal, he writes: 'To cultivation of the ground they are utter strangers, and wholly depend for food on the few fruits they gather, the roots they dig up in the swamps, and the fish they pick up along shore or contrive to strike from their canoes with spears.'[12]

Trench was not alone in dismissing what he observed. It is a view that has persisted until recent years, when thorough reviews of early colonial records and later anthropological studies clearly show widespread practices with food plants that are by any measure cultivation. Bruce Pascoe, an Indigenous Australian farmer, fisherman and writer of Bunurong/Tasmanian heritage, puts the position succinctly in his book *Dark Emu*:

> the economy and culture of Aboriginal and Torres Strait Islander people had been grossly undervalued . . . [journals and diaries of explorers and colonists] revealed a much more complex Aboriginal economy than the primitive hunter-gatherer lifestyle we had been told was the simple lot of Australia's First People . . . I came across repeated references to people building dams and wells, planting, irrigating and harvesting seed, preserving the surplus and storing it in houses, sheds or secure vessels, creating elaborate cemeteries and manipulating the landscape.[13]

Plants formed as much as half of the diet of First Peoples in many areas.[14] The range of plants from which fruit, seeds or roots were collected is extensive. Central Desert people collected 'bush tomatoes' (*Solanum* spp.), quandong (*Santalum acuminatum*), native plumbush (*Santalum lanceolatum*) and the desert fig (*Ficus platypoda*). The roots of *nalgoo* (*Cyperus bulbosus*), a nut-grass, often called 'bush onion', were eaten. Across southern Australia plants eaten included *cumbungi* (*Typha* species – water-rushes) of which young shoots and flower stems were eaten; water-ribbons (*Triglochin procera*), of which the rhizomes were eaten; marsh club-rush (*Scirpus medianus*), sea club-rush (*Scirpus caldwellii*) and ground orchids.[15]

Yams were also a substantial part of many diets, the desert yam (*Ipomoea costata*, whose tubers may weigh as much as 2.6 kg (5.7 lb), and *murnong*, or yam daisy (*Microseris lanceolata*), among them. An 1850 description of women digging up tubers of the yam *warran* (*Dioscorea hastifolia*) and replacing part of the stem in the hole is the earliest record of deliberate planting, and it is known that this was also a practice for two other yams.[16] Yam digging could be conducted over a wide area of land:

> We now crossed the dry bed of a stream, and from that emerged upon a tract of light fertile soil quite overrun with warran plants the root of which is a favourite article of food with the natives. This was the first time we had seen this plant on our journey and now for three and a half consecutive miles traversed a piece of land, literally perforated with holes the natives made to dig this root; indeed we could with difficulty walk across it on that account whilst the tract extended east and west as far as the eye could see.[17]

Quandong: picked and eaten fresh by Aboriginal Australians, it became a popular fruit for jam-making among rural settlers.

Extensive yam digging like this had benefits for their cultivation. 'Over the yearly round,' Beth Gott, a botanist specializing in Aboriginal plant use, writes,

> most areas productive of tuberous species would be covered. Since most of these species are found growing in locally abundant patches, gathering thinned out the plants and made room for further growth. The benefits of this cultivation are that the soil was aerated, and litter and ash were turned into it. Early settlers remarked on the loose absorbent nature of the soils, contrasting it with the compaction produced by the hard hoofs of sheep and cattle.[18]

Nardoo (*Marsilea drummondii*) is a water fern with clover-like leaves that grows in shallow waterholes. It is one of the plants whose seeds were collected and ground into a flour, then mixed with water into a dough to make flat cakes cooked over a fire. Wattleseeds were collected from some of the 120 species of Australian acacia and either eaten green or roasted, dried and ground into flour. Thomas Mitchell observed the harvesting of the native pepper grass *Panicum laevinode*: 'Dry heaps of this grass, that has been pulled expressly for this purpose of gathering the seed, lay along our path for many miles, I counted nine miles [14.5 km] along the river, in which we rode through this grass only, reaching to our saddle-girths.'[19]

Regular firing of bushland at three-year intervals is necessary for the propagation of several food plants, allowing nutrients to return to the soil, removing shade, and creating clear areas to allow seed germination and regrowth from tubers.[20] Mary Gilmore, a poet, journalist and memoirist who spent her childhood in rural southwestern New South Wales in the late 1800s, was a close observer of the foodways of Aboriginal people. She describes women planting grass seeds after fire:

> This was done at the direction of the chief, who, when the earth was cool enough to walk upon, went first to one shrub and then to another, testing and examining the burnt capsules, and where these had been destroyed directing the attention of the women

Nardoo sporocarps (seed cases) were ground, mixed with water and cooked in flat cakes over a fire.

Finger limes were one of the first fruits to be cultivated in the resurgence of interest in native foods in the 1990s.

> to them. The women gathered fresh ones from untouched shrubs and planted them where the destroyed ones once stood . . . I had often seen [them] set individual seeds as well as replace where the plant grew, those of what they ate. But the former was usually done where they themselves first made a small fire of twigs in order to prepare the earth by heating it . . . this alone shows that the natives had a knowledge of their own in regard to conditions of soil, shade and moisture in relation to seed.[21]

Fruits and nuts were collected in season. Fruits included quandong, *kutjera* (*Solanum centrale*, the desert raisin), muntries (*Kunzea pomifera*), riberries (*Syzygium luehmannii*), Davidson's plum (*Davidsonia jerseyana*) and finger limes (*Citrus australasica*). The Waka Waka and Gubbi Gubbi peoples in the Blackall Ranges and Bunya Mountains of southeastern Queensland would gather every three years, some travelling as far as 300 km (185 mi.), to feast on bunya nuts, the seeds of the *Araucaria bidwillii*, shaking the nuts out of their cones, then eating them fresh or roasting them like chestnuts. They would also store them in the mud of running creeks until they had fermented and then eat them.

Yams, fruit and seeds were often collected in coolamons, a section of hardwood that has been hollowed out and dried into a distinctive oblong with curved sides. The coolamon also served as a water carrier. Women wove grass into twine to make net bags for carrying small game, yams and fruit.

Nutritional Values of Australian Native Food

In the early 1980s staff of the Armed Forces Food Science Establishment at Scottsdale in Tasmania carried out an extensive evaluation of Australian survival foods, in effect an assessment of Aboriginal foods. With a slightly different emphasis, a study of the nutritional composition of dozens of Australian Aboriginal bush foods was undertaken almost simultaneously in the Human Nutrition Unit, Department of Biochemistry at the University of Sydney. Fruits, vegetables, animals, seeds and nuts were analysed, and in general the composition and nutritive values found were similar to those of comparable Western foods. Witchetty grubs, larva of *Cossidae* spp., were found to be high in protein (15 per cent) and fat (19 per cent). There were some surprises. The green (or Kakadu) plum, *Terminalia ferdinandia*, was found to have very high levels of vitamin C, up to 5 per cent. High thiamin (vitamin B) values were found in cooked candle nut (*Aleurites molucanna*) (4 mg per 100 mg) and in wild cucumber or bush banana (*Leichhardtia australis*) (3 mg per 100 mg), and many seeds were found to be nutrient-rich – high in fat, protein and minerals (the seeds of *Grevillea leucopteris* were reported to be up to 1.5 per cent calcium).

The Bogong moth (*Agrotis infusa*), gathered and eaten in the Australian Alps in springtime for at least 1,000 years, is highly nutritious. The edible portion, the abdomen, contains about 22 per cent protein and 39 per cent fat and is thus a high-energy food. The bunya pine in the hinterland of Queensland's Sunshine Coast has starchy kernels that are eaten raw or toasted and are nutritionally similar to chestnuts.

Overall, the traditional Aboriginal diet, low in fat and high in polyunsaturated fatty acids, is demonstrably healthier than a Western diet.[22]

Coolamons were an all-purpose carrier of everything from yams and seeds to babies.

Methods were also developed for dealing with plants that, if left untreated, could have an impact on physical health and in some cases be fatal. Nardoo must be ground and soaked in water to remove an enzyme called thiaminase, which destroys thiamine (vitamin B1). Thiamine deficiency can lead to fatigue, reduced appetite, muscle weakness, blurry vision and other conditions. Seeds of the burrawang (an Australian cycad, *Macrozamia communis*) contain a toxin that can lead to severe gastrointestinal irritation and abdominal cramps, with vomiting and nausea, diarrhoea and, in severe cases, liver damage. To avoid this, they are pounded and washed in running water for several days. The pulp is then made into flat cakes and roasted. The Dyirbal people eat the seeds of the *mirrañ*, the black bean or Moreton Bay chestnut (*Castanospermum australe)*. The beans are removed from their pods, baked in a hole filled with coals and covered with tree bark and sand, with another fire then lit on top. After several hours the beans are removed, cooled, then thinly sliced with a sharpened snail shell, put into a dilly-bag (a traditional bag woven from plant fibre) and left in running water for two to three days to completely leach the toxins.[23] Evidence from the remains of plant matter at Madjedbebe in the Northern Territory shows that techniques for the sophisticated preparation of food over several days to make it fit for consumption, such as cooking, leaching and pounding, were known as far back as 65,000 years ago.[24]

Working out how to deal with these foods took considerable observation and trial and error. This knowledge was passed down through the generations by watching and practising alongside those who held it, and sometimes through songs and dances performed at corroborees, ceremonial meetings that can last for days.

Food from Rivers, Lakes and Seas

All manner of fish, crustaceans and other riverine and ocean-dwelling animals were a substantial part of the diets across Australia and the ways of capture were many and varied.

Thomas Mitchell, on his 1835 Darling River expedition, described osier twigs inserted into the bed of the Gwydir River to form a trellis with small openings across. He concluded that 'some bag or netting might be applied there to receive the fish, while the natives in the river above should drive them towards it.'[25] Mary Gilmore recalled that 'the aboriginals made balks, so that, when flood currents took water back up creeks and gullies, as the water fell the up-taken fish remained impounded behind . . . Besides holding fish where these had been carried upstream from a junction, the aboriginals would bring fish caught in coolamons, water-filled hollow logs, and in baskets, and put them in places where rains were held.'[26]

The two most extensive river-fish management systems were the Budj Bim eel traps in southwestern Victoria, and the Brewarrina fish traps on the Barwon River in northwest New South Wales. At Budj Bim, the Gunditjmara excavated channels and made basalt block dams to direct eels from Lake Condah into shallow depressions, which served as holding ponds. The system, the oldest part of which is dated to 6,600 years ago, is one of the earliest examples of aquaculture in the world. The system runs over 2 km (1¼ mi.) and covers an area of about 6 ha (15 ac). The system extended the range of the eels, allowed them to grow and ensured availability for much of the year.[27]

At Brewarrina rocks were placed as low walls, forming rounded pens in the riverbed itself. Each pen could be opened at one end by moving the rocks. Fish coming downriver would enter the pens and be unable to exit at the other walled end. The entry would then be closed, and the fish held for use over a long period. Pens were set at different heights along the river to catch fish at various stages of their journey downstream. The pens were strong enough to withstand the force of torrential flood waters. Young fish that had managed to get downstream were caught with nets and carried in coolamons back to the pens to grow until ready for catching. Another method was to twist grass into a moveable dam that could be pushed from one end of a waterhole to the other, trapping fish while letting water flow through.[28]

Other fish traps were made from woven reeds. The Kininjku of Maningrida in the Arnhem Land region of the Northern Territory made two sorts of conical fish trap. A *mandjabu* is large and strong, made from a vine called *milil*, and used in tidal reaches of creeks to catch large fish. The smaller *manylik mandjabu* is used in flowing freshwater creeks to catch smaller fish and freshwater prawns. It can take three or four weeks to make a fish trap.[29]

Where water was deeper, for example in lakes, canoes were used, together with either nets or spears. Canoes were sometimes worked in tandem. A man in each canoe would hold the end of a net trailing down into the water. Men in other canoes would beat the water with sticks, driving the fish towards the net, where they would be speared. At other times, fish were speared as they were sighted. Canoes were usually made of bark. The shape was marked out on a suitable tree. Ropes were tied around it to keep the bark together, and the bark loosened by tapping with stone axes and then prised off carefully. The bark was then inverted over a fire, which evaporated the sap, making it curl inwards. It was caulked with clay and gum and waterproofed with several rubbings of fat. Often spearing was carried out at night by the light of torches or fires on the riverbank, or from a fire in the canoe itself.

Inland, fishing lines were made from possum hair or by twining lengths of the inner bark of trees, reeds, grasses or fibrous roots. Hooks

Low rock walls across the Barwon River at Brewarrina allowed the trapping and releasing of fish.

were made of wood or bone. Peter Beveridge, a grazier from southeastern Victoria writing in the 1870s, described men diving underwater to spear fish that they would bring to the surface wriggling about on their spears like great entomological specimens on immense pins.[30] Tom Petrie, a grazier in Queensland in the late 1800s who developed strong ties with Aboriginal communities, saw people fishing by poisoning water with a plant they called *tanggul*, which he identified as water pepper (*Polygonum hydropiper*). The plant, which produced highly pungent oils and acids, was pounded with sticks and thrown into a waterhole, stunning the fish, who would then rise to the surface to be picked up by hand. Petrie also saw people eeling in drought times by muddying water and feeling for the eels with their feet, then grabbing them by hand. Rivers were a source of more than fish. Women would dig in the mud and the banks for freshwater mussels and crayfish. Woven baskets were used to scoop up small fish and tadpoles, the water draining through the perforations in the weave.[31] Water birds – ducks, black swans, geese – were speared, trapped in nets or hunted with boomerangs. Ducks could also be caught by the hunter camouflaging their head with reeds and swimming carefully towards them until he could grab a duck and pull it under the water.[32]

Shellfish, prawns, crayfish and lobsters formed a significant part of the diet of coast-dwellers. Shellfish were a reliable source of food and available all year. The Mandu Mandu Creek rockshelter, in northwestern Australia, shows evidence of human occupation around 25,000 years ago, and the material gathered shows little difference between the fish, turtle, molluscs and crabs eaten then and those still eaten in the area now.[33] Abalone was collected on the southern and southeastern coasts. Skeletons of women from coastal Victoria show a thickening of bone in the ear that is thought to have developed to protect the eardrum from extreme cold when diving for abalone, a condition now sometimes called 'surfer's ear'.[34]

Sharks, stingrays, dugongs, turtles, mulloway, tuna, flathead and mullet were all hunted in their season at different areas of the coast. Seabirds were hunted and turtle eggs collected from the nests in beaches. Fish were speared from canoes in shallow water in estuaries and lagoons, or caught with hook and line from the shore and from rock platforms. Fish were trapped in the shallow pools using the same technique as in lakes and billabongs inland, by creating a barrier of sticks to prevent them returning to the ocean. Berleying, scattering shellfish, whole or ground, on the water to attract fish, was widely practised. Fishing lines were made from tender bark fibres – soaked and pounded, and sometimes chewed, then worked into thread. Hooks were made from wood, fish bones, bird bones and talons, and carved from abalone and other suitable shells. In coastal communities in New South Wales, women removed a part of their little finger in a practice called *malgun* to make it easier for them to handle lines from canoes.[35]

On the eastern coast, dolphins and porpoises were hunted. The Yugambeh people of southeast Queensland and northeast New South Wales have a story about Gowonda, a great hunter who left the people and entered the sea, where he was transformed into a porpoise. Now he teaches porpoises to lead fish onto the beach where they can be caught.[36] Whales that beached provided an opportunity for feasting. Watkin Tench observed one such occasion:

> On drawing near the shore, a dead whale in the most disgusting state of putrefaction was seen lying on the beach, and at least two hundred Indians surrounding it, broiling the flesh on different fires and feasting on it with the most extravagant marks of greediness and rapture . . . Their demand for hatchets being reiterated, notwithstanding our refusal, they were asked why they had not brought with them some of their own. They excused themselves by saying that on an occasion of the present sort they always left them at home and cut up the whale with the shell which is affixed to the end of the throwing stick.[37]

Joseph Lycett, Aborigines cooking and eating beached whales, Newcastle, New South Wales, c. 1817.

Food from Land Animals and Insects

At the time of the arrival of the First Peoples Australia was populated by many species of megafauna, animals weighing more than 40 kg (6 st.). Globally, megafauna are thought to have evolved after the extinction of dinosaurs and to have reached their peak distribution around 2.5 million years ago. Many species became extinct after the last ice age, replaced by other species better adapted to the warmer, drier climate that followed. Among the Australian megafauna herbivores there was the marsupial *Diprotodon optatum*: wombat-like, it was around 2 m (6½ ft) high at the shoulder, 3.5 m (11½ ft) long and weighed as much as 2 tonnes. *Procoptodon goliah* was the largest kangaroo that ever existed, standing 2 m (6½ ft) tall and weighing as much as 240 kg (37 st.). The family Meiolanide were herbivorous horned turtles of immense size. *Genyornis newtoni* was a flightless bird of around 200 kg (30 st.), resembling an emu but in fact related to chickens and ducks. A cave painting in the land of the Jawoyn people in the Northern Territory depicting a bird with the features of *Genyornis* has been dated to 40,000 years ago. Among the carnivores were a marsupial lion (*Thylacinus cynocephalus*), a land crocodile (*Quinkana fortirostrum*) and a giant monitor lizard, *Megalania prisca*, like today's goanna.

Human stone artefacts have been found together with megafauna bones at several sites around Australia. At Cuddie Springs near Brewarrina, in northwestern New South Wales, megafauna remains date to between 30,000 and 19,000 years ago. At Willandra Lakes bones of *Zygomaturus trilobus*, another wombat-like marsupial, have been dated to as recent as 17,000 years ago.[38]

Why the megafauna became extinct is the subject of ongoing debate. Tim Flannery, in 1994, argued that the First Peoples 'were spectacularly successful predators, for they appeared to have killed off all of the Australian land-based creatures larger than themselves'.[39] But as evidence emerges about the length of time during which humans cohabited with megafauna, opinion now is that it was a combination of human hunting and environmental change that led to the extinction.

Boomerangs and spears were the weapons of choice on open ground. Cross boomerangs and returning boomerangs were effective for knocking down birds in flight. *Nulla nullas*, long, thick rods that were bulbous at the end, were effective in clubbing an animal once it had been brought down by a spear. Spears were made of hardwood and sometimes fire-cured to make them stronger and straighter. Flints were tied to the tips with grass or bark twine. *Woomeras* used leverage to throw a spear up to three times further than by hand. They were made by shaping a piece of hardwood into a long, thin handle and attaching a string to the base to hold a spear. Young men learned how to use weapons by practising on small animals. Dyirbal youth practised on a *gugandal*, a long length of bark joined up and fashioned into a not-quite-circular wheel. This was thrown into the air and the young men tried to throw their spears through the moving target.[40] The Yaraldi of the Murray River used branches of thick foliage as camouflage to come within easy spearing range of kangaroos without them becoming aware and bounding off. [41] Several members of a tribe might form a line and make noise by hitting spears against shields and calling out to startle herds of kangaroos, wallabies or emus, chasing them towards pits covered by leaves and twigs or into huge twine nets strung between trees. After their arrival about 5,000 years ago, dingoes became part of hunting practices in much the same way as domestic dogs would later: detection and tracking of difficult-to-see animals; flushing game out of cover and into the waiting hunters; and capturing and killing smaller animals.[42]

Goannas and other lizards, crocodiles, snakes, frogs and echidnas were all hunted. Women poked digging sticks into burrows and holes to expose small marsupials and other animals for capture. Emu eggs were gathered. Possums and stick-nest rats (*Leporillus conditor*), so called for the metre-wide nests of interlocking sticks they built high in the tops of trees, were smoked out. Axes were used to cut deep into trees to collect honey from native stingless sugarbag bees (*Tetragonula carbonaria*). Witchetty grubs are the larvae of the cossid moth (*Endoxyla leucomochla*) found across Western Australia, South Australia and the Northern Territory and were an important source of food, particularly for people living in desert areas. Digging sticks were used to pry them and other moth larvae out of the ground or tree barks. The bogong moth (*Agrotis infusa*) is renowned for its annual migration from south Queensland and western New South Wales to the Australian Alps, a part of the Great Dividing Range that straddles New South Wales and Victoria, where they stay semi-dormant in the cooler climate before returning to their breeding grounds. Their presence in the Alps drew people from many parts of southeastern Australia to collect them off the walls of caves, roast them and eat them whole, or make them into flattened cakes that could be taken back to home territories.

The western grey kangaroo (*Macropus fuliginosus*), one of the many macropods hunted in Australia.

Mary Gilmore recorded the creation of areas set aside

> to remain as breeding-places or animal sanctuaries. Where there were plains by a river, a part was left undisturbed for birds that nested on the ground. They did the same thing with lagoons, rivers, and billabongs for water-birds and fish . . . the law of sanctuary in regard to large or wide breeding-grounds, such as Ganmain and Deepwater, where once there were miles and miles of swamps (as also near Deniliquin) was that each year a part of the area could be hunted or fished, but not the same part two seasons in succession.[43]

A similar practice is recorded for people of the South Alligator River in the Northern Territory, who set aside parts of the country for two or three years to allow game numbers to increase.

Cooking, Storage and Preservation

Food not eaten raw was cooked with fire. Large furred animals – kangaroos, wallabies, possums and the like – were skinned with stone flakes and either placed whole or roughly butchered with stone axes on the coals of a low fire. Skins were used to make watercarriers or cloaks. Birds, fish and small animals were eviscerated with a stick and then tossed onto the coals without plucking, scaling or skinning. There are no records of Aboriginal people boiling food.

At Budj Bim earth oven mounds containing faunal remains have been found near swamp margins. The Yaraldi people of the lower Murray River in South Australia cooked by the *maramin* method. This method is like the *muu muu*, common in the Pacific Islands.

> A fire was made in a scooped-out depression and stones were thrown in so that they could be heated to the extent of retaining their heat. When the fire burned down, the stones were moved about with a wooden poker to form a level base . . . *kinyera* and *pilbala* grass was strewn over the stones to keep the meat clean and unburnt. Either portions of meat or the whole trussed up would be put on the grass bed . . . The oven was then covered with *yalkura* or other grass, followed by the skins and finally sand so that the heat of the oven would be retained . . . Shortly after cooking, a pointed stick would be thrust through the sand, between the skins, so that it reached the bottom stone base, and was then withdrawn; water was poured into the whole to increase the intensity of the steam . . . Finally, when it was cooked, the coverings were removed, and the meat taken out and distributed according to the obligations of kinship . . .[44]

Food not immediately eaten was stored as it was or was prepared in some way to preserve it for later use. Caches of seeds, tubers and other food were kept in protected locations: in trees, in caves or buried in sand. The Kukatja and Pintupi of the northern part of the Great Sandy Desert in Western Australia kept acacia pods and eucalyptus seeds covered by spinifex for the lean months of the year. Some seed hordes were so big as to be described as granaries by early colonial explorers. Ossified caches have been found in stone chambers, preserved by tight-fitting stone plugs.[45] Seasonal food was stockpiled in preparation for large gatherings as in the case of bunya nuts.

Fruit like quandongs, bush plums and figs were skewered on sticks and dried. Large fish were sometimes cut into pieces and smaller fish eviscerated before being cooked on the coals. They were then smoked on beds of grasses that had been set alight, the fish covered by other leafy materials that created a lot of smoke, such as *parangum* (samphire) and *witjeri* (fig bush). Other scale- and shellfish were dried and kept in pieces or made into fish meal or fish flour. Ground seeds and tubers were made into flour or cakes and balls that could be kept for long periods and were easy to carry while travelling. Caterpillars, witchetty grubs, grasshoppers and meats were coated in the ashes of particular woods and later mixed with seed flour before cooking.[46]

Food was distributed according to totem and custom, which designated certain portions to different sexes and ages within family groups.

Food surpluses were not only stored but traded between nations. This may have happened through regular formal social and kin relations between nations, through occasional encounters or at times of coming together for corrobborees. In the Corners Region of the Central Desert there was trade in caterpillars, witchetty grubs, grasshoppers, nardoo, *panicum* seeds, bush onions and fish meal. Overlapping linkages meant that some trade webs extended for thousands of kilometres across the mainland. *Pitjuri*, a plant containing nicotine and nicotine-related compounds, when prepared, was extensively traded over large areas of central Australia, reaching into southern Australia. At Budj Bim, an analysis of the soil at the base of trees showed it contained eel fat and the trees showed signs of being used as smokehouses that would have produced enough quantities to trade.

Water and Other Drinks

In a country as arid as Australia, knowing where to find good water and how to access it was crucial. Where rivers, waterholes and lakes were more or less permanent, good water was readily at hand. In more arid areas and where the water was not as clean, other methods had to be used. Thomas Mitchell described Aboriginal members of his exploratory group getting 'a cool and clean draught' by 'first scratching a hole in the soft sand beside the pool, thus making a filter, in which the water rose cooled but muddy. They next threw into this some tufts of long grass, through which they sucked the cooler water thus purified also from sand and gravel.'[47] The Yankunytjatjara of central Australia would dig up the roots of the *ilpara* (*Grevillea nematophylla*, silver-leaved water bush), pierce each end of a tuber, put them in a wooden dish and drink the water that came out of them.[48] Water was carried in pouches of animal skin or intestines. Water was sometimes flavoured by steeping flowers in it, such as those of the honeysuckle grevillea (*Grevillea juncifolia*).

Three fermented drinks are recorded. In the southwest of Western Australia *mangaitch* was made from the flowering cones of banksia

Ultukun(pa) (Honeysuckle grevillea) Drink

Pompey Everard

Ka ultukunpa katantara kapingka tjunkupai.
You break off some honeysuckle grevillea and put it in water.

Munu tjalatjura – tjunyintja wiyangku – purtinytju marungku nyurmintananyi, alatjinanyi.
After immersing a good deal of it – without squashing it around at all – you squeeze it gently with the hands, like this.

Munu nyanganyilta. 'Nyangatja maruringu.'
And watch it. 'It's gone dark.'

Munu kulini 'Tjinguru tjinkintjakulta wamalta, wirulta. Nganana tjikintjaku ngaranyi.'
And think: 'Maybe it's got sweet enough to drink. It's ready to drink.'

Munu tjanpi piyuku tjunkula, katu tjunkula, raputji tjikilpaingka, kilinananyi.
And you put some grass in on top as a strainer, in case you should drink the rubbish.

Munu palunytjanungku, panya paluru pulka kutjupa, paluru purinypa tjikilpaitu.
And after that, you drink the other big one just the same.

Tjunyira, tjalatjura tjunkupai. Mumu wati tjuta 'Panya, mapalkiungku! Rawangku tjunkunytja wiya!'
Squish it around, immerse it and put it aside, and the men would say 'Come on! Quick! Don't let it sit for too long!'

Paluru ngarira panya nyaaringkupaingka – unaringkupaingka, raputjiringkupainngka. Uwa, tjuwita wiyaringkupaingka.
Lest it stand and go off. In case it spoils. Yes, lest the sweetness disappear.[49]

Grevillea flowers were soaked to release their nectar in order to make a sweet drink.

fermented in water to what was described as a mead-like drink. The Tasmanian Palawa people tapped sap from cider gum trees (*Eucalyptus gunii*) that was left to ferment to make *way-a-linah*, which British settlers described as tasting like cider. The Yanyuwa people of the Borroloola region of the Northern Territory pulped the ripe red nuts of the spiral pandanus and left the juice to ferment to make *yambuda*. All three were reported to produce 'exhilaration' by settlers who observed them being imbibed.[50]

Torres Strait Islander Foodways

Current archaeological scholarship puts the arrival of the first people to the Torres Strait Islands from Melanesia at around 3,000 years ago, when ocean levels has stabilized after the flooding of the Strait.[51] At the time of the first European contacts, a transition in foodways was evident from north to south across the Strait, with islands closer to Papua New Guinea having more evidence of agricultural practice and those further south mainly relying on fishing and gathering.[52] Starchy root vegetables – *kumala* (*Ipomoea batatas*, sweet potato), cassava, taro and yams – were introduced into the diet around 1,900 years ago using the cultivation system known as ditch-and-mound. They may have been brought with the second wave of migration by people from Papua New Guinea before the arrival of the British in Cape York. Pigs were also introduced through trade.[53] In the southern islands the diet was primarily marine animals: fish, dugong, turtle, crayfish, octopus, squid and bivalves were the main sources. On some islands, families had intertidal clam beds and fish traps built from low walls of coral and rocks. Small outriggers were the common sea craft. The Torresian imperial pigeon (*Ducula spilorrhoa*) was hunted. Fruits were also gathered: *wongai* (*Manilkara kauki*, native plum), beach almonds (*Terminalia catappa*) and coconuts.

Terra Nullius

In 1768 the British Admiralty commissioned Lieutenant James Cook to sail to the South Pacific to observe the transit of Venus and to investigate the southern landmass Dutch explorers had described, and to which one of them, Abel Tasman, had given the name Nieuw Holland in 1644. After observing the transit, Cook sailed south on the *Endeavour*, stopping briefly at New Zealand, then proceeding east. On 19 April 1770 Lieutenant Hicks sighted the east coast of Nieuw Holland. Cook continued up the east coast and on 29 April harboured in a sheltered area he named Stingray Bay, after the fish in its waters that most caught his attention. He made brief contact there with the Gweagal people. The botanists Joseph Banks and Daniel Solander, who accompanied Cook, collected samples and made drawings of the unique flora. Cook later renamed the bay Botany Bay because of the number of new species they collected. After a week Cook sailed north, charting the east coast, then foundered on the Great Barrier Reef. He managed to get the ship to a coastal river for repairs. Here he had several untroubled encounters with the Guugu Yimithirr. At some point on the journey from there to England – when and where is disputed – Cook claimed possession of the eastern coast of the southern land-mass for King George III, first calling it New Wales and then New South Wales. Despite his encounters with Aboriginal Australians, he took possession on the basis that the land was *terra nullius* – a land without owners.

But Australia emphatically was not *terra nullius*. At the time of Cook's act of possession, at least 400,000 – and as many as 1 million – people were living in over five hundred nations across the southern landmass. They had survived the last glacial maximum and the dry, hot millennia that followed; had observed the final separation of the continent from its partner land masses; had seen the seas invade and recede to form the land; and had gone on to populate every environmental niche in Australia. They were actively involved in agriculture and aquaculture, were managing food stock for sustainability and had developed sophisticated strategies for turning fire, a significant environmental hazard, into a powerful tool for resource management. The consequences of this act of possession reverberate through the rest of this book.

THREE

Settlers to Squatters, 1788–1850

Cook was not the first Englishman to step onto Nieuw Holland soil and meet its Indigenous peoples. In January 1688 William Dampier was travelling on the *Cygnet*, a ship engaged in pirating in Southeast Asia. The ship put into what is now named the Dampier Peninsula in north Western Australia. There he had brief contact with the Bardi nation. In his 1697 book *A New Voyage Around the World* he described them as 'the miserablest people in the world'. He was also disparaging of the Martuthunira, whom he met on a second voyage in 1869 taken under commission from the British Admiralty to explore Nieuw Holland.[1]

Dampier's views arguably shaped the perspective with which Cook and those who followed viewed the Indigenous nations they encountered. The impact of this on Indigenous Australians in the first sixty years of the British colonial enterprise is part of the story of this chapter, which opens as the British Admiralty sends Arthur Phillip to establish a colony in the land now in the king's possession. Settlers began transforming the land into another Britain, introducing agricultural practices, plants and animals at odds with the land and its flora and fauna. These introduced practices had a disastrous impact on Indigenous Australians, native flora and fauna and the land itself.

A Colony Established

In the late eighteenth century the British government faced a dilemma. The American Revolution had put an end to transporting convicts to the American eastern seaboard in 1775. Convicts were subsequently held on decommissioned naval vessels – 'hulks' – anchored in the Thames, but this option also was now becoming untenable. Transportation to the southern land that Cook had claimed for Britain presented itself as a solution. Support for establishing a colony there also came from British merchants like James Maria Matra:

> Part of it lies in a climate parallel to the Spice Islands and is fitted for the production of that valuable commodity, as well as the sugar-cane, tea, coffee, silk, cotton, indigo, tobacco and the other articles of commerce that have been so advantageous to the maritime powers of Europe . . . [and] the New Zealand hemp or flax plant, an object equally of curiosity and versatility.[2]

Cook had taken some flax back from Norfolk Island and New Zealand. Matra, Sir George Young, who was Attorney General at the time, and others also suggested the colony could serve to break the Dutch hold on trade with China, Japan, Korea and the Spice Islands, the name then given to the Indonesian Molucca archipelago, which were the main sources of cloves, nutmeg and mace. Britain was also viewing French activity in the Indian Ocean with anxiety.

The task of establishing the colony was given to Admiral Governor Arthur Phillip. On 13 May 1787 a fleet of eleven ships – two Royal Navy vessels, three store ships and six convict ships carrying 1,300 marines with their wives and children, civil officers and convicts – set out for what was now named Australia. Three of the ships were chartered by the British East India Co. to sail to Canton to purchase tea and other trader goods after disembarking their passengers.

The ships were provisioned with beef, pork, bread, butter, pease (dry peas) and fresh water. However, carrying enough food for a long sea-voyage, plus all they would need to begin to feed themselves between reprovisioning from later ships, would have been impossible. The fleet stopped along the way to buy fresh meat and vegetables for the voyage and to stock up for the colony. Captain-Lieutenant Watkin Tench, who had volunteered for a three-year tour of duty at the settlement, noted in his account published after his return to England that at Tenerife, their first port of call, they 'completed our stock of water and [took] on board wine', but while figs and mulberries were plentiful there, they did not purchase any.[3]

At the next port, Rio de Janeiro, they stocked up on rum, which would have a significant role to play as a medium of exchange in the colony. They also collected banana plants, coffee (both beans and plants), guava seeds,

Lieutenant Watkin Tench's diaries describe the colony of New South Wales in rich detail.

indigo plants, lemon seeds and plants, orange seeds and plants, and the prickly pear plant bearing the cochineal beetle. The Cape of Good Hope was the last port before the passage across the Indian Ocean and here the fleet bought 'a considerable quantity of flour, and the principal part of our livestock, which was to store our intended settlement . . . [The latter included] two bulls, three cows, three horses, forty-four sheep and thirty-two hogs, besides goats and a very large quantity of poultry of every kind.'[4] The fleet was already carrying some young fruit trees and cuttings, corn, seed-grains and tubers. Here they also collected apple, pear and quince trees and seed, fig trees, maize, sugar cane, strawberries, grape vine cuttings, and rice, wheat and barley for seed to replace what might be damaged on the voyage.[5] Spades, hoes, axes, hatchets, wheelbarrows and butcher's knives were also part of the cargo.

All these provisions were based on what Matra and Sir George Young had proposed. The expectation was that what they had brought

Sydney Cove, Port Jackson, 1788.

was sufficient to feed the colony until it could be self-sustaining with the produce from vegetable and fruit gardens, beef and dairy, based on the European foods that formed their familiar diet. They brought rifles, fishing hooks and lines, expecting that some part of the diet would be met by hunting and fishing native fauna.

On 24 January 1788 the First Fleet, as it came to be called, anchored in Botany Bay, of which Cook had given excellent reports. Then came the first of several disappointments. The land was marshy, beset with flying insects and had little fresh water. Phillip upped anchor and headed further along the coast. A few kilometres north he found what Cook had sailed past: a harbour Phillip described as the finest in the world, one in which a thousand ships could dock with perfect security. On 26 January 1788 Phillip raised the British flag in what he named Sydney Cove. There was fresh water here from a stream that ran down into the cove (named the Tank Stream after three or four holding tanks were cut into the sandstone over which it flowed). Fish were plentiful. A public garden was planted in an area he called Farm Cove (now the Royal Botanic Gardens); marines began another garden on a small island (Garden Island, now a naval dockyard); and free settlers and convicts were encouraged to build their own gardens, the convicts returning to nurture these after they had completed the day's work for the marines and settlers to whom they were assigned.

A Precarious Year

The settlement soon hovered on the brink of disaster. The crops failed to flourish. Tench wrote: 'the spots we have chosen for experiments in agriculture, in which we can scarce be supposed adepts, have hitherto but ill repaid our toil, which may be imputable to our having chosen such as are unfavourable for our purpose.'[6] The soil was too sandy and lacked the nutrients needed for the crops being planted. He was also right about their farming skills. The marines knew nothing of farming and among the convicts only a handful had any background as farmhands. Adding to their woes they had arrived during an El Niño event, which though mild was sufficiently dry and hot to have an impact on plants suited to the cooler, damper English conditions.

Phillip had initially placed marines and convicts on the same weekly rations per male: 7 lb beef, 4 lb pork, 3 pts pease, 7 lb flour for bread, 6 oz butter, ½ lb rice. Female convicts and wives of marines got two-thirds the male ration.[7] As the plight of the colony sank in, he began reducing the rations.

In May, as the food situation worsened, Phillip sent the *Supply* to collect turtles from Lord Howe Island off the east coast, but without success. Tench was despondent: 'The unsuccessful return of the *Supply* cast a general damp on our spirits, for by this time fresh provisions were become scarcer than in a blockaded town. The little livestock, which with so heavy an expense and through so many difficulties, we had brought on shore, prudence forbade us to use.'[8] Phillip had been told to prevent the slaughter of the cattle he purchased until such time as the herd was big enough to be sustainable. Before this happened, however, another blow fell. The cattle they had brought with them went astray and no amount of searching located them. They were eventually found accidentally in 1795, by two convicts 65 km (40 mi.) from the settlement, along the Nepean River in an area that subsequently was named, perhaps with tongue in cheek, the Cowpastures. The herd by this time had swelled to three hundred beasts and proved difficult to recapture.

The colonists did supplement their produce with native fruits, plants and animals. Tench mentions hunting kangaroos with rifle and dogs, the taste of a young kangaroo being like veal; shooting ducks and emu, which tasted like beef; a 'small purple apple', probably the blue lilly pilly (*Syzygium oleosum*) whose colour ranges from a pale mauve to deep blue; and a fruit that looked like a grape but tasted sour like a green gooseberry, which was probably the native grape (*Cissus hypoglauca*) whose deep blue berries, while edible, have a bitter taste.[9] Warrigal greens (*Tetragonia tetragonioides*) are probably the plant that Tench writes led to a convict who ate it raw 'falling a sacrifice in twenty-four hours afterwards'.[10] A ground-hugging creeper also called native spinach, its leaves are high in oxalates and are best blanched or cooked in some way, as Tench observed Aboriginals doing.

When scurvy hit the colony, native greens were particularly sought. Foraging by the settlers was not always taken well. Tench writes of two convicts who were 'peaceably engaged in picking of greens' being speared, one escaping and the other never being seen again.[11] In March 1789 sixteen convicts raided a group of Aboriginals at Botany Bay, intending to steal fishing tackle and spears. One of the convicts was killed and the others ran back to the settlement. When questioned by Phillip, they first maintained they had been 'quietly picking sweet-tea' but later admitted intending theft. Phillip had them all flogged. The Aboriginal fishing party had long gone by the time an officer arrived at the Bay.[12] These incidents were early indications of the conviction that Indigenous Australians had no ownership of land or its resources.

Sweet tea was the native sarsaparilla (*Smilax glyciphylla*), used by the marines and convicts in lieu of tea, which was not part of the provisions

Warrigal greens may have been the plant that Watkin Tench wrote of when he said that eating a native plant made one of the settlers ill.

Watkin Tench wrote of eating a 'small purple apple', which may have been the midgen berry (*Austromyrtus dulcis*), above left. 'Sweet tea', the native sarsaparilla (*Smilax glyciphylla*), above right, used by marines and convicts in lieu of tea.

sent with the Fleet.[13] The leaves and berries were used medicinally by the Gadigal and other Aboriginal clans. While the Fleet surgeons claimed to have discovered the medicinal uses of the leaf themselves, the food historian Jacqui Newling wonders whether it was rather through observation or direct communication with the Aboriginal peoples that knowledge of this and other useful plants was gained.[14] Settlers did not always credit their dependence on the knowledge of Aboriginal people, though it often meant the difference between survival and starvation.

Supplementing their rations with native produce, however, was not a viable strategy in the long term. Phillip realized the depth of the danger they were in. In October 1788 he dispatched the *Sirius* back to the Cape for supplies. It returned at the beginning of May 1789. Tench wrote, 'The day of famine was at last procrastinated by the supply of flour and salt provisions she brought us.'[15] Further relief came with the arrival in June 1890 of the *Justinian* with provisions for the colony, one of six ships that formed the Second Fleet.

Phillip had been sent out with clear instructions to have the colony off rations within two years. The desultory results of the attempts at farming in

The high street at Parramattta from the gates of Government House, *c.* 1804–5.

the area around Sydney Cove were a spur to him sending out exploratory parties to find more suitable land. By mid-1791 good land had been found along the Hawkesbury and Nepean rivers to the northwest of the colony, and at Parramatta along the upper reaches of one of the two rivers that flowed into the harbour.

Settling In

A new government farm was established at Rose Hill near Parramatta under the management of Henry Edward Dodd. Dodd had accompanied Phillip as a personal servant, but his background as a farmhand was of more value to the Governor. When Tench visited Rose Hill in November 1790, Dodd reported that he had cleared and planted 70 ac. (30 ha.) and expected a barley yield of four hundred bushels and thirteen or fourteen bushels of wheat per acre. Dodd had successfully also grown a vegetable crop, maize, oats and a small quantity of flax. Dodd intended to use this first harvest mainly for seed. Of Dodd's farming methods, Tench wrote:

> The plough has never yet been tried here, all the ground is hoed and (as Dodd confesses) very incompetently turned up. Each convict labourer was obliged to hoe sixteen rods a day, so that in some places the earth was but scratched over. The ground was left open for some months, to receive benefit from sun and air; and on that newly cleared the trees were burnt and the ashes dug in. I do not find the succession of crops has yet been attempted; surely it would help to meliorate and improve the soil.[16]

The lack of crop rotation is odd. Dodd was a farmhand in an England deep in the Agrarian Revolution of the eighteenth century, the period of transformation of British agriculture characterized by land enclosures and technological advances. He would have been familiar with the Norfolk four-course rotation system, which was standard practice by the end of the century. Under the system wheat was grown in the first year, turnips in the second, followed by barley, with clover and ryegrass in the third. These were grazed or cut for feed in the fourth year. The system had the benefits of providing feed for cattle and sheep in winter – turnips – and the beasts provided manure for the soil as they grazed. As for using hoes only, which Tench says was common among the other farmers, it is unfathomable why no plough was included with the First Fleet. The British-designed Rotherham plough was in common use at the time. Jethro Tull's seed drill, another advance during the Agrarian Revolution, may have been too bulky to transport in sufficient numbers. In 1795 John Macarthur imported the first plough to the colony, but it was not until 1806 that Governor King, the third governor of the colony, could report that 'the plough is getting into general practice by the really industrious.'[17]

Macarthur, his wife Elizabeth and their son Edward arrived on the *Scarborough* in June 1790. He did not get on well with Phillip but did get on with his commanding officer Major Francis Grose. On Phillip's return to Britain in 1793, Grose became Acting Governor and Macarthur was one

The residence of John Macarthur Esquire near Parramatta, New South Wales.

of the first to benefit from Grose's largesse in allocating land and labour, being given 40 ha (100 ac) at Parramatta and unlimited convict labour. Macarthur named the property Elizabeth Farm. Elizabeth Macarthur's letters to friends give an indication of the fruit that was being grown in the colony:

> Our climate is delightful, and we have in high perfection and in great abundance the fruits of warm and cold climates. In our garden, which is large, we have Oranges, Lemons, Olives, Almonds, Grapes, Peaches, Apricots, Nectarines, Medlars, Pears, Apples, Raspberries, Strawberries, Walnuts, Cherries, Plums. These fruit you know. Then we have the Loquat, a Chinese fruit, the Citron, the Shaddock and the Pomegranate, and perhaps some others that I may have forgotten to enumerate, such as the Cherry and Guava . . . I have, I perceive, omitted to mention the Fig, of which we have many varieties and in abundance.[18]

The garden is an interesting mix of both fruit trees that she would be familiar with from English orchards and others that are tropical. There are no native fruiting trees, however. Elizabeth doesn't refer to vegetables, perhaps thinking them too ordinary to mention, but among those commonly grown were beans, beetroot, broccoli, carrots, cabbages, cucumbers, cauliflowers, potatoes, pumpkins, turnips and radishes.

By the early 1800s farmers in the Hawkesbury area were producing fruit and vegetables and breeding livestock for sale. An informal market began at the Hospital Wharf, on the west side of Sydney Cove, where their boats docked and produce coming by road from Parramatta was offloaded. The market moved to the Old Parade grounds site in 1809. In 1833 the Hay, Corn and Cattle Market was established near the Campbell Street cattle yards, the area that is now the Sydney suburb of Haymarket.[19] By the 1820s preserved fruits were being sold on the streets of Sydney, suggesting that orchards were bountiful.

Goods that could not be produced in the colony were imported, offloaded at warehouses and sold in bulk either to families who could afford to buy in large quantities or through small retailers. Imported cheeses, preserved goods such as mustards, relishes, sauces, tea, rice, sugar and some spices found their buyers both among those who could make regular purchases and those who might buy them in small amounts as

Paddy's Market became the central market for Sydney from 1834 and was situated next to the cattle market.

occasional treats. Early retail shops were usually the front room of private houses, as was the case for small shops in eighteenth-century Britain. Shops advertised new goods that had arrived in their windows or in the *Sydney Gazette and New South Wales Advertiser*, an official government publication first published on 5 March 1803.[20] For those too far away to make a daily trip to the market, hawkers plied their trade through the streets with fruit, vegetables and fish that they had grown or caught themselves, or bought at the market.

Meat and Dairy

More cattle for the New South Wales colony were purchased from Bengal in India, the Cape of Good Hope, Madagascar, Spain and St Helena. Tench wrote of the growing herd: 'The cattle look in good condition, and I was surprised to hear that neither corn nor fodder is given to them. The enclosures in which they are confined furnish hardly a blade of grass at present. There are people appointed to tend them who have been used to this way of life, and who seem to execute it well.'[21]

Not all households had their own cow and in 1805 Dr John Harris, a former colony surgeon, built the first commercial dairy to plug the gap. The wealthier settlers with larger landholdings like the Macarthurs had dairy rooms to make butter and other milk products for the household. Some with sufficient excess milk began producing small amounts of butter and cheese for sale. The first commercial dairy herds were established in the 1820s in the Illawarra district along the coast to the south of Sydney, within a day's travel by packhorse.

Meat was at risk of spoilage, and salt for it, particularly pork, remained an important part of the rations in the colony. Solar salt pans were established in Sydney in 1790, but imported salt was preferred for salting meat and in 1801 Governor King sought to find a nearer supplier than England. He found it in Tahiti, where pigs were plentiful, and curing was done with salt from Hawai'i. In January 1813 colonists at Windsor suggested that excess meat should be salted and sold to Britain, but the project did not proceed at that time. In 1843 the Sydney Salting Co. was established to salt meat for the domestic and export market.[22] In 1847 the Joseph brothers opened the Patent Preserved Provision Manufactory in Camperdown, stocking locally canned soups, meats and milk. Then, in February 1848, Henry Dangar in Newcastle began to produce canned soups and meat for the commissariat in Sydney and for export. The product won a medal at the Great Exhibition of 1851 and was rated highly in *The Lancet*'s *Analytical Sanitary Commission*. By 1851–2 the sale price had fallen, and exporting ended in 1855.[23]

Bring Your Own Bread

'If a lucky man who had knocked down a dinner with his gun, or caught a fish by angling from the rocks, invited a neighbour to dine with him,' Tench wrote, 'the invitation always ran, "bring your own bread." Even at the governor's table this custom was constantly observed. Every man when he sat down pulled his bread out of his pocket and laid it by his plate.'[24]

The supply of wheat remained unstable. The granary of the colony shifted to the fertile river flats of the Hawkesbury, but floods in 1801, and a particularly catastrophic flood in 1806 that inundated more than 14,000 ha (3,460 ac), destroyed crops, livestock and seed reserves and caused further stringent rationing. Grain had to be imported from Calcutta.

When there was grain, milling became a problem. Four water-driven millstones were included in the equipment brought with the First Fleet, but there was no millwright or reliable stream to use them efficiently.

Colonists had to grind wheat in iron hand mills, and when they were blunted had to resort to querns and pestles and mortars.

In January 1794 John Hunter was appointed to succeed Phillip and brought with him the working parts for a windmill. The first began operation at what is now Millers Point in Sydney in January 1797. Sydney's first successful watermill began operating in 1812. In 1815 Governor Macquarie opened John Dickson's steam-driven mill, which could grind ten bushels of wheat per hour. By 1840 Sydney had about a hundred mills, many of which were steam driven. Watermills made up nearly half the mills in Van Diemen's Land as colonists took advantage of its regular rainfall and large number of suitable streams.

A public bakery was built in Sydney in early 1788. Colonists could exchange flour for a baked loaf here. An order in May 1801 brought both milling and baking under direct government supervision. The extraction rate, or percentage of flour obtained from the wheat ground, was fixed at 76 per cent and a loaf of 2 lb 1 oz (936 g) was to be bartered for 3 lb (1.3 kg) wheat. The first instance of food adulteration was reported when a woman was found to have given over a quantity of flour for baking that was 40 per cent powdered stone. Bread was also baked at home in a camp oven or as a flat bread over the coals. Baking tins came on the market in the 1830s. There is no record of what the first yeasts in the colony were.

New Colonies

While the colony based on the Sydney settlement was expanding, new strategic settlements were established in other districts of New South Wales, and new colonies grew up around them. Settlements were also established in western and northern parts of the country, in lands not included in the eastern Australian coast claimed by Cook.

In 1803 Governor King, alarmed by the presence of two French vessels in the waters around Van Diemen's Land, dispatched Lieutenant John Bowen with fifty settlers, crew, soldiers and convicts to establish a settlement at Risdon, on the Derwent River. The site was abandoned for lack of a suitable supply of fresh water and in 1804 Lieutenant David Collins established a settlement at Hobart on the opposite side of the river. On 19 October 1812 the *Indefatigable* brought the first convicts transported there directly from England.

In 1824 Governor Brisbane commissioned Hamilton Hume and William Hovell to look for grazing land in the south of New South Wales.

James Ruse

James Ruse was the first emancipist (a convict whose term had expired) to be given land by Governor Phillip. In 1791 he was granted the colony's first land title. Watkin Tench met him at his farm and wrote this account of Ruse's farming practice, which contrasts markedly with Dodd's:

> I have now an acre and a half in bearded wheat, half an acre in maize, and a small kitchen garden. On my land I sowed three bushels of seed, the produce of this country, broad cast. I expect to reap about twelve or thirteen bushels . . . My land I prepared thus: having burnt the fallen timber off the ground, I dug in the ashes, and then hoed it up, never doing more than eight or perhaps nine, rods in a day; by which means it was not like the government farm, just scratched over, but properly done. Then I cold-moulded it and dug in the grass and weeds. This I think almost equal to ploughing. I then let it lie as long as I could, exposed to air and sun; and, just before I sowed my seed, turned it all up afresh. When I shall have reaped my crop, I purpose to hoe it again, and harrow it fine, and then sow it with turnip seed, which will mellow and prepare it for the next year. My straw I mean to bury in pits and throw in with it everything which I think will rot and turn to manure. My opinion of the soil of my farm is that it is middling; neither good nor bad. I will be bound to make it do with the aid of manure, but without cattle it will fail. The greatest check on me is the dishonesty of the convicts who, in spite of all my vigilance, rob me almost every night.[25]

In October 1793 he sold his farm to Dr John Harris for £40, intending to use the money to pay for passage back to England, but spent it instead, possibly in gambling. He sought a new grant and in January 1794 was one of the 22 settlers responsible for beginning the settlement of the Hawkesbury

River area. There he grew the first successful commercial crop of wheat in the colony.

The James Ruse Agricultural High School in Carlingford is a leading high school in New South Wales today. Agricultural high schools combine a general curriculum (usually mathematics, English and science as core subjects) with compulsory classes in farming theory and practice. They tend to have some land, providing students practical experience with crops and animal husbandry, and some offer on-campus boarding for rural and remote students. In rural areas, generalist high schools often offer elective agriculture subjects.

They travelled as far as Western Port Bay on the edge of Bass Strait, which separated Van Diemen's Land from the Australian mainland, reporting favourably on land they found. The news attracted the interest of Hobart grazier John Batman and his partner John Wedge, who formed a syndicate, the Port Phillip Association, and in May 1835 landed in Port Phillip Bay, looking for a suitable site for a settlement. They struck an agreement with the Kulin Aboriginal nation in exchange for food, tools, blankets and clothing. This is the only record of anyone making any kind of treaty with the Indigenous peoples in an area of settlement. Governor Bourke was opposed to the settlements and in August 1835 issued an order that the settlers were trespassers, declaring the agreement with the Aboriginal group void. He was too late to stop the flood of other pastoralists to the area. Bowing to the inevitable, Bourke began to allocate land to settlers as if it were Crown land, that is, land owned by the government. In March 1837 the settlement at the head of the Yarra was proclaimed a town and named Melbourne.

In 1824 John Oxley established a penal settlement on Moreton Bay at Redcliffe. A year later he moved it to a site on the Brisbane River where fresh water could be better guaranteed. The settlement, first named Edenglassie, was where Brisbane now stands. Free settlers began moving into the area in 1838 but Brisbane remained a penal settlement until the end of transportation in 1839.

Also in 1824, the British built a fort on Melville Island off the northern coast of Australia, near what is now Darwin, in the hope of engaging the Makassans in spice trading. No contact was made in five years and the fort

The Makassan Trepang Trade

For at least two centuries before the British settlement at Sydney Cove, traders from Makassar on the southwest coast of Sulawesi sailed to northern Australia to collect trepang (bêche-de-mer, *Holothuroidea*). Fleets of between thirty and sixty craft crewed by dozens of men took advantage of the winds of the northwest monsoon to sail to northern Australia, making landing in the Kimberley region in the north of Western Australia and in Arnhem Land in the Northern Territory. Trepang were speared in the shallow waters of the coast. They were then boiled, dried and smoked in smoke-houses of bamboo matting and palm leaves. They were carried back to Makassar for the lucrative markets of Southeast Asia.

The Makassan fleets were from the same group of families each year and formed ongoing relationships with the Aboriginal peoples of the region. The Makassans exchanged tools and food for pearl shells, beeswax and ironwood. Aboriginal people were employed to help gather and process trepang. The Makassans are credited with introducing praus – dugout canoes with sails – to the Aboriginal peoples both here and in the Torres Strait, where they also sourced trepang. The Yolŋgu words for canoe, knife and matches are all derived from the Makassan equivalent. Some Aboriginal people are said to have accompanied the trepang hunters back to Makassar and settled there. The Makassans also are credited with the introduction of tamarind trees into the Kimberley and Arnhem Land regions. The Arnhem Land word for alcohol is *nganitji* or *anitji*, both of which are similar to *anisi*, the Makassan word for an alcohol that they distilled from palm flowers.

In 1906 the South Australian government, under which the Northern Territory was at that time administered, restricted trading licences to locally owned businesses. The Makassan trade collapsed.[26]

Drying trepang, Caledon Bay, Northern Territory, c. 1934.

was abandoned. Two other attempts were made and also abandoned: at Raffles Bay on the Cobourg Peninsula in 1827, abandoned in 1829; and at Port Essington in 1838. Finally in 1869 George Goyder, Surveyor General of the colony of South Australia, established a settlement at Port Darwin.

In 1827 James Stirling, a British naval officer and colonial administrator, reconnoitred the Swan River on the west coast of Australia and proposed it as a site from which to monitor French activity in the Indian Ocean and also as a possible port from which Britain could enter into independent trade with the spice merchants in the East Indies. Under pressure from speculators such as the Sydney emancipist Solomon Levey and Thomas Peel in London, the British government agreed to allot land to investors in proportion to the capital they put forward. On 8 June 1829

Stirling proclaimed the territory of Western Australia, covering land not then included within the boundaries of New South Wales.

In England in 1829, Edward Gibbon Wakefield, a former diplomat turned social reformer, began pressing for establishing a new colony on the southern coast of Australia, where explorer Charles Sturt had found a large river flowing to the sea. Wakefield believed that Britain's social problems were a result of overpopulation and that encouraging migration to the colonies would alleviate the problem. In response to his lobbying and that also of land speculators the British government passed the South Australian Colonisation Act in 1834. In December 1836 Governor Hindmarsh proclaimed the colony of South Australia on the shore of Holdfast Bay in Gulf St Vincent, now the suburb of Glenelg.

Dining In and Out

Until permanent homes were built, the colonists cooked on an open fire using a large pot, something to hang it from and something to stir it with. Pots could be raised or lowered or moved to hotter and cooler areas of the fire as needed. Soups and one-pot stews were the most convenient meals to cook. Some root vegetables were directly cooked in the coals, as was flatbread. A sturdy pot nuzzled into the coals, with more coals on the lid, formed a simple oven for a bigger loaf. A griddle or flat iron and a frying pan sometimes supplemented the cookware. Wood was the common fuel for the better part of the nineteenth century. The food was a melange of English, Irish and Scottish dishes, reflecting the makeup of the settlers.

Permanent dwellings incorporated a fireplace of some kind, usually with a mantel and a chimney to channel the smoke out of the room. Bigger hearths may have had a spit built into the walls. Dining room, kitchen and at times sleeping quarters were usually in one room in simpler homes. Wealthier settlers built houses with separate sleeping quarters. With wealth also came the capacity to equip a kitchen with more than the basics.

In 1803 two eating houses opened in Sydney. Rosetta Stabler advertised in the *Sydney Gazette* that she 'prepares Boiled Mutton and Broths every day at 12 o'clock and a Joint of meat Roasted Always ready at One, which, from its quality and mode of serving she flatters herself will attract the Notice of the Public'.[27] A month later the paper carried an advertisement for Mann's Rooms, which provided both in-house dining and 'Dinners at home on the shortest notice; and soups, made dishes, pastries, jellies etc. sent out in a superior style.'

Water

Maintaining clean freshwater sources was a common problem as the colonies grew. In Sydney Governor Hunter issued an order to prevent people building houses and keeping hogs near the Tank Stream as early as 1795, but the area continued to be used as a rubbish dump and sewer. In 1827 the mining engineer John Busby was appointed to design and supervise construction of a tunnel to bring water from the Lachlan Swamps southeast of the settlement to a tank in Hyde Park, a distance of 4 km (2½ mi.) through rock and loose sand. The project, named Busby's Bore, took ten years to complete. Water carts carried water to householders. A severe drought in 1838–9 reduced the supply to a trickle and at its height, water from the bore cost sixpence a bucket, half the average weekly wage at the time. In 1844 the first seventy houses were connected by reticulation pipes directly to the bore at a yearly fee of 10 shillings. People could also buy water from public fountains supplied from the bore.[28]

Melbourne was established upriver from Port Phillip Bay, where fresh water could be drawn from the Yarra River at low tide. Water carters delivered water here also. Pollution of the river became an issue, as it was used for bathing and cesspits disgorged their contents into it. In Adelaide the River Torrens, too, was degraded within a matter of years. Perth was built on a series of freshwater lakes, but these were subject to flooding and the water was often described as brackish. The need for a reliable supply of clear water for drinking was one of the reasons for the abandonment of the Risdon settlement in Van Diemen's Land for the better supply coming from Mount Wellington at the Hobart site. In 1831 an aqueduct was constructed to bring water to the town. The government passed the Water Act (1835) to ensure the supply of water to Hobart after a very hot summer in 1834–5. It was the first such Act in Australia. Water was also extracted in rural and remote areas in mainland Australia from wells where the groundwater was fresh and sufficiently convenient to access, and rainwater run-off was collected in household tanks.

Alcohol

The first beer in the colony arrived with the Second Fleet in 1790, a shipment of porter, and Phillip issued the colony's first alcohol licence to its commander, Captain E. H. Bond. He, along with his first officer Thomas Reibey, began selling imported spirits and porter in Parramatta and Sydney. In 1794 John Boston, a free settler who practised as a surgeon and apothecary, was the colony's first successful brewer, using maize instead of barley and the leaves and stalks of the Cape gooseberry in lieu of hops. But it is James Squire, transported as a convicted highwayman, who is credited with being the first to brew on a commercial scale. He began with small amounts based on maize and barley, which he sold at fourpence a quart. In 1875 he was granted 12 ha (30 ac) at Kissing Point on the Parramatta River, where he planted hops and built a brewery and tavern. John Mills, an emancipist, was Melbourne's first brewer. The quality of these beers was variable: the first hops and barley were of poor quality, higher temperatures accelerated fermentation, and contamination was a risk in the rough conditions in which beer was brewed. Until the advent of refrigeration it was difficult to keep beer cool.[29]

The climate in the Sydney colony was not conducive to hop growing, but it was in Van Diemen's Land. Hops had been grown there before the 1820s, and in 1825 William Shoobridge, a free-settler hop-grower from Kent, England, set the industry there on its feet from his Providence Valley farm with his first marketable crop. Peter Degraves and his brother-in-law, Major Macintosh, established the Cascade Brewery in Hobart in 1832.

In 1790 James Larra was given land at Parramatta on his emancipation and established an inn there serving French-inspired food. Melbourne's first public house was established by J. P. Fawkner, who imported his beer from Launceston, Van Diemen's Land. Sarah Bird, an emancipist, became the first woman licensee in 1797. She opened the Three Jolly Settlers in Sydney. By 1815, twelve of the 96 public houses in Sydney were in female hands.[30]

In 1791 Philip Schaffer, a German free settler, was granted 56 ha (140 ac) of land outside Parramatta, which he called The Vineyard. His father was a vigneron in Germany and Shaffer planted wine grapes along with the

The Melbourne Brewery and Distillery, 1875.

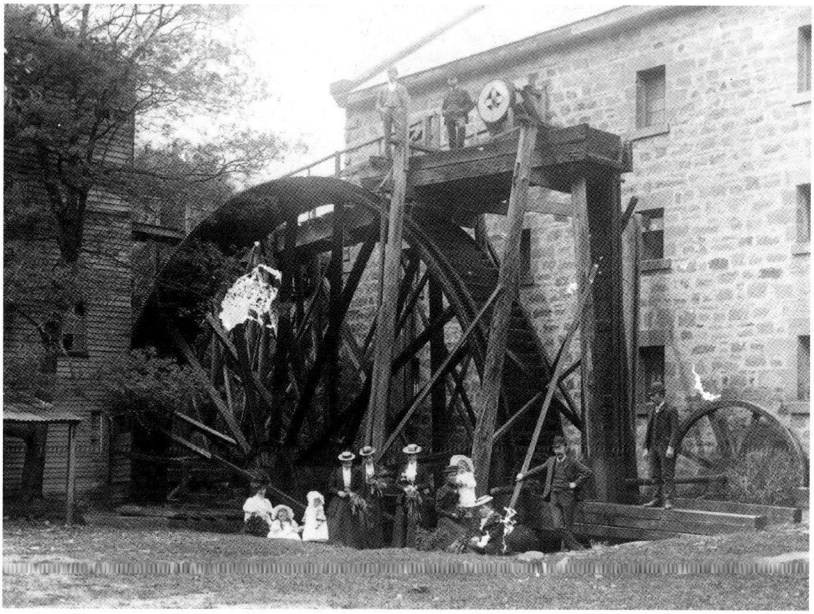

Waterwheel at Degraves' and Macintosh's Cascade Brewery, Tasmania.

usual mix of grain crops. In 1795 he produced 10 litres of wine, the first in the colony. He sold his property two years later and stopped making wine. The property would eventually be bought by the Catholic Church, whose nuns grew grapes and made altar wine there until the 1960s.

In 1816–18 Gregory Blaxland planted vines at Brush Farm near Parramatta. He was awarded a silver medal by the Royal Society for the Arts in 1823 for his fortified wine and won a gold medal in 1827. The Macarthurs had planted vines at Camden and Penrith and were producing as much as 20,000 gallons by 1827.[31] By 1823 some 8 ha (20 ac) of vineyards had already been planted on the northern banks of the Hunter River to the north of Sydney. In 1825 James Busby, who had studied viticulture in France, wrote *A Treatise on the Culture of the Vine and the Art of Making Wine*. Busby's brother-in-law was the winemaker on his property in the Hunter Valley. Australia's first wine-growing association, the Hunter River Vineyard Association, was established in 1847.

Orchardists in the other colonies were also planting vines in the 1820s. In Van Diemen's Land Bartholomew Broughton had a small vineyard at Prospect Farm on the banks of the Derwent River. Vines were planted at Fremantle soon after colonists arrived in Western Australia. They were planted in the Yarra Valley in Victoria from 1838. In the 1840s German settlers planted the first vines in the Barossa Valley in South Australia.

The 'Rum Rebellion'

When Arthur Phillip and his men hoisted the British flag to proclaim the colony of Sydney, their toast to King George III was made with rum. Rum was an entrenched part of the British navy diet, with sailors guaranteed a daily ration. British currency was scarce in the colony, and rum became the preferred means of payment for food, clothing and other goods. Control of the rum trade was in the hands of the New South Wales Corps under the command of Francis Grose, who had charge of the colony on Phillip's departure.

John Macarthur was a member of the Corps and had become wealthy and influential. Grose granted Macarthur large areas of land and appointed him to several important positions in the colony when he retired from the Corps. The next two governors, Hunter and King, both clashed with Macarthur and also unsuccessfully tried to stop the Corp's monopoly of trade. William Bligh became governor in 1806 and immediately sought to curb Macarthur's power and threatened to take back his lands. Matters came to a head when Bligh sought to have Macarthur brought to trial over an incident involving one of Macarthur's trading ships.

The jury of Corps officers refused to recognize the authority of the court. Bligh countered by saying he would charge them with treason. The Commanding Officer of the Corps, George Johnston, wanted Bligh removed from office.

In the first decades of colonization it was not illegal to supply alcohol to Aboriginals. Alcohol was frequently used as payment for work and sex, and to encourage drunkenness and fighting for the colonists' amusement. In 1838 the first law was passed prohibiting the supply of alcohol to Aboriginals.

Squatters and the Frontier Wars

By the late eighteenth century, settlers were urging the government to expand the Sydney settlement. Its long-term viability depended on finding

The arrest of Governor Bligh, 1808.

On the evening of 26 January 1808 the men of the Corps marched to Government House and arrested Bligh, who, legend says, was found hiding under a bed. Johnston took over command of the colony.

The situation rapidly descended into farce. Bligh was under house arrest for a year, refusing to return to Britain until a new governor arrived. In March 1809 he agreed to return but instead sailed to Hobart where he hoped Lieutenant-Governor Collins would help him. Collins refused; Bligh sailed back to Sydney arriving just when Governor Macquarie had taken control of the colony.

better soil than at Sydney Cove. New and larger pasturelands were needed for the burgeoning flocks of sheep, which were beginning to be a lucrative industry following John Macarthur's success breeding high-quality merino sheep for export to a wool-starved Britain. The cattle-herds were growing both to provide the meat and dairy products that the colonists saw as essential to their survival and for salting and canning for export. In January 1794 Governor Grose approved the settlement of the Hawkesbury River area by a group of emancipists and free settlers.

At that time the colony was rife with rumours of vast well-watered plains on the other side of the Great Dividing Range, the mountain range stretching along the eastern coast of Australia. In 1813 Gregory Blaxland, William Lawson and William Charles Wentworth made a successful crossing of the mountains and confirmed the rumours, leading to a land grab on the Macquarie Plains and the establishing of Bathurst, the first inland town. In 1828–9 Charles Sturt explored the courses of the Macquarie, Bogan and Castlereagh rivers, tracing them to where they joined the Darling, so answering a question that had long been pondered by the colonists as to where the inland rivers went and further encouraging dreams of wealth creation from large runs for sheep and cattle.

Up until the 1820s it was possible for someone to set out with a small herd, find a vast acreage, chart it, leave the herd there with a caretaker, return to Sydney and claim the land for free. Those who did became called squatters. For agricultural workers displaced by the British Enclosure Acts the lure of this unfettered land-grab is clear. Successive governors became alarmed at the loss of revenue to the Crown. Governor Darling was attracted to Edward Gibbon Wakefield's proposal for establishing a colony in South Australia through the sale of land and subsidized selective migration. However, he saw that this could not be rolled out in New South Wales, where charging a premium for land would have halted the wool industry. Yet the basic outline was attractive, and in 1831 he set about putting it in place. A great arc surrounding the established colonies at a distance was drawn on the map declaring the area within it Crown land – that is, land belonging to the monarch and controlled by the monarch's representative, in this case the governor of a colony – with 5 shillings an acre as the purchase price. The area was limited because while the government wanted to gain revenue from the land it also needed to be able to maintain control of the settlers and so had to enclose the land within reasonable horse-travel time from the main towns.[32]

The government and squatters were proceeding to claim land in the first instance on the same basis that Cook had proclaimed Australia for Britain in 1770: that Australia was *terra nullius*, a land belonging to no one. The Indigenous clans whose land was thus stolen of course saw it differently. What they saw was the loss of grassland as fodder for cattle and sheep and being cleared for wheat fields, waterholes and rivers being fouled by the herds, the clearing of open forests they had built up over millennia as part of their management of their marsupial meat sources, competition for that meat at times, disregard for long-established clan-based ownership of the land and so the resources on it, and disregard for their cultural and social practices.

It was inevitable that these competing claims would lead to conflict. In September 1794 a Hawkesbury settler and his servant were killed by a party of Aboriginals and food and clothing was taken. A few days later the settlers retaliated, killing seven or eight of the Aboriginals they hunted down.[33] The Frontier Wars had begun. In 1814, at Appin, south of Sydney, Gandangara people from the Blue Mountains came to their traditional foraging lands. A fight ensued and four were killed. Governor Macquarie ordered the capture of the Gandangara. Instead, at least fourteen Aboriginal men, women and children were killed.[34] In 1861 at Parachilna, in the Flinders Ranges of South Australia, a party of Aboriginals had gathered at a waterhole. A shepherd came to the waterhole with a large flock of sheep. The Aboriginal men stopped the sheep from fouling the water, killing three sheep. In retaliation, settlers from the nearby town killed three Aboriginal men.[35]

Estimates of the number of Aboriginal peoples killed in the Frontier Wars between 1788 and the mid-1930s range from 20,000 to 30,000. Estimates of colonists killed range between 2,000 and 5,000. The weaponry used were disproportionately effective: the settlers had rifles, while the Aboriginals had only spears and clubs. In some cases settlers poisoned waterholes; in others, poison-laced flour was given directly to Aboriginals, or left out as bait.

In the single most calculated attempt at control, Governor George Arthur in 1830, with a force of more than 2,200 settlers, military and convicts, began to march across the whole of the settled area of Van Diemen's Land to force the Palawa, the Aboriginal people of the island, onto the Tasman Peninsula in the southeast of the island. The Black Line, as it was called, was a spectacular failure: only two Aboriginals were reported captured and two more were killed of an estimated three hundred living on the island at the time. By 1832 those who remained were relocated to Flinders' Island in Bass Strait, ostensibly for their protection, but mainly under pressure from the settlers. In 1847 some ninety were still surviving, and they were repatriated to mainland Tasmania.

In 1988 a group of archaeologists led by John Mulvaney estimated that in 1788 there were between 750,000 and 800,000 Aboriginals living in Australia. There is a consensus that by 1850 this had been reduced to 200,000. Deaths due to resource loss – both the loss of productive members of Aboriginal groups and of land from which food was obtained – is estimated at 120,000. Other major causes of deaths were European-introduced diseases, particularly smallpox and chickenpox.[36]

FOUR

Golden Soil and Wealth for Toil, 1851–99

When Peter Dodds McCormick wrote the words of this chapter's title in his song 'Advance Australia Fair' in 1878, he was lyrically capturing what many Australians undoubtedly felt about the country. Improvements in transport dispelled what the historian Geoffrey Blainey called the 'tyranny of distance', both within the country and to world markets.[1] Australian pastoralists and farmers were able to capitalize on the latter, aided by Australian-pioneered freezing and farming technologies. Australia's Gross Domestic Product was outstripping even that of Britain. And it all began with gold.

Gold

The assistant surveyor James McBrien reported the first gold in Australia in 1823 in the sand of the Fish River east of the inland town of Bathurst in New South Wales. Two subsequent finds were reported by Pawel Strzelecki in 1839 near Hartley and in 1841 by Reverend W. B. Clarke at Cox's River, both sites being on the way to the inland town of Bathurst. By June 2,000 prospectors had headed to the Bathurst-Orange area. The first claim to be recognized in Victoria was that of James Esmond at Clunes in 1850. In quick succession gold was found at Ballarat (1851), Castlemaine (1851) and Bendigo (1852), all in the Central Highlands of Victoria. In Queensland, the major finds were at Canoona near Rockhampton (1858) and the Palmer River on the Cape York Peninsula (1873). Gold was discovered at several sites in Western Australia during the 1890s and by the end of the decade a third of its population were prospecting.

Life on the goldfields was as varied an experience as the backgrounds of the prospectors. Tents were the most common form of accommodation, usually a piece of canvas thrown over a rough timber frame and pegged to the ground. Cooking took place on an open fire outside the tent. The wealthier prospectors had roomier tents with a mudbrick fireplace and chimney at one end. Others built rough bark shacks. Most prospectors lived on basic staples of flour, mutton or beef, sugar and tea. Fresh vegetables were rare and expensive when in stock. But for the monied there were stores where they could buy luxury goods. William Kelly, one of the many migrants to Victoria who flocked to the goldfields, dined on 'the beef and mutton of Victoria, the bread of South Australia, the butter of ould Erin, the coffee of Ceylon, the sugar of Mauritius, the tea of China – while the ham of York, the marmalade of Scotland, the sardines of France, the condiments of India, were only waiting for a beckon to jump down our throats from the surrounding shelves'.[2]

The impact of this sudden surge of population was felt in the cities and towns that supplied the goldfields. Agricultural labourers headed for the goldfields and between 1851 and 1853 land under cultivation was reduced by 40 per cent. The impact of this was to create shortages in basic foods such as wheat.[3]

When the prospectors hit the colonies' capitals the distinction between those who had done well and those who had not spilled over

Mine shaft at the Victorian goldfields.

into where, and what, they ate. The more cashed-up could dine at restaurants where the bill of fare was heavily influenced by French chefs. At the Union Hotel in Melbourne, writes the food historian Charmaine O'Brien, 'Patrons enjoyed a menu of classical French dishes; julienne soup, potage a la reine, fricassee, vol-au-vent, salamis du perdreau, omelettes, souffles, and truffles au vin champagne.'[4] For those with less cash in their pockets there were the fourpenny and sixpenny restaurants where 'the diner received a full meal, which usually comprised a generous quantity of meat, gravy and bread. The meat was either grilled steak or chops, roast mutton or beef, corned beef, curried mutton, Irish stew or sausages. Vegetable accompaniments, when offered, were usually limited to potatoes and cabbage.'[5]

The Chinese On and Off the Goldfields

The earliest recorded Chinese migrant to the colony of New South Wales was Mak Sai Ying (also known as John Shying) who arrived from Canton (Guangdong) in 1818 as a free settler. He bought land in Parramatta and worked as a carpenter and cabinet maker. He subsequently became the publican of the Golden Lion Hotel in Parramatta.

While there may have been other individual Chinese people resident in the colony, the first significant migration was between 1848 and 1853, when indentured labourers from Fujian (Xiamen) arrived to work for private landowners. By 1854 opposition to them as cheap labour was

Mei Quong Tart

Mei Quong Tart migrated from Canton to New South Wales at the age of nine with his uncle, who was bringing a group of Chinese miners for the goldfields at Araluen and Braidwood in the Southern Highlands of New South Wales. In Braidwood he first lived with Thomas Forsyth, a Scottish storekeeper, in the village of Bells Creek, where he acquired a love of all things Scottish, including affecting the accent, dressing in kilts, playing the bagpipes, and dancing the Highland fling. He was a successful investor in the local goldmines, converted to Christianity and became a British subject in 1871.

In 1881 he returned to China and made connections with tea merchants there. Returning to Sydney, he began importing tea and silk. He started to hold tea tastings in his shop, giving customers attractive Chinese crockery as gifts. The tastings became so popular that he opened the first tearoom in Sydney, serving tea, cakes, sandwiches and scones. He did not serve any Chinese dishes. By 1885 he had six tearooms in Sydney – one of which, the Loon Shan Teahouse, had marbled fountains and ponds with carp as features. In 1898 he opened the Elite Dining Hall, which sat five hundred in the newly completed Queen Victoria Building, a grand sandstone and stained-glass shopping edifice in the centre of Sydney.

In 1886 he married Margaret Scarlett, an English woman. They had four daughters who were the first non-European students at the prestigious Presbyterian Ladies College at Croydon, near where the family lived in the gentrified suburb of Ashfield in Sydney.

Mei Quong Tart and his wife Margaret.

sufficiently strong in Victoria that a Select Committee on Asiatic Labour of the Legislative Council of Victoria was tasked with investigating the impact. The Committee concluded that there was no need for any action at that time.

News of gold in New South Wales and Victoria found its way back to the rural communities in the Canton Delta, the large area of fertile land around the estuary of the Pearl River (Chu Kiang). The region was coming under increasing pressure from overpopulation, heavy taxation levied on the farmers and food shortages. The goldfields held out the lure of a quick fortune. The Chinese who arrived at the goldfields were overwhelmingly male (it was culturally not acceptable for wives or single women to leave the family) and were expected to remit money back to their families. Passage could be paid for by families pooling finances or borrowing, or by advances from Chinese merchants in the colony who often would exploit the migrant.

In 1854 the first census in Victoria counted only 2,341 Chinese. By mid-1855 numbers had swelled to 17,000. By 1860 there were around 40,000 Chinese migrants across all the colonies. Accommodating, provisioning and feeding the new arrivals presented opportunities on and off the goldfields. In Melbourne and Sydney, lodging houses, importers and cookshops concentrated in what would become their Chinatowns. On the goldfields, too, cookshops opened serving not only the Chinese miners but those looking for an alternative to mutton and damper. John Alloo (Chin Thum Lok), who had arrived in Australia in 1844, established a restaurant at Bakery Hill, Ballarat, serving European-style dishes to the mining community. On the goldfields some Chinese migrants began small market gardens, providing one of the few sources of fresh vegetables to the prospecting communities. Others ran 'sly grog shanties', unlicensed liquor outlets selling poor-quality beverages. In Melbourne the Chinese began a trade in salting and drying fish not considered edible by non-Chinese residents of the Australian colonies. Salted and dried fish were packed in hessian bags and pickled fish were stored in timber casks ready for transport to Chinese communities of miners, market gardeners and businesspeople throughout the Australian colonies.

Resentment towards the Chinese population, who were seen as competition for employment, continued to fester. The Victorian parliament passed legislation levying £10 on every Chinese migrant and restricting the number of Chinese migrants that ships entering Port Phillip could carry. The Chinese got around both regulations by disembarking in Robe, on the coast of South Australia, and walking overland to the central Victorian goldfields.

Resentment turned to violence. On 4 July 1857 European miners in the Buckland Valley in Victoria attacked the Chinese settlements there, beating and robbing the settlers and destroying a joss house. The ringleaders were tried but acquitted of all charges. On 30 June 1861 a 2,000-strong party of European miners attacked Chinese miners at Lambing Flat and Back Creek in New South Wales. No one was killed. In both states, governments tried to resolve the tensions by quarantining the Chinese prospectors into separate areas of the goldfields.

With the end of the gold rushes in the 1860s most of the miners returned to China. Some went to the new goldfields in Queensland. When that rush ended, many headed to the coast at Cooktown, Cairns and Innisfail. Here they were the first to plant bananas, pineapples and sugar cane, beginning what would become major rural industries in Queensland and northern New South Wales. Others set up small businesses and became market gardeners or cooks on outstations and with droving teams. Chinese hawkers shouldering panniers of fresh vegetables became a common sight in Melbourne and Sydney.

Paddlewheels, Steamers and Rails

For the first 75 years of settlement the colonists relied on horses and carts, or bullock teams for carriage. However, as settlement pushed inland, the cost of sending goods by bullock team rose: the time taken to get goods to the ports grew longer, and the teams had to contend with the vagaries of the weather.

Australia has only one river system navigable into the interior, the Murray–Darling system. In 1853 William Russell and Francis Cadell successfully won the South Australian government's competition to navigate the Murray stretch of the river, showing that goods could be transported along its length. Soon paddle steamers were carrying wool, hides, tallow, timber, bulk station supplies and farming equipment back and forth from the Murray mouth in South Australia 2,735 km (1,700 mi.) up the river, near the goldfields of northeastern Victoria, and 3,220 km (2,000 mi.) up the Darling River in New South Wales. Additional cargo was carried in barges towed behind. Some were set up as travelling stores serving isolated properties. But the usability of the system was limited: the rivers were shallow, meandering, with big fluctuations in flow and navigable

The paddle steamer *Shannon* operated on the Murray river from 1877 to 1894.

for only seven to eight months each year. Boats were stranded upriver waiting for flood waters to re-float them. They also were held up for weeks at a time when trees fell into the river and the snags had to be cleared. The ongoing battle with the weather, the unpredictability of the rivers and the coming of railways led to decline in the river trade. By the 1930s there were about thirty steamers left, and the trade had stopped entirely by the 1960s.

In the early 1850s Australia had no inland pastoral town or farming area important enough to justify a railway to the coast.[6] By 1850, however, with the squatting of the sheep- and cattle-grazing lands, rapid growth in the size of herds and the establishment of inland towns with populations needing goods and services, the economics of building rail links between these towns and the major ports was now attractive. 'The first railways built from a port to serve a pastoral area reached Echuca (Victoria) in 1864, Toowoomba (Queensland) in 1867, and Goulburn (New South Wales) in 1869.'[7] Tracks were laid to the goldfields at Ballarat and Bendigo in 1862.

It wasn't only pastoralists and gold prospectors who benefited from railway construction. In South Australia, ports on Spencer Gulf and Gulf St Vincent had short spur lines into the wheatbelt that made the state the major granary for Australia from the 1850s to the 1870s. Similarly, rail opened up wheatbelts in the northern and western plains of Victoria, the western plains of New South Wales, and those in southern Queensland and in southwest Western Australia. As the yield increased and could be transported speedily to ports, Australia became a major supplier of wheat to European markets.

Where the rails did not go, camels did. Some 25 camels had arrived in the country in 1860 to carry supplies for the ill-fated expedition of Robert O'Hara Burke and Edward Wills to the Gulf of Carpentaria in northern Australia. (Both died on the return journey.) Then, in 1866, a shipment of 127 camels and their handlers arrived in Port Augusta, South Australia, marking the beginning of commercial South Asian merchants' ventures into the remotest areas of central Australia. While most came from Afghanistan, others were Bengali with businesses in Calcutta.[8] Camels were better suited to the arid centre than horses and bullocks: trains of as many as seventy animals carried food, furniture, medicines, and mining and building materials, including material for the north–south railway now called The Ghan. The cameleers lived in Ghantowns, separated parts of small remote settlements like Marree in South Australia. A camel-breeding station was established at Beltana in the Flinders Ranges, north of Adelaide. Abandoned tin mosques still stand in some towns. By the early 1920s motor vehicles had replaced camel trains.

When goods for export got to the ports, the challenge was to overcome Australia's isolation from the European markets. The sailing time to Australia from Britain in 1850 on average, weather permitting, was four months. Ship owners looked for shorter routes and faster ships. The watchmaker-turned-armchair-navigator John Towson published *Tables for Facilitating the Practice of Great Circle Sailing* in 1849, showing that the

Camel train in Sylvester Street, Coolgardie.

shortest route across the Atlantic and directly to Melbourne was to follow the Great Circle of the 68th parallel of latitude and get the benefit of the Roaring Forties, gale-force winds that blow from the west throughout the year between the latititudes 40 degrees and 50 degrees in the Southern Hemisphere. At the same time American clipper ships were breaking all records for sailing vessels. The two, when combined, dramatically cut the sailing time to Australia. In 1854 the *James Baines*, operated by the Black Ball Line, made the journey from Liverpool to Melbourne in 65 days and the return trip in 69½ days. But it was when the first fully steam-powered ships began plying the routes that time and distance began to be of little consequence. The *Aberdeen* sailed from England in 1881, called at Cape Town for coal, and reached Melbourne after only 42 days.

The Goyder Line

The pushes to open up more and more land for farming often resulted in disaster. In November 1864, in the middle of a severe drought, George Goyder, Surveyor General of South Australia, was tasked with mapping a boundary in the state demarking areas that received good rainfall from those that were more likely to be affected by drought. In 1872 the Waste Lands Alienation Act drew a boundary from east to west based on areas with an average rainfall of 250 mm (10 in.). Good rains in the early 1870s led to pressure on the South Australian government to release more land. The Act was repealed in 1874 and farmers could buy land on credit in the drought-prone areas above the Goyder Line. When rainfall failed in the 1880s, so did the farms. By the end of the century they had been abandoned.[9]

From Drip Safes to Refrigeration

Keeping food for any length of time in the colonies, particularly meat and dairy products, was challenging. Salting and drying meat was one option. Another option was using a drip-safe to keep raw meat and other perishable products cool. These were made of an upright wooden frame covered with hessian, kept damp by soaking its ends in a tray of water. As the water evaporated from the hessian, heat was drawn from the inside of the safe, keeping the meat cool.[10] In the late 1890s Arthur Patrick McCormick developed this into the iconic Coolgardie Safe, which kept food cool as well as protecting it from insects and scavengers.

In 1839 the *Tartar* carried to Sydney 250 tonnes of ice (reportedly 400 tonnes had been sent, with nearly half melting on the journey) and 22 ice boxes. The ice came from Boston, one of the American eastern seaboard cities which engaged in what was called the 'frozen water trade'. The whole cargo was bought by Thomas Dunsdon, a confectioner, who began selling the ice at threepence per pound but increased the price to sixpence as the ice melted and became a rare commodity. Ice was transported upriver to Parramatta and by small boat to Newcastle, the port to the north of Sydney at the head of the Hunter River. The end of the imported frozen-water trade in Australia came with the first successful ice-making plant, built by James Harrison at Geelong, Victoria, in 1851. But most people lived too far from ice suppliers to make carting ice practicable. Ice was also expensive. Philip Muskett, writing in 1893 in *The Art of Living in Australia*, wrote:

> The mass of the people – I am not referring to those who are well endowed with worldly gifts – are apt to look upon the ice chest as a luxury which is altogether beyond their means. But, as I have said elsewhere, I am firmly persuaded that if the price of ice were brought down to one half-penny per pound . . . it would be a great boon.[11]

The Coolgardie Safe kept food cold using evaporation.

In the 1890s the Newport freezing works in Melbourne exported as many as 5,000 meat carcasses a day.

In the mid-1870s the merchant Thomas Mort and French engineer Eugène Nicolle developed a domestic ice-making machine, and in 1884 Hudson Brothers Ltd, also in Sydney, introduced a domestic refrigerator. But it was not until after the First World War that domestic refrigerators began to take their place in Australian kitchens.

Frozen meat from Australia being unloaded at Millwall Docks, London, late 19th century.

As transport by sea became faster, Mort's thoughts turned to how the emerging technology could be used to keep food frozen for export. In 1872 Mort and Nicolle installed an ammonia refrigeration system on the *Northam* to send frozen beef to England as part of its cargo. The project failed when the ammonia proved difficult to control, and the ship sailed without the meat. In November 1880 the Melbourne-based Australian Frozen Meat Co. successfully transported 4,000 frozen carcasses of sheep and 100 tonnes of butter on the SS *Protos* from Melbourne to London using compressed air technology. In 1885 W. D. Peacock of Hobart was successful with cool storage of fruit and was soon shipping apples to England. Soon, other entrepreneurs were installing refrigerating machines and cold chambers to carry chilled and frozen goods from Australia and New Zealand to England. Freezing works and cold stores were built at ports.

Meat Three Times a Day

Philip Muskett was among the first to publish dietary advice to Australians. 'It is evident,' he wrote, 'that the natural dietary of the earth's inhabitants is controlled largely by the particular region in which they dwell.'[12] Comparing the mean annual temperature of Australia's principal cities of the time with cities at corresponding latitudes in Europe, he concluded that the Australian diet, with its preponderance of meat, was out of keeping with what should be its climate-appropriate diet, one more like those of southern European and Mediterranean locales.

It was no wonder that meat, both beef and mutton, should figure so prominently in the diet of the colonists; it was plentiful and cheap. Richard Twopeny, in his 1893 book *Town Life in Australia*, wrote: 'A working-man whose whole family did not eat meat three times a day would indeed be a phenomenon. High and low, rich and poor, all eat meat to an incredible extent, even in the hottest weather.'[13] However,

Australian meat canners played on the fears of Britain's rinderpest outbreak in 1863 to increase sales of their products.

> While the working man's food is here immeasurably better and cheaper . . . the richer man who asks for more than soundness in the quality of his food, finds himself worse off than in London. Meat of the same quality as he gets at his club in Pall Mall is not to be got in Collins Street [Melbourne] for love or money.[14]

He put the inferior quality of the meat in the cities down to the sheep and cattle having to be driven on hoof long distances to the slaughterhouses. Twopeny was scathing about Australian cookery:

> The meat is roast or boiled, hot or cold, sometimes fried or hashed. It is not helped in mere slices, but in good substantial hunks. In everything the colonist likes quantity . . . I once heard a colonist say 'I don't like your nasty little English slices of meat: *we* want something that you can put our teeth into.'[15]

By 1880 there were 7.5 million cattle and nearly 100 million sheep.[16] There was plenty for domestic consumption and plenty left over for export. In another of those serendipitous moments in Australian food history, the year 1863 saw European cattle herds devastated by rinderpest, a viral disease of cattle and other ruminants, and England was no exception. Charles Grant Tindal, a highly successful Australian cattle and horse breeder, had returned to live in London in 1862 where he was following developments in canning meat. Seizing the opportunity provided by the rinderpest outbreak, he set up the Australia Meat Co. and began importing canned meat from Australia and meat extract (or 'beef tea', a type of broth). By 1871 the company was exporting 5 tonnes of canned meats each week to Britain. Other meat-canning companies quickly followed in capital cities around Australia, also producing meat extract, tallow and other side products. The Sydney Meat Co., established in 1869, exported tendons to Japan and manufactured blood and bone fertilizer, most of which went to Mauritius.[17]

As European herds recovered, demand for Australian meat declined. It was cheaper and quicker to import canned meat from America. By the end of the 1880s refrigerated meat also was becoming a more competitive product.

Acclimatization Woes

By 1880 every state had formed an Acclimatisation Society to import into the country plants and animals from across the British Empire that would, in their members' views, beautify the landscape and provide opportunities for hunting and fishing familiar game. The impact on foodways was in several instances disastrous.

The blackberry (*Rubus fruticosus*) is a declared noxious weed: its invasive habits have deleterious impacts on watercourses, orchards, pastures and plantations. It also increases fire hazard as it collects large amounts of dead material that is difficult to clear. Lantana (*Lantana camara*) is similarly destructive.

Prickly pears (*Opuntia stricta*) arrived with the First Fleet, along with the cochineal beetle (*Dactylopius coccus*), to establish a dyeing industry. The industry failed and the prickly pear began to be used as fencing and quickly became widespread, turning land unproductive. The cactus moth (*Cactoblastis cactorum*), whose larvae eat prickly pear, was introduced in 1925 to eradicate the cactus, with limited success.

The fox was introduced for hunting in the 1860s and quickly became established in the wild, where it continues to

Motor lorry loaded with 1,760 pairs of rabbits.

Prickly pear (*Opuntia stricta*), introduced for the cochineal-dye industry, soon spread, destroying valuable pastureland.

destroy sheep and native fauna. The most successful import was also the most disastrous – the rabbit. Wild populations were released in Tasmania, Victoria and South Australia in the 1820s but rapidly spread. By the 1920s it is estimated that there were 1 billion rabbits. Rabbit warrens led to soil erosion, with its associated impact on vegetation and watercourses, and were a hazard for cattle and sheep. The rabbits also selectively grazed some plant species on which native and domesticated animals fed. In 1907 a six-year project to build a rabbit-proof fence 3,256 km (2,025 mi.) across Western Australia was completed. The fence was made of timber posts and wire netting that extended 150 mm (6 in.) into the ground. In 1950 a strain of the *Myxoma* virus was released into rabbit populations, with lethal results. However, in a short space of time rabbits developed a resistance to the virus. The RHDV1 strain of the rabbit haemorrhagic disease virus (*Calicivirus*) was first released in Australia in 1996. Over time its effectiveness also decreased, and a new strain was introduced in 2017.

Cookery Instruction

The first cookery book published in Australia was by Alfred J. Wilkinson, chef de cuisine at the Athenaeum Club in Melbourne, who published *The Australian Cook: A Complete Manual of Cookery Suitable for the Australian Colonies with Special Reference to the Gas Stove* in 1876.[18] The recipes do not reflect any attempt at an Australian cuisine, however, containing dishes like those that could have been found at a gentlemen's club in Britain. The book enthusiastically supported the new gas cookers, introduced to Melbourne in 1873 by R. A. Walker and to Sydney by the Australia Gaslight Co. at about the same time. The latter company was the first of its kind, founded in 1837 by Ralph Mansfield. At the Intercolonial Exhibition in Melbourne in 1875, five Australian manufacturers displayed gas cookers. Gas supply companies began to hold public demonstrations promoting them as clean, convenient, labour-saving and economical. Having cookbooks that showed women how to cook pre-existing recipes using gas became part of the promotional tools.

Mina Rawson began writing cookery books to supplement the income her family was making from a fishing business in Mackay, Queensland. She

'Australian Kitchen' from Mrs Isabella Beeton, *Mrs Beeton's Book of Household Management* (*c*. 1880).

was canny enough to have her first book, the 1878 *Queensland Cookery and Poultry Book*, sell for 3 shillings, which she said in her preface was for those who could not afford a 'Mrs Beeton'. In *The Antipodean Cookery Book and Kitchen Companion* (1895) she empathized with the 'far Bush housewife [who] is very often at her wits end to know what to do for a change of diet. If a time of drought, or should there be no vegetable garden attached to the station, she has generally to fall back upon preserved and tinned vegetables.' Her suggestion was that the bush housewife turn to native produce – young pigweed for salads, witchetty grubs, locusts, iguana, snakes and marsupials. She wrote that she was 'beholden to the blacks for nearly all my knowledge of the different edible ground game'.[19] 'There were endless experiments in preparing "bush tucker"', Mary Durack recalled in her history of the Durack pastoralist dynasty. 'Grandmother did her best with kangaroo, emu and even under strong persuasion, with lizard, but she put her foot down when it came to snakes, frogs and witchetty grubs, which Grandfather insisted were delicacies if cooked on hot coals as the blacks advised.'[20]

The first half of Philip Muskett's *The Art of Living in Australia* is taken up with what would these days be called gastronomic essays. In Chapter Nine, 'Australian Food Habits and Their Faults – A Plea for Their Improvement', he seeks to 'direct attention to the great neglect there is of vegetables, especially those of the more unknown varieties, as an agreeable, desirable, palatable, and salutary element in the Australian food life'.[21] He

Trade card for the Queen's Hotel run by Hannah and Donald Maclurcan during the 1890s.

The Granny Smith Apple

In 1868 Mary Ann Smith found an interesting seedling coming up among the apples in her backyard in Ryde, a suburb of Sydney, which she believed had grown from the remains of some French crab-apples she had tossed out. Unbeknown to her the seeds were mutants that would surprise her with a completely new form of apple: a hard, light-green-skinned, crisp and tartish variety that yellows as it ages.

Smith began growing the cultivar and shared her find with other orchardists in Sydney. Edward Gallard was one of them. When Smith died in 1870, Gallard bought her farm and began to market the apple. In 1890 Gallard exhibited apples called 'Smith's Seedlings' at the Castle Hill Agricultural and Horticultural Show, and in 1891 the fruit won first prize for cooking apples under the name 'Granny Smith's Seedling'. It was the fruit's high acidity and ability to hold its shape when baked that were its winning features.

Its popularity as a cooking apple spread and in 1895 the New South Wales Department of Agriculture began growing trees at its Bathurst Experiment Farm with a view to exporting it. The apple remains a favourite Australian fruit.

The Granny Smith apple is valued for its slight tartness and holds its shape well when cooked in a pie.

Jugged Wallaby

Hannah Maclurcan

1 small wallaby
Butter
2 small onions
Bunch of sweet herbs
Black pepper
Cloves
1 tablespoonful red currant jelly
2 glasses of port wine
1 lemon

Cut the wallaby into nice sized pieces, flour and fry them in a little butter until nice and brown, put them in a jar with the herbs (tied together), the onions sliced, and the cloves (about a dozen), half a teaspoonful black pepper and a teaspoonful of salt, cover with water, slice half the lemon and add the juice of the other half, put the jar in a saucepan of water, keep it closed very tight and allow it to cook for four hours; be sure you keep the saucepan full of boiling water. Melt the jelly, add to the port wine, and about half an hour before serving put in in the jar, thicken with a little browned flour. Serve with red currant jelly.[22]

goes on to list and describe the uses of vegetables he thinks should be taken up: Jerusalem artichokes, asparagus, Brussels sprouts, cardoon, eggplant (aubergine), kohl rabi, salsify, scorzonera (a Spanish plant he describes as similar to salsify), sea kale and sweetcorn. He is also critical of 'the crude cookery that is bestowed on the ordinary vegetables . . . monotony in an endless recurrence of boiled potatoes, boiled cabbage, boiled this and boiled that'.[23] The second half of Muskett's book is a collection of recipes from Mrs Harriett Wicken, who at the time of publication was lecturing in cookery at the Technical College in Sydney. Her recipes for vegetables suggest that what was available was far removed from this adventurous list: potatoes, cabbage, green peas, French beans, cauliflower, marrow, beetroot, tomatoes, onions, parsnips, haricot beans, celery, leeks and lentils. And despite Muskett's decrying, Wicken advances little past the 'monotony' of boiling, often for as long as twenty minutes. Even when she includes globe artichokes and tender pumpkin leaves as 'imitation' spinach, she boils them. If not boiled, vegetables are baked, sautéed or drowned in white sauce.[24]

Hannah Maclurcan, the author of *Mrs Maclurcan's Cookery Book*, published in 1898, also stays generally with the familiar vegetables and ways of preparing them, with three interesting exceptions: brinjaw or egg fruit (aubergines here given a corruption of the Hindi word for them – brinjal), which she bakes or grills; just off-ripe pawpaw, which she bakes, boils or makes into a pie; and chokos, the choyote or vegetable pear, which she suggests should be sliced, crumbed and fried. Maclurcan was a hotel proprietor in Townville, north Queensland, and undoubtedly the inclusion of these vegetables reflects the influence of Indian and Pacific Islander communities who had come to Townsville to work on the sugarcane plantations.

Cookery books would have been of little use to the young Irish women being employed as domestic staff in middle-class households. Many of them were orphaned by the Great Famine of 1845–9 and recruited from workhouses where they eked out a living. Their passage to Australia was paid by colonial governments through the funds raised by the sale of Crown lands. They were subject to sustained prejudice by the free settlers residing in the colonies. Richard Twopeny voiced the popular opinion: 'Unfortunately, four-fifths of our servants are Irish – liars and dirty . . . Your Irish immigrant at eight and ten shillings a week has as often as not never been inside any other household than her native hovel, and stares in astonishment to find that you don't keep a pig on your drawing-room sofa.'[25] It was true that the girls were not generally educated and had little or no experience in the kind of domestic service required of them. They were unlikely to be literate enough to make much of the cookery books.

Likewise they were unlikely to attend the government secondary schools and technical colleges at which domestic economy and cookery were now being taught as elective subjects for young women and girls.[26] Domestic economy had been included in the training for all new women teachers since 1869, though it was not part of the prescribed curriculum in government schools.[27] In 1882 the New South Wales Department of Public Instruction began classes in Sydney. The fee of 10 shillings for ten lessons proved a barrier to attendance. Fees were abolished but the cost to the government of running the classes for free became

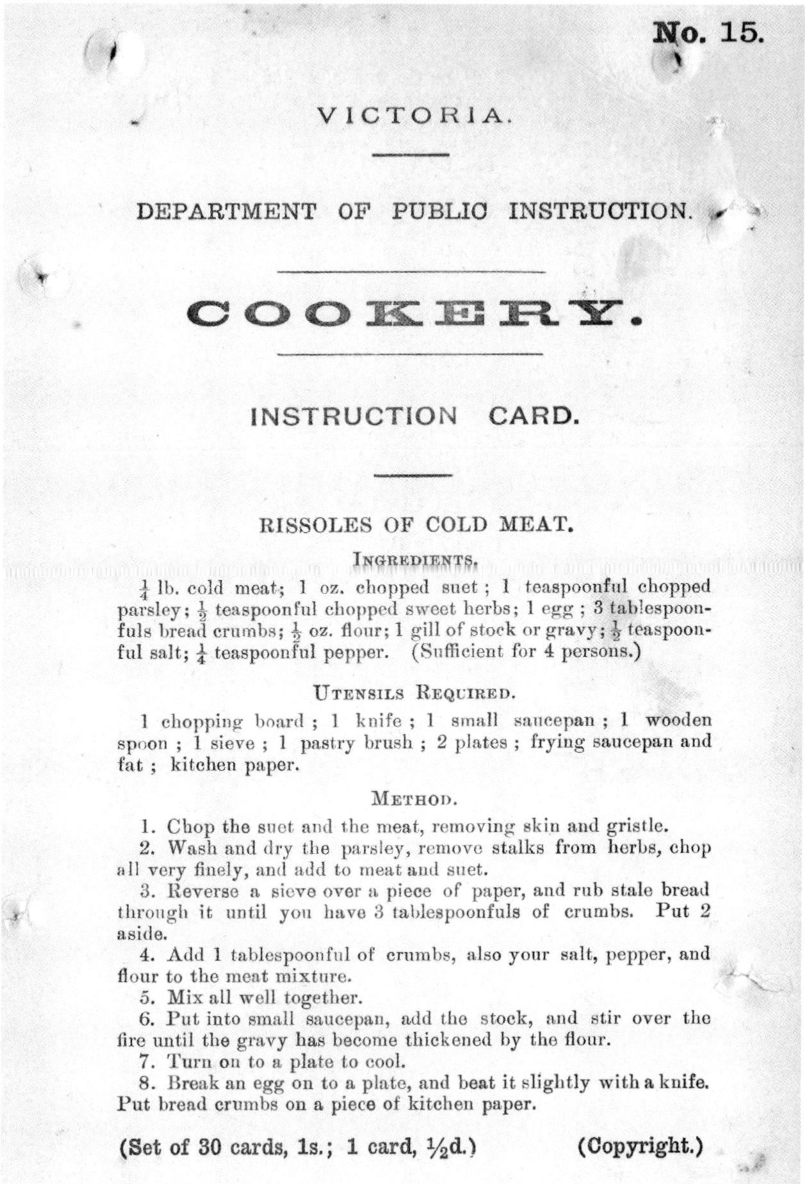

No. 15.

VICTORIA.

DEPARTMENT OF PUBLIC INSTRUCTION.

COOKERY.

INSTRUCTION CARD.

RISSOLES OF COLD MEAT.

INGREDIENTS.

¼ lb. cold meat; 1 oz. chopped suet; 1 teaspoonful chopped parsley; ½ teaspoonful chopped sweet herbs; 1 egg; 3 tablespoonfuls bread crumbs; ½ oz. flour; 1 gill of stock or gravy; ½ teaspoonful salt; ¼ teaspoonful pepper. (Sufficient for 4 persons.)

UTENSILS REQUIRED.

1 chopping board; 1 knife; 1 small saucepan; 1 wooden spoon; 1 sieve; 1 pastry brush; 2 plates; frying saucepan and fat; kitchen paper.

METHOD.

1. Chop the suet and the meat, removing skin and gristle.
2. Wash and dry the parsley, remove stalks from herbs, chop all very finely, and add to meat and suet.
3. Reverse a sieve over a piece of paper, and rub stale bread through it until you have 3 tablespoonfuls of crumbs. Put 2 aside.
4. Add 1 tablespoonful of crumbs, also your salt, pepper, and flour to the meat mixture.
5. Mix all well together.
6. Put into small saucepan, add the stock, and stir over the fire until the gravy has become thickened by the flour.
7. Turn on to a plate to cool.
8. Break an egg on to a plate, and beat it slightly with a knife. Put bread crumbs on a piece of kitchen paper.

(Set of 30 cards, 1s.; 1 card, ½d.) **(Copyright.)**

Victorian Department of Public Instruction cookery card from the 1880s.

prohibitive and the classes stopped in 1895. Annie Fawcett Story was also a graduate of the English National Training School for Cookery. She arrived in Sydney with her husband in 1882 and by 1883 was giving cookery classes. In 1886 she joined the Department of Public Instruction as a lecturer in domestic economy at Hurlstone Training College, Sydney. In

1889 she began teaching cookery at the city's Fort Street Model School for girls in the fifth year of primary school. The classes were successful and in 1892 portable kitchens were bought to take the classes to rural towns. However, when the colonies were hit by the 1890s depression, funds were reduced and enrolments fell. Numbers would not recover until the early twentieth century.

Flour, Sugar and Tea

'Many children had bread only once a day,' Mary Gilmore wrote of rural families.

> The morning meal was porridge; with or without salt or black sugar, and no milk; at midday there was a hunk of meat or a leg of possum; at night with sop for the little ones, there was bread and dripping (or more meat) for tea. Sop was bread soaked in black tea and sweetened . . . Nothing was watched so anxiously as flour.[28]

While the first attempts at growing wheat in the colonies had been disappointing, by the mid-nineteenth century the opening up of the inland plains of Victoria, South Australia and Western Australia brought more land under cultivation. Three technological improvements were particularly important in increasing the yield of wheat. The first was the Ridley Stripper. Invented by John Ridley in 1843, it was a mechanical harvester that reaped and threshed the grain directly from the standing crop instead of by laborious hand-scything. The second was the stump jump plough. Land being brought under wheat cultivation was bedevilled with mallee scrub, a eucalyptus species with multiple stems growing from lignotubers underground that made land clearing challenging. After the scrub-like trees were cut down the roots regrew energetically, causing damage to the ploughshare. In 1876 Robert Bowyer Smith invented a plough that rose up out of the ground when it hit an underground obstacle. Attached weights forced the blade back into the ground after the root was passed. The third technological improvement was the combination stripper-harvester developed by Hugh McKay in 1885. McKay initially partnered with the plough-makers McCalman, Grade & Co. in Melbourne to build the machines. A new company, the McKay Harvesting Machinery Co. established in 1890, bought the patent and operated successfully until 1894. McKay had shares in the company and formed a syndicate to revive it. He built an improved harvester and named it the 'Sunshine'. By 1901 the company was producing five hundred Sunshine harvesters annually.

While the technology was improving, the wheat being grown was still from the original varieties brought with the First Fleet. Soon after the first crops were harvested black stem rust, a fungal disease that thrives in warm humid conditions, hit the crops. The move inland to drier climates protected the wheat from the disease but the varieties of wheat used were not suited to the new conditions and the yield diminished between 1840–60. William Farrer, the son of a tenant farmer, had migrated to Australia in 1870 hoping to buy pastoral land but could not afford it. He became a surveyor and maintained an interest in agricultural improvement. In 1889 a catastrophic outbreak of rust cost the wheat industry an estimated £2 million. Farrer by this time was experimenting with cross-breeding wheat to produce a variety that was disease resistant and had improved baking qualities. He worked on this with the chemist F. B. Guthrie. They hybridized Indian and Canadian varieties. The first successful result was a strain called Yandilla, but it was the Federation variety that became the most popular, arriving as it did at the same time as the creation of Australia as a nation.

Sugarcane had been experimentally grown by T. A. Scott at Port Macquarie, 500 km (310 mi.) north of Sydney on the coast of New South Wales, in 1823. But it wasn't until Captain Louis Hope planted 8 ha (20 ac) of cane at Ormiston, south of Brisbane, in 1863 that the sugarcane industry can be said to have begun. Until then sugar in the colony had come from refining raw sugar from the Philippines, first in 1839 by the Australian Sugar Co. established by Francis Kemble and W. K. Child. In 1855 Edward Knox took over the assets of the company and another refinery, Robey & Co., and established the Colonial Sugar Refinery, which would dominate the industry through a virtual monopoly for the next 130 years. Following Hope's success at Ormiston, plantations spread to the north coast of Queensland, each with its own mill for extracting the raw sugar. In 1898 there were eighty mills in Queensland, producing about 1 million tonnes of sugar per year.[29] Sugarcane farming was established on the north coast of New South Wales from the 1870s.

'Tea,' Richard Twopeny wrote, 'may fairly claim to be the national beverage. A large majority of the population drink it with every meal, and you find cases of this even in the metropolitan middle classes.'[30] While in the first half of the eighteenth century tea was imported from China, after the First Opium War (1839–42) it began to be cultivated in India and Ceylon (now Sri Lanka). From that time the price of tea steadily fell, and it remained low for the rest of the century. Tea became an indispensable accompaniment for middle-class women entertaining guests. Tearooms became part of the department stores and arcades that were changing the way the middle class in particular shopped.

Wherever tea was served, sugar and flour joined it via biscuits and cakes. For many women, cake- and biscuit-making was both a break from the tedium of making meat-and-three-vegetable dinners and a chance to gain admiration from their peers for their skills and inventiveness. To help them there were cookery books like the *Presbyterian Cookery Book* of 1895, produced to raise funds for missionary work. This was a precursor of the Church and community group recipe books that would become a feature of charitable fundraising in the twentieth century. These books contained recipes contributed by members of the local congregation or charity organizations. Cakes and biscuits took up as much as half the recipes in some. The Agricultural Shows held in each state at different times of the year were also an opportunity for women to show their skills in making cakes and biscuits, pickles and jams. Strict guidelines were enforced on the shape into which fruit and vegetables could be cut, the proportion of whole fruit to syrup, and the density of the finished cake. There was much kudos in taking home the ribbons for first and second prizes.

Dining Out, High and Low

What to eat as a change from home-cooked meat three times a day increasingly was not a problem for those reaping the rewards of wool and wheat. The gentlemen's clubs provided the fine dining their members read about in the imported British papers. At the Athenaeum Club in Melbourne, Alfred Wilkinson presented an Anglo-French eleven-course dinner beginning with hors d'oeuvres of caviar on toast, oysters and stuffed olives. Soup and fish followed, then an entrée of sweetbreads or chicken fillet. The relevé (main course) was roast mutton, turkey and ham. Then came roast snipe, a red wine sorbet, asparagus, a selection of entremets (sweets served between courses), bouchées (small savoury pastries), and finally a selection of sweet titbits such as confectionary and fresh and dried fruits.[31] In Sydney in 1854, 'Messrs Budin and Mellon advertised the opening of the Aux Frères Provençaux Café Restaurant de Paris in George Street. Dinner cost 8 shillings and consisted of two hors d'oeuvres, a soup,

Keen As . . . Curry

Curry powders were first advertised in the *Sydney Gazette* in 1814, but it is likely they were available before that year. Curries by then were a popular British dish, having been introduced by merchants of the British East India Co. in the mid-1700s. Governor Macquarie served duck curry to guests shortly after he arrived in the colony in 1810.[32]

In 1844 a 22-year-old former carpenter, Joseph Keen, and his wife Annie set up shop in Hobart, from which they sold home-produced sauces and condiments. Among them was a curry powder made from a mix of turmeric, coriander, salt, fenugreek, pepper, chilli, black pepper, rice flour, allspice and celery powder. The virulently turmeric-yellow mix won a medal at the 1866 Intercolonial Exhibition in Melbourne. Keen's Curry Powder became a standard item in the spice racks of Australian households.

In 1954 the formula and rights to manufacture and sell were bought by Reckitt & Colman Australia Ltd, long established as spice manufacturers.[33]

Keen's Curry Powder, first made in 1844, found its way into every Australian larder by the early 20th century.

two "plates", one entremets, two desserts, a half bottle of fine wine and "bread at discretion."'[34] The French influence in these menus is clear. It extended to grand dinners at public occasions. For example, the menu of the Centennial Dinner held on 26 January 1888 was almost entirely composed of French dishes. This would be a feature of Australian fine dining well into the latter part of the twentieth century.

Those wanting less expensive fare could head to a public house and have oysters and pig trotters at the bar, both calculated to be briny enough to require several pots of ale as an accompaniment. Author Henry Lawson's character One-eyed Bogan, when he came to Sydney town, went to Pfahlert's Hotel, 'where a counter lunch – as good as many dinners you get for a shilling – was included with a sixpenny drink'.[35] At Adam's Café, operating in 1895 in George Street, you could dine on Scotch Finnan haddock, Vancouver salmon, New Zealand whitebait and Tasmanian trumpeter all accompanied by Australian claret and hock.[36]

To Drink or Not to Drink?

Wine growing had continued in the Hunter Valley and was underway in South Australia by the 1850s. But it was the Rutherglen area of Victoria that led the growth of the industry in the second half of the nineteenth century. Lindsay Brown planted just over 1.5 ha (4 ac) of vineyard in the area in the early 1850s and others soon followed. By the 1880s more than 1,215 ha (3,000 ac) were under cultivation in fifty vineyards, making it the largest wine region in the country, and Rutherglen was producing nearly a third of all wine in Australia. In 1896 the Victorian government built the Rutherglen Viticultural College to service and promote wine growing in the area.

Then in 1877 phylloxera, an aphid-like root louse that destroys grapevines, was detected in Geelong, Victoria. It spread rapidly, causing severe damage in Victoria and New South Wales. South Australia banned the importing of vine material into the colony in 1874 and so avoided the infestation. Tasmania and Western Australia also were unaffected. The disease was halted in the eastern colonies by grafting onto American rootstock, which was resistant to the louse.[37]

In the bush, wine was unknown. Drovers, prospectors, teamsters and the free settler escaping the monotony of eking out a living at his farm headed for the sly grog shanties. Flagons of spirits would have half their content removed, be topped up with water and a dash of turpentine and be

Peter Bond Burgoyne & Co. imported Australian wines to Britain in the 1870s.

re-coloured with tobacco juice. The men in Henry Lawson's short stories are frequently described in ways that now would be seen as characteristics of depressed alcoholics:

> Shepherds and boundary riders, who are alone for months, *must* have their periodical spree, at the nearest shanty, else they'd go raving mad. Drink is the only break in the awful monotony, and the yearly or half-yearly spree is the only thing they've got to look forward to: it keeps their minds fixed on something definite ahead.[38]

Nights in the grog shanties frequently ended with drunken brawls. Drunkenness also was a feature of the goldfields and the public houses in the cities and towns. Joseph Bleasdale, a Catholic Doctor of Divinity, among others, believed drinking wine to be 'the one efficient cure for spirit-drinking and drunkenness'.[39] Bleasdale's case, however, may have had more to do with his role in the promotion of viticulture through papers he wrote to the Royal Society of Victoria and chairing the wine jury at the Intercolonial Exhibition of 1866–7.

For others, temperance was the only solution. The Independent Order of Rechabites established a chapter in Australia in 1847 and the Sons of

Sly grog shanty, Victorian goldfields, 1852–3.

Not all establishments selling coffee were 'palaces'.

Temperance began in 1864. In 1885 the Woman's Christian Temperance Union set up branches in Queensland, New South Wales, Tasmania, South Australia and Victoria. By the 1890s there were 70,000 members of these organizations in Australia.

One of the strategies of the temperance groups was to set up 'coffee palaces' to counter the bed-and-board services provided by public houses.

The Federal Hotel and Coffee Palace, built in 1888, opposite busy Spencer Street railway station.

Businessmen could enjoy a quick cup of coffee from street stalls.

In Melbourne, the Grand Hotel, built in 1884, was turned into the Grand Coffee Palace in 1886, operating under this name until 1897. In Sydney, the Grand Central Coffee Palace, the Hotel Metropole, the Town Hall and the Sydney Coffee Palace were among the most elaborate. Coffee palaces were also established in inland centres, like the one at Echuca, the port on the Murray River, 'an institution which can be sincerely recommended as a first-class hotel to stay at. [It] is splendidly laid out, handsomely furnished, well ventilated, and in every way is a model of comfort, cleanliness and general excellence. The two dining rooms are nice cheerful apartments with plenty of light.'[40]

By the 1890s, as a result of campaigning by temperance organizations, every Australian colony except for Western Australia had introduced a local option policy whereby those paying rates to the local council could decide not to have a public house in their district, or to ban the issuing of new alcohol licences.

Depression, Recovery and the Push for Federation

'From the second half of the 1860s until the end of the 1880s,' writes the economist George Megalogenis, 'it was not unusual for Australia's Gross Domestic Product per capita to be at least 20 per cent larger than the next ranked nation, which was often the United Kingdom.'

> The new boom in national income was due to technology . . . Adelaide, Melbourne, Sydney and Brisbane were connected by telegraph cable in late 1861 . . . The colonies were becoming more accessible for trade through the steam engine, as the development of railways brought people and goods together across the continent. New machines increased the productivity of the worker, so living standards continued to grow as the population expanded.[41]

Wealth encouraged speculative investment in both the cities and the burgeoning pastoral lands, most of it funded through Australian trading banks lending funds borrowed from banks in England. When the Baring Brothers & Co. bank failed in England as a result of a crash in investments in Argentina, the crisis rapidly spread. Between April and May 1893 thirteen banks closed in Victoria, New South Wales and Queensland. The banks recovered quickly but the economy was slower to do so. Business and consumer confidence was low, wheat and wool prices had fallen, and property was offloaded to repay loans. It would take nine years for a full recovery.

The banks and financial companies had been shaken, however, and began lobbying for a federal parliament with the power to legislate banking and currency. In May 1893 premiers of the colonies meeting in Melbourne resolved that 'recent events prove that laws require to be enacted with respect to banking in all colonies, and that legislation should be uniform'.[42]

This was not the first stirring of the view that some level of federalism was necessary. In 1883, at an earlier intercolonial meeting, Samuel Griffith, premier of Queensland, concerned at growing French territorial ambitions in the Pacific, had proposed establishing a federal council to manage maritime defences outside the colonies' territorial waters. It did not proceed because New South Wales refused to join.

Industrialists were also unhappy with the limits inter-colony tariffs put on the expansion of their markets. Victorian tariffs were hampering farmers from the Riverina in New South Wales selling wool and wheat across the border. Food and textile producers in Melbourne and Geelong were faced with tariffs on goods being sent interstate by rail to New South Wales. Edward Abbott, a self-described 'Australian aristologist' and author of *The English and Australian Cookery Book: Cookery for the Many, As Well As for the 'Upper Ten Thousand'*, found it 'a curious custom-house anomaly at present [that] one of the Australias cannot use the wine of the adjoining colony without paying a similar duty to that extracted from wines of foreign growth'.[43]

In 1897 delegates from all the colonies met to draft a federal constitution. Debate was heated. Difficulties were identified as to which level of government would have the power to raise revenue in particular, the states worrying that if the power to tax was handed over to the federal body, they would have few, if any, sources left from which to raise revenue. The outcome was not assured.

FIVE

Federation, 1900–1913

Notwithstanding concerns from delegates wanting to ensure that states must be left to make their own legislation, the 1897 conference on federation came to an agreement. A federation would be established called the Commonwealth of Australia, with the six existing colonies to be called States. There would be a division of powers. The Commonwealth would hold 'specific powers' to legislate in areas of national importance: trade and commerce with other countries and among States; taxation, posts and telegraphs, banking; marriage, divorce and matrimonial causes; invalid and old-age pensions; immigration and emigration; external affairs; and conciliation and arbitration for the prevention and settlement of industrial disputes extending beyond the limits of any one State. The States would have 'residual powers' to legislate in such areas as education, health and railways.[1]

Over the next decade, Australia would work to entrench what the historian Manning Clark called 'this feeling of being one people with one destiny'.[2] New schemes for releasing more Crown land for settlement and harnessing rivers seemed to offer promise of this greater national destiny. In a ground-breaking inquiry, a new national industrial body established the principle of the basic wage that has been at the core of industrial action ever since. But even as this feeling was being instilled, many living in Australia and contributing economically and culturally to its foodways were excluded from sharing in that destiny.

Australia for the Australians

On 21 August 1886 *The Bulletin* magazine published an article that described in detail the houses and shops of Chinese residents in Sydney:

> It has show windows on either side of the front door. That on the left hand side contains oranges, bananas and sugar-cane; that on the right is entirely and completely empty. Within the shop a deeply pock-marked Chinaman, sitting on a low stool, sells the fruit over a rough counter in dimensions something like an elongated gin case, or a shortened coffin, and this is the only honest trade carried on in the premises. On the right hand side the back of the show window is boarded over and there is no pretence to any sort of trade except in pak-ah-pu tickets.[3]

Anti-Chinese sentiment had continued in the late 1800s. In 1878 members of the Seaman's Union walked off the job on ships of the Australian Union Steamship Navigation Co., declaring they would not return until the company ceased its practice of replacing European members of their crew with Chinese. The company agreed to reduce the number of Chinese employed and the men returned to work. It wasn't only workers who attacked the Chinese. At the second intercolonial union congress in 1884, delegates discussed restrictions on Chinese labour. 'The bourgeoisie feared competition from Chinese importers and furniture manufacturers. They were obsessed with the evils of miscegenation and the problem of permitting Chinese, Japanese, Pacific islanders, or Indians to live in Australia when they did not share the political tradition of bourgeois or liberal democracy.'[4]

First published in January 1880, *The Bulletin* had become a strident voice of anti-Chinese sentiment in Australia. The August article continued:

> What do the general public of New South Wales think of the Chinese? They buy cabbages from them, never asking how these cabbages have been grown; they occasionally buy cigars from them, without enquiring whether those cigars have paid any duty or not; they buy furniture not troubling to consider by what class of workers that furniture has been made . . .[5]

Another group of labourers in Australia also came under fire. From its inception, the Queensland sugar industry relied on labour from the Pacific Islands. No European was prepared to undertake the backbreaking work at the wages that were being offered to make the local product economically viable against imported raw sugar from Fiji, Mauritius and other tropical areas. Labour agents would sail schooners first to Vanuatu (then called the

New Hebrides) and later to the Solomon Islands. There they would recruit, or take involuntarily, men indentured for an initial period of three years. The practice became known as 'blackbirding'. Initially the Islanders were brought in to labour across a range of industries, but with the passing of legislation in Queensland in 1884 they were restricted to field labour in tropical agriculture, mainly sugarcane. Sickness was prevalent and in the years 1867–1907 an average of fifty in every 1,000 died from infectious diseases, with dysentery and respiratory tract infections (tuberculosis, bronchitis and pneumonia) being the main killers.[6] Some remained for further terms; some went home and then came back again. In the 1890s the majority were those who had stayed past their initial indenture. 'They were able to bargain for higher wages and shorter contracts,' writes the historian Henry Reynolds, 'move within and between districts, take time off for holidays and were much more likely to work for small farmers than on large plantations. Independent, self-confident "time-expired boys" became the subject of increasing European anxiety.'[7]

As opposition to the Pacific Islanders in the cane fields of Queensland also grew, *The Bulletin* went even further. Its masthead now declared 'Australia for the Australians', and in 1887 it made clear what it meant:

> By the term Australian we mean not those who have been merely born in Australia. All white men who came to these shores – with a clean record and who leave behind them the memory of class distinctions and the religious differences of the old world; all men who place the happiness, the prosperity, the advancement of their adopted country before the interests of Imperialism are Australian . . . No nigger, no Chinaman, no lascar, no kanaka, no purveyor of cheap coloured labour, is an Australian.[8]

As discussions continued towards federation of the various colonies, representatives of the colonial governments looked for a way to legislate against Chinese immigrants and Pacific Islanders. For the former, they had to work out a way of discriminating without bringing down on their heads the rancour of the British government, which was opposed to anything that would threaten the free trade agreement with China after the Second Opium War (1856–60). The solution was for the new parliament of the federation to introduce the Immigration Restriction Act 1901, a provision that anyone who failed to pass a fifty-word dictation test in a European language would be declared a prohibited immigrant. Any immigrant who had been resident in Australia for less than five years could also be subject to the test. In 1905 the words 'European language' were changed to 'prescribed language' to avoid giving offence to Japanese and Indian business interests.[9]

There were no such niceties to be concerned about when it came to the Pacific Islanders, however, and the Pacific Island Labourers Act 1901 legislated that all Pacific Islanders who had migrated to Australia were to be deported by 1905, an amendment for some exceptions on compassionate grounds being passed a year later.

Further entrenching what was to become known as the 'White Australia Policy' were two other Acts. The 1901 Posts and Telegraph Act prohibited any contract for service development or provision that did not contain a condition that only white labour would be employed. The Commonwealth Franchise Act in 1902 legislated that no Australian Aboriginal, Asian or African could have their name placed on the electoral role unless they were also legally able to enrol in the state in which they were resident. The White Australia Policy significantly shaped Australian foodways until it was abolished in 1973.

The Quarantine Act of 1908

While labour protectionism led to discriminatory Acts, protection in another area was to have lasting benefit for Australia. Livestock – cattle and sheep – had been imported to Australia since the first British settlement. As Australia established its own herds, they became exposed to outbreaks of disease caused when infected stock were imported for breeding or otherwise increasing local stock. Contagious bovine pleuropneumonia killed an estimated 1.5 million cattle between 1858 and 1864. While inoculation was available from the mid-1870s there was no compulsion to use it or to report new infections. In 1872 foot and mouth disease was identified in a small number of cattle and pigs on two properties in Werribee, Victoria. The potential for devastation of Australia's growing pastoral industries caused concern enough to consider putting quarantine measures in place.

Federation provided the ideal time and vehicle through which to do this nationally under the separation of powers, which gave the Commonwealth the power to legislate quarantine measures. The 1908 Quarantine Act provided for inspection of all vessels (which would later include aeroplanes) from overseas, and for the quarantine, isolation and continued surveillance of infected or suspected vessels, persons, goods, animals and plants. Fisheries outside territorial waters were also under Commonwealth control. Australia's isolation from other livestock raising and its stringent quarantine procedures would serve it well in significant outbreaks of illness in the later years of the twentieth century.

Selectors: The New Yeomen

As the gold rushes ended in New South Wales and Victoria in the 1860s, the new free and subsidized immigrants-turned-prospectors began to lobby for governments to unlock more land. Pressure was also coming from the second and third generations of free settlers – descendants of both the emancipated convicts and the non-convict migrants to the colonies. They wanted to break the hold of the squatters – those who in the late eighteenth century had established extensive sheep and cattle stations prior to the passing of controlling legislation – had over large holdings of land. Over the 1860s and 1870s all the colonies, except Western Australia and Tasmania, passed legislation that allowed selectors, as they became called, to purchase small acreages of government-held land other than that which was already part of cities and towns and proclaimed goldfields. In some cases, certain areas were specifically set aside as agricultural lands. The price of the land varied across the colonies and on the categories of land the selector was buying. In Victoria the Duffy Act of 1862 proclaimed over 4 million ha (10 million ac) as agricultural land and people could select between 16 and 240 ha (40–600 ac) for £1 an acre. In Queensland the Selection Act of 1868 provided for two classes of land for selection: agricultural land at 15 shillings an acre and pastoral land at 5 shillings an acre. A condition of the sales in all states was that selectors had to show, within a reasonable frame of time, that they had some of the land under cultivation, had erected a habitable dwelling and had enclosed their selection with a fence. Henry Lawson described a selector's property in his short story 'Water Them Geraniums':

> It was a small oblong hut built of split slabs, and he had roofed it with shingles which he split in spare times . . . At the end of the house was a big slab-and-bark shed, bigger than the hut itself, with a kitchen, a skillion for tools, harness, and horse-feed, and a spare bedroom partitioned off with sheets of bark and of bark and old chaff-bags. The house itself was floored roughly, with cracks between the boards; there were cracks between the

Selector's hut, Gippsland, Victoria, 1880s.

> slabs all round – though he'd nailed strips of tin, from old kerosene-tins, over some of them; the partitioned off bedroom was lined with old chaff-bags with newspapers pasted over them for wall-paper, There was no ceiling, calico or otherwise, and we could see the round pine rafters and battens and the under end of the shingles . . . There was one small glass window in the 'dining room' with three panes and a sheet of greased paper, and the rest were rough wooden shutters. There was a pretty good cow-yard and calf-pen and – that was about all.[10]

The take-up rate post-bidding for a selection was variable. In New South Wales by 1880 only 18,000–20,000 legally compliant homesteads had been established. In Victoria 30,000 had taken up selections by 1869 and were engaged in sheep and cattle raising and/or agriculture.[11] This low take-up rate was partly due to the selectors' financial failures. They often had to borrow money to carry out the improvements the laws required. They bought seed and supplies from stock and station agents and general stores on credit at usurious interest rates. When they could not make their repayments, creditors foreclosed and amalgamated properties into larger holdings. The selector would become a farm-wage worker or return to the cities in search of work.

Others took to domestic industry to supplement what could be earned from the farm, selling egg, milk and butter, for example. The soldier/farmer autobiographer A. B. Facey worked on his uncle's selection of 400 ha (1,000 ac) in the wheat bowl of Western Australia in the early 1900s. He recounted his grandmother's small dairying venture:

> The old lady used to put the milk into flat tin trays, each one holding about two gallons. She would then put these into a large bag cooler and let them stand like that for about twelve hours. By that time the cream would have come to the top of the milk and she would skim it off and make it into butter. Her daughter's children used to come and take it away and sell it, and the money from this and the eggs that she sold were her only cash income.[12]

'But the more success eluded the selectors of the 1860s and 1880s,' writes Marilyn Lake in her study of the soldier settlements after the First World War (discussed in Chapter Five of this book):

The Harvester Case and the Minimum Wage

From the mid-1800s Australian 'anti-sweating leagues' (based in religious social-reform groups) and workers increasingly became concerned about the working conditions in factories, particularly those that employed women and younger adolescents. In 1873 the Victorian government passed the Supervision of Workrooms and Factories Act, which prohibited the employment of women in factories with no fewer than ten persons for more than eight hours a day. However, the lack of enforcement of the Act led to calls for further action and a Royal Commission was established in 1882. The Commission led to the 1896 Factories and Shops Act under which Boards were established with representatives of employers and employees to negotiate industrial disputes and determine the lowest rate of payment for factory work. The Bread-making Board, for example, set the minimum wage in that industry at 1 shilling an hour. Industrial tribunals were established in other colonies that also set minimum wage levels across various industries.

In the second Commonwealth Parliament, Prime Minister Alfred Deakin, who favoured protection of Australian industries, sought to extend tariffs. The Free Trade Party, formed in 1887, held the second largest number of seats in parliament. To counter their influence, Deakin garnered the support of the pro-protection Australian Labor Party, and in 1906 parliament passed the Customs Tariff (Agricultural Machinery) Act, which placed a tax of £12 on imported stripper-harvester machines, so protecting the industry that had begun with Hugh McKay's combined harvester, and also protecting the jobs of Australian workers. The second part of the deal was the Excise Tariff (Agricultural Machinery) Act, which imposed a £6 tax on locally produced stripper-harvesters that would be dropped if the local manufacturer paid their workers a fair and reasonable wage.

Employers began applying for exemptions, which raised the question of what a fair and reasonable wage in the industry was. Hugh McKay's new business the Sunshine Harvester Works was the largest agricultural machinery plant in the country, employing around five hundred, and sought an exemption. As the Act was a Commonwealth Act the case was heard in the newly established Commonwealth Conciliation and Arbitration Court. Justice Henry Higgins presided and sought evidence of the living conditions of people in Victoria. He collected information on what they were paid but also their expenses, including rent, food, education and clothing. He determined a fair and reasonable minimum across all industries to allow the average employee to live adequately.

McKay was paying less than this and so was determined as not exempt. He appealed to the High Court and won on the grounds that the legislation under which the matter had been determined was unconstitutional. But the principle of an across-the-board minimum wage would continue to be central to Australia's industrial relations.

> the more vigorously it seems did policy makers pursue the yeoman ideal. Under the terms of the 1869 Victorian *Land Act*, for example, the upper limit for holdings was not increased, but reduced to 320 acres . . . When a witness [to the 1878–9 Royal Commission into the Act] offered his opinion that areas of 1,000 to 1,500 acres would be more suitable for farming than the standard 320 acres, the commissioners responded: 'instead of a yeomanry on the soil you would have the landlord and tenant system?'[13]

The push for small holdings continued unabated at the start of the new nation and it was now tied up, Lake writes, with

> [the] related pre-occupations – the standard of the race, the character of the Australian people and the future greatness of the new nation . . . The great problems of the day were how to turn back the human tide from 'the enfeeblement of the streets to the breeding grounds of health and wealth . . . and the raising of a sturdy producing race'. The yeoman ideal was invoked with a new urgency: It is the profitable commodities that come from the small holding and it is on the small holding that the country must depend to populate its territory and win its riches.[14]

In 1910 the Commonwealth Labor government, led by prime minister Andrew Fisher, introduced a Land Tax Act, imposing a tax on unimproved land that aimed to break up large holdings of underutilized arable land secured by squatters.

Enriching the Soil

Cattle manure was the main means for enriching the soil over the nineteenth century. 'I am decidedly of the opinion,' Watkin Tench wrote,

> that many large tracts of land between Rose Hill and the Hawkesbury, even now, are of a nature sufficiently favourable to produce moderate crops of whatever may be sown in them. And provided a sufficient number of cattle be imported to afford manure for dressing the ground, no doubt can exist that

> subsistence for a limited number of inhabitants may be drawn from it.[15]

James Ruse and other farmers also burned the trees and grasses they cleared on their land and dug the ashes back into the soil. The results in reasonable soil were positive.

But as selectors pushed the boundaries of the agricultural belt further and further inland, the soil on which they hoped to grow their bounty was more and more lacking in necessary nutrients and was in areas that were hotter and drier, putting crops at greater risk of failing during drought. For cereal crops, the lack of phosphorus was a problem. Phosphorus is essential for seedling vigour, better root development – essential for taking up what little moisture and nutrients there was – and for higher yields, by encouraging more grains per head. Yields declined throughout the 1870s as overcropping further depleted the soil. When a field was no longer productive most farmers simply broke new ground and hoped for natural recovery of the now fallow soil. A drought that lasted from 1895 to 1903 (commonly called the Federation Drought) was the result of three successive El Niño events and added to the wheat farmers' problems. In 1902 wheat yields in New South Wales and Victoria were the lowest on record.

The South Australian government was alarmed at the situation in what was by then the Grain Bowl of Australia and in 1883 brought out J. D. Custance to head Roseworthy Agricultural College. There he was tasked with researching and improving the productivity of South Australian soils. Custance and his successor William Lowrie experimented with superphosphate, which had been patented in England in 1842 by John Bennet Lawes. Lawes's fertilizer was made by treating phosphates with sulphuric acid. The trials were successful, and superphosphate became widely used. 'The contractor would bring back a load of superphosphate after delivering each load of wheat,' Facey wrote.

> He would bring sixty bags back each time and charged one shilling a bag. The superphosphate (super it was commonly called) was a new kind of artificial fertiliser subsidised by the Government and delivered to the settler's nearest railway siding . . . It was a boon to the settlers, in some instance improving the crop by forty percent.[16]

In 1897 Cuming Smith & Co. began importing rock phosphate from Tennessee and Florida, but by 1900 it was being imported from Ocean Island (a Pacific Island now called Banaba and part of the Republic of Vanuatu), its near neighbour Nauru and Christmas Island (an Australian Territory in the Indian Ocean). Australia became one of the largest users and producers of superphosphate in the world with dire consequences for both the sources of the phosphate and for Australia's ecology. By the 1980s the phosphate stocks in both Banaba and Nauru were exhausted and the island's environments were irreparably damaged. In Australia, nitrates and phosphates used in the Queensland sugarcane fields are flushed down to the coast, enriching algae that threaten the ecology of the coral reefs, including the Great Barrier Reef.

The Irrigation Settlements

In 1885 Alfred Deakin, at the time a minister in the Victorian colonial government, went to California to study irrigation systems there. Victoria had recovered from a severe drought in the years 1877–84 and Deakin was heading up a Royal Commission into the water supply of the colony. In California he met George and William Chaffey, pioneers in the Santa Ana River irrigation settlement. Deakin was impressed with the brothers and discussed with them the possibility of developing irrigation settlements in Victoria. In 1886 George Chaffey arrived unprompted in Melbourne, hoping to get a land grant to replicate the Santa Ana project. Deakin suggested he investigate the areas bordering the Murray River. George Chaffey was enthusiastic about the prospects and Deakin assured him that the government would make available 8,000 ha (250,000 ac) of Crown land on favourable terms, with the Chaffeys committed to spending £300,000 over twenty years on improving the land and building irrigation infrastructure. George Chaffey selected an abandoned sheep station at Mildura, near the confluence of the Murray and Darling rivers. At the same time John Downer, premier of South Australia, offered the brothers 8,000 ha in South Australia. They chose land on the Murray River at Renmark, 140 km (90 mi.) from Mildura.

Under the purchase deals, the Chaffeys were able to sell land in their holdings. They advertised widely in England and Australia and by December 1890, 3,300 people had settled at Mildura and 1,100 at Renmark, of which almost half were English immigrants. What began as a grand vision failed in the face of the Depression years of the early 1890s and the familiar combination of poor rainfall, increasing salinity of the land through poor water management, the inexperience of the settlers, poor fruit and vegetable crop choices, and the cost and difficulty in transporting the produce to Melbourne. A promised railway line to nearby Swan Hill did not eventuate and low water made Murray River transport untenable.

Complaints were also made to both governments about the Chaffey brothers' management of their business and the impact of that on those who had bought properties from them. Investigations in both states found enough of substance to set up public trusts to take over the businesses. William Chaffey settled in Mildura and made a success of his orchard. He established the Mildura Winery Pty Ltd and went on to be a significant player in the dried fruits industry. Both Mildura and Renmark built on the early work of the Chaffeys and remain important centres of citrus, grape and nut production in Australia. In 2000 the Murray River Salt company near Mildura turned the salinity of the Murray River to its advantage by producing gourmet-targeted pink salt flakes.

In New South Wales in May 1887, the Royal Commission on the Conservation of Water handed down its final report, which called for

An irrigation pump designed by the Chaffey brothers for their irrigation settlement in Mildura.

One of the network of irrigation canals in the Murrumbidgee Irrigation Area.

surveying the Murrumbidgee River for irrigation purposes. This suited the plans of Samuel McCaughey, a grazier at North Yanco who was eager to extract more water from the Murrumbidgee for his growing herd. In 1900, using Irish immigrant labour, he constructed an irrigation system of some 320 km (200 mi.), which fed a steam pump that extracted the river's waters. In 1899 he had been appointed to the New South Wales Legislative Council and he used his experience and position to lobby for action on the Royal Commission's findings. It bore fruit in the Barren Jack Dam and Murrumbidgee Canals Construction Act 1906. Construction began in March 1907 of the Barren Jack (now Burrinjuck) Dam capable of holding enough water to irrigate 65,000 ha (160,000 ac). The Murrumbidgee Irrigation Trust was established to administer the project and to buy or resume land on which to construct the irrigation works, build towns and sell lots to prospective farmers. The first land release of 120,000 ha (300,000 ac) was in May 1922.

Assistance to settlers here included the erection of houses, supply of building materials, fencing posts, ploughing and grading of 4 ha (10 ac), and ditching, with repayments over a ten-year term. Settlers could also buy lucerne seed and horticultural stock at cost price. The lessee or purchaser was provided with a contour plan of the farm and implements could be rented. A small nursery at Yanco Experimental Farm was established with a larger nursery at Leeton prepared for construction. Agricultural research encompassed fodder grass, fruit growing, and trees for timber.[17] By 2019, the Murrumbidgee Irrigation Area covered 670,000 ha (1.6 million ac) of which around 140,000 ha (345,000 ac) is irrigated on 3,300 agricultural holdings. Water is now captured from the Burrinjuck Dam and the Blowering Dam, completed in 1964 as part of the Snowy Mountains Hydro-electric Scheme. The area produces rice, wine grapes, almonds, citrus and vegetables, and the major towns provide ancillary processing.

Aboriginal Labour: The Station Workers

'All the people round there,' Aboriginal station worker Arthur Corunna recounted to his grandniece Sally Morgan, 'we all belonged to each other. We were the tribe that made the station. The Drake-Brockmans didn't make it on their own. There were only a few white men there, ones that fixed the pumps and sank wells by contract. The blackfellas did the rest.'[18] Corunna Downs (Arthur took his surname from the station on which he was born) was a sheep station in the Pilbara area of northwestern Western Australia, established by the Drake-Brockman brothers in 1890. The brothers and other squatters had followed the lead of the Duracks and Costellos into the rich grazing lands of the Kimberley and Pilbara regions. Throughout the Northern Territory and western Queensland, too, squatters had established vast cattle and sheep stations from the 1880s. These were the 'Kings in Grass Castles', to quote Patrick Durack's memorable phrase, which gave the title to his grandniece Mary's family history.

The corollary of this is that the Aboriginal people of the areas occupied were the serfs. As the pastoralists set up their properties, they looked for ways to access labour and protect their herds. The solution they came to was to bring the Aboriginal group whose land they now occupied onto the stations, where they lived in rough campsites providing a labour force when needed. Workers were fed rations, often done as a weekly dole out for each family of a quantity of flour, tea, sugar and perhaps some jam. The workers were expected to continue to hunt for their own meat from whatever native and feral animals they could (rabbits and pigs mainly) and harvest native fruits and vegetables. While all the stations had their own small vegetable plots, the Aboriginal workers and their families were often forbidden to pick the produce. 'When I was little,' Daisy (Talahue) Corunna, Arthur's sister, recalled, 'I picked the grubs off the caulis and cabbages at the back of the garden. I got a boiled sweet for that. Now the blackfellas weren't allowed to pick any vegetables from the garden. You got a whipping if you were caught. Old Pompee [one of the Aboriginal workers], he used to sneak us tomatoes. And so he should have, he was eatin' them himself.'[19]

Four Aboriginal stockmen on their horses, Cox River, Northern Territory, 1928.

On some stations, like Corunna, rations were doled out as regular meals that sometimes included meat. Providing meat was an attempt to stop raids on sheep and cattle. Arthur Corunna recalled:

> We used to call Sam Moody backwards. Moody Sam. He was a white man and a good cook. He'd cook bread, cut it in big slices and give it to the natives through the small kitchen window. He cooked meat too. We'd all get bread and slices of meat. We'd poke our billies through and get tea too. Moody Sam didn't cook, we'd get slices of mutton make a fire outside and cook it ourselves. For extra meat, my people used to catch kangaroo and wild turkeys and fish from the creek. We'd go down to the creek and we'd stand with our legs bent and apart, then we'd catch them between our knees. We'd grab them with our hands and throw them on the bank.[20]

Daisy and other girls also supplemented their rations by bartering tin they had panned on the property in exchange for sugar and flour. Daisy occasionally also supplemented their rations by raiding the food store.

The Canning Stock Route

Having reliable sources of water each day was essential for those seeking new pastures, along the droving tracks that criss-crossed the country from the stations to towns and ports where cattle and sheep could be sold.

In 1906 Alfred Canning, who had previously surveyed the route for the rabbit-proof fence, was commissioned by the Western Australian government to survey a route from Wiluna, in central Western Australia, to the Halls Creek goldfields. Canning set out along routes previously travelled by the explorers David Carnegie and Lawrence Wells on separate journeys in the late 1800s. Both Carnegie and Wells had used ropes to tie Aboriginal men in a line and forced them to identify sources of water along the tracks. Carnegie fed his trackers salt beef to make them thirsty. Canning, setting out in 1906, went further in his enslavement of members of Aboriginal nations through which he travelled, including Martu and Wangkatjungka peoples. He used neck-chains and handcuffs to stop the trackers and their wives from escaping, chaining them up also at night. On the party's return to Perth in 1907, Canning's camp cook, Edward Blake, raised Canning's treatment of the Aboriginal men and women with the government. A Royal Commission was established in 1908 but Canning was not charged as Blake's was the only testimony against him.

Sporadic droving continued along the Canning Stock Route until 1959 but it did not achieve the outcome that was intended.[21]

> It had tin walls, tin roof and a tiny window near the top covered with flywire [a fine metal mesh]. You wouldn't believe the food they had in there, sacks of apricots, potatoes, tobacco, everything. It makes my mouth water just thinkin' about it. When it was siesta time, the other kids used to lift me up and poke me through the window. I'd drop down inside quiet as a mouse when the cat's after him. Then I'd pick up food and throw it out the window. If they heard someone coming they'd cough, then run away, I'd hide behind the sacks of potatoes and wait for them to come back for me. I had a good feed on those days.[22]

The practice of rationing came under debate by policy makers with responsibility for Aboriginal affairs. The argument, conducted entirely by non-Aboriginals, was about whether rationing was leading to 'pauperizing' Aboriginal people, making them dependent on rations. Baldwin Spencer, appointed as Special Commissioner to advise on Indigenous welfare in 1912, came down on the side of pauperizing, advocating that it was better for Aboriginal people to be settled on supervised reserves where they could continue to hunt and gather and so survive without rations. Rationing continued nonetheless. The debate about the appropriate form of Indigenous welfare would continue into the twenty-first century and access to food would be central to it.

Fowler's Vacola jar became an indispensable part of Australian households, who preserved fruit and vegetables for the lean times.

Estimates of the number of Aboriginals employed as stock workers and domestic servants on the stations vary on where the count was taken and when, as stock work was largely seasonal and men were often employed for short periods of time. The historian Henry Reynolds has suggested there may have been as many 10,000 working in the pastoral stations across the north of Australia in the early 1900s.[23]

Dining In

There was little change in the diet of town-dwellers as the twentieth century began. The range of fresh fruit and vegetables was still largely seasonal. Commercial canning of vegetables was underway but still in its earliest stages. Bottling, pickling and curing continued to extend availability beyond the season. Those who couldn't afford to buy commercial products bottled fruit and vegetables at home. Joseph Fowler began selling his home-bottling kits in 1915, hawking them from a cart in the streets of Sydney. The system used glass jars, single-use rubber ring seals and pressed, unthreaded metal lids. During the preserving process the lids are secured by metal tension clips. The bottles are then submerged under water in a preserving unit. The unit is turned on to heat the water to a temperature of 92°C (198°F). The bottles are left in the unit for 60–70 minutes destroying any food spoiling enzymes or microbes which may cause illness. Oxygen is forced from the bottles, creating an anaerobic vacuum that also seals the bottles as they cool. Rebranded as Fowler's Vacola, its place was assured in Australia's food history.

As towns grew and farms were pushed further and further to the urban fringes, access to daily fresh milk for town-dwellers became more difficult as it was liable to spoil during transportation. In the 1870s Thomas Mort began sending milk from his New South Wales south coast dairy in refrigerated rail cars to the Southern Highlands from which it could be carried to Sydney within a day. In 1888 David Wilson was appointed the first Victorian Dairy Expert and in the early 1890s he visited Europe to study pasteurization. While he advocated for it to become standard practice, pasteurization did not become widely used in Australia until after the Second World War. Victoria became a major dairy area and by 1895, there were two hundred butter factories and three hundred creameries there. In 1890 the Bacchus Marsh Concentrated Milk Co. was established, and within a few years began to export their product. Cheddar became the favoured cheese across Australia because it stored and carried well.[24]

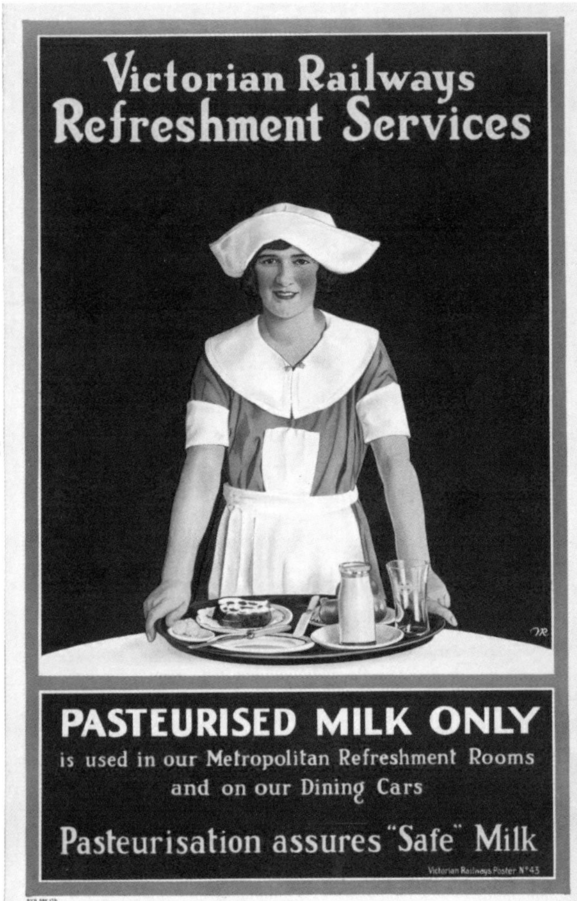

A poster from the 1920s promoting pasteurized milk as a unique selling point. Pasteurization was not common until after the Second World War.

Until refrigeration became economical, ocean fish continued to be consumed in the communities that caught them, where the fishing families could barter for meat and vegetables. In cities like Sydney and Melbourne fish was still brought to the central markets where people either made time to go and purchase them or waited on hawkers carting small amounts of fish through the suburbs early in the day to prevent them spoiling. Crayfish could be kept longer, and oysters could be kept up to two weeks and became a major source of seafood consumption. Oysters 'bars' opened in capital cities, with hotels and cafés serving freshly shucked oysters. Oysters were harvested by dredging, with iron-mesh bags slung off the end of boats, which resulted in whole areas of oyster beds being denuded.[25] Fishing on inland waterways again was generally for local consumption, though Murray cod sustained a large commercial fishery on the Murray and Murrumbidgee rivers.[26]

On farms and stations, without easy access to groceries and butchers' shops women continued to use what was at hand and preserve what could not be eaten straight away. Mary Durack's grandmother, Mary (née Costello):

> made a creative art of her homely hospitality . . . There were exclamations of wonder and delight at the feast she produced – the kangaroo tail soup demanded by Grandfather, fish from the now brimming Kyabra Creek, spiced and pickled beef, home cured bacon and ham from pigs that had mightily increased and were now running wild among the Cooper channels. She had mastered the delicate art of extracting rennet from the carcasses of calves for making cheeses which she kept in store with a variety of queer sausages that festooned the rafters between hanging bladders of lard while the greenhide shelves below groaned under rows of pickles and preserves, some of the produce of the kitchen garden, some from wild oranges and bright red rosellas [*Hibiscus heterophyllus*, the native hibiscus] that grew along the river bank.[27]

Mary Durack Senior, like other women on the stations, continued to cook on wood-fired stoves or open fires. In the towns, women could use any of the increasing range of gas, wood or coal stoves. G. E. Crane & Sons advertised as the sole agents for the 'celebrated "Up to Date" Cooking Range Specially Made for Australia' with either a single or double oven in three styles: New Mistress, Aidress and Dover.[28] The Welsbach Light Co. of Melbourne promoted their gas cooker as consuming 25 per cent less gas than other cookers.[29]

In November 1905 David Curle Smith, the Municipal Electrical Engineer of Kalgoorlie, Western Australia, patented an electric stove with an oven and a hotplate, and a grill tray between them. Production was limited to fifty, which were hired out to residents of the municipality. His wife Nora wrote a cookbook with operating instructions, *Thermo-electrical Cooking Made Easy*, published in March 1907. The cost proved prohibitive and production ceased.

This was also the time when dietary reform was receiving increased attention. The Australian Health Society was founded in Melbourne in 1875, and over the next ten years presented lectures on 'Food and What Becomes of It', 'The Art of Preserving Health', 'Cookery and Health'

The Welsbach Gas Cooker, a real friend to the housewife.

and 'On the Adulteration of Food and Drink'.[30] In 1910 Professor W. A. Osborne, professor of physiology and histology at the University of Melbourne, published his *Primer of Dietetics*, and in 1914 Dr J. W. Springthorpe published *Therapeutics, Dietetics and Hygiene: An Australian Textbook*. Both books were influential in the nutritional guidance given to mothers in the newly established Baby Health Clinics, the first of which opened in Alexandria, Sydney, in August 1914.

By the time of their publication, however, William Arnott had already realized the benefit of selling to the infant- and child-health market. Arnott was a Scottish baker and confectioner who had migrated to Australia in 1844. In 1865 he set up business in Newcastle, north of Sydney, and began baking bread and cakes and ship's biscuit, also known as hardtack (a simple mix of flour and water and salt made firm to last on

Robert Edgell

In 1906 the former civil engineer Robert Gordon Edgell bought land near Bathurst, New South Wales. On it he planted apples and pears, cool-climate fruit trees favoured by orchardists in the area. He also planted 1.2 ha (3 ac) of asparagus and other vegetables. The asparagus, planted in rows rather than the traditional beds, thrived, and soon Edgell had saturated the Sydney market with fresh produce and was left with an excess on his hands.

He turned to canning, but lacking knowledge in how best to can vegetables his early efforts were not successful. In 1925 he sent his son Maxwell to America to learn canning techniques. On Maxwell's return the Edgells set up a small cannery at their property Bradwardine, undertaking the process from making the cans through to sealing and marketing the produce. In 1930 Edgell registered Gordon Edgell & Sons as a public company. The company continued trading successfully through the 1930s Depression and extended the range of fruit and vegetables being canned during the Second World War as demand increased to supply American and Australian armed forces. In 1943 he set up a second cannery at Cowra, 100 km (60 mi.) from Bathurst, to meet the demand. The one-millionth can of vegetables rolled off the now mechanized production line in 1944.

In 1955 the company merged with Birds Eye, the American company that had pioneered the technique for quick-freezing vegetables, fish and meat. Birds Eye products had been first imported into Australia in 1940, and in 1949 vegetables were being grown locally specifically for Birds Eye. In 1956 Birds Eye rolled out its frozen, crumbed Fish Fingers, which would go on to become a staple at the Australian dinner table throughout the next two decades.

The Lamington

While arguments rage about the origin of the meringue-based pavlova (Australia and New Zealand both lay claim), there is no doubt that the Lamington originated in Queensland around the turn of the century. Its creation is generally ascribed to the Frenchman Armand Galland, chef to Lord Lamington, Governor of Queensland from 1895 to 1901.

The Lamington is a cube of sponge-cake dipped in chocolate icing and rolled in grated coconut (fresh, while best, was rare for much of the Lamington's life, and rehydrated desiccated coconut regularly substituted). It may have begun life as a way of using up leftover sponge-cake as an alternative to trifle, but it soon established itself as an entity in its own right.

Miss K. Ayers of Mount Lofty and Mrs L. T. Maund of The Rectory, Crafers, provided the following recipe for the *Kookaburra Cookery Book of Culinary and Household Recipes and Hints*, produced by the Lady Victoria Buxton Girls' Club, Adelaide, South Australia, in 1912. It does not, however, use chocolate in the icing.

long journeys). Sometime in the 1880s he had the brilliant idea to create a soft biscuit in an oval shape using arrowroot flour and milk – the prosaically named Milk Arrowroot. The biscuit was promoted as 'The Children's Food'. An early advertisement shows a young boy trying to give a young girl milk from a large jug. The tagline is 'Out of the Jug a drink under difficulty,' implying it was easier to get milk via a biscuit. Arnott's would go on to produce some of Australia's best-loved biscuits in the following years.

War

As 1914 began, Australia was settling into its new federated structure. Then, in August, Britain declared war against Germany. Australia, as part of the British Empire, was automatically at war. The Australian Imperial Force was formed in August 1914 and deployed to Turkey, where it fought with British, New Zealand, French and Indian troops on the Gallipoli Peninsula

Lamington Cake

1 cupful butter; 1½ cupfuls sugar; 1 cupful milk; 3 cupfuls flour; 1 teaspoonful carbonate of soda; 2 teaspoonfuls cream of tartar; 4 eggs. Melt the butter, pour it over the sugar and eggs, then add the milk with the soda dissolved, and the flour with cream of tartar mixed. Beat all well together with the essence of lemon to taste. Bake in a meat tin, lined with buttered paper, half an hour or a little more in a fair oven. When cold, cut into squares and ice.

Icing for above Cake: – 1 lb icing sugar; ¼ lb butter; crush sugar fine, melt butter, mix both together; add 1½ tablespoonfuls of boiling water and 4 teaspoonsful of cocoanut.

If too thick for spreading, add another teaspoonful of water.

Spread all over little squares and roll in grated cocoanut. Half the quantity is sufficient, if the cake is not cut into squares.

Three Lamingtons.

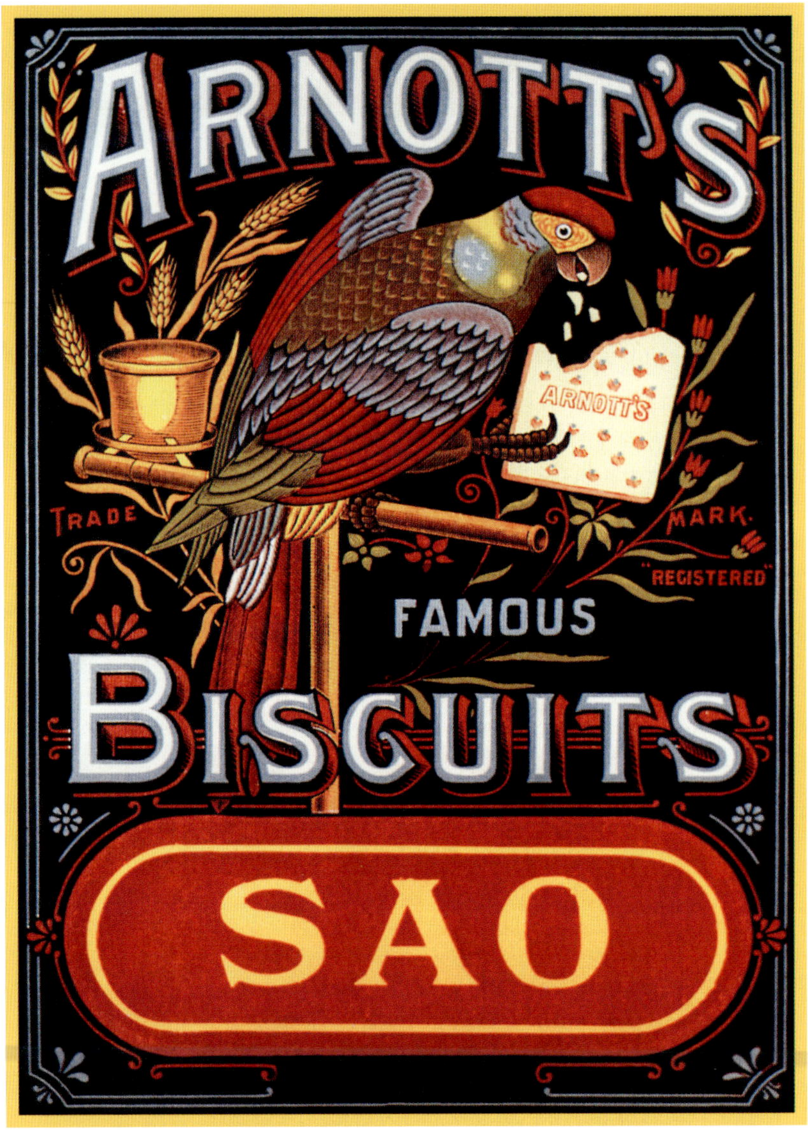

The logo for Arnott's Sao Biscuits featured the Australian rainbow lorikeet developed from a sketch by Arnott's daughter-in-law Leslie Arnott in 1888.

Anzac Biscuits

Australian women baking Anzac biscuits and sending them to the troops overseas is an abiding story of the First World War. Food historian Barbara Santich suggests it was far more likely that these biscuits were a commercial product, even those sent by charitable organizations such as the Australian Comforts Fund. The biscuit that was in oversupply was the Arnott's Anzac Wafer or Tile, its popular hard tack or ship's biscuit, which was part of the regular ration of the troops. Santich identifies possibly the earliest printed recipe for 'Anzac Biscuits or Crispies' in the Melbourne paper *The Argus*, 15 September 1920, specifying that John Bull oats be used, which Santich suggests may well have been part of a publicity campaign for the popular oats.[31]

Anzac Biscuit or Crispies

Josephine (E. Brunswick) has been kind enough to contribute the following recipe for Anzac biscuits: – two cups John Bull oats or flaked oatmeal, 1 cup flour, 1 tablespoonful golden syrup, half-cup of sugar, 1 teaspoonful carbonate of soda, 1 good pinch salt, 2 tablespoonfuls boiling water, 1 half-cup melted butter. Put oatmeal, flour, sugar and salt together. Pour on the melted butter, mix syrup and boiling water, and stir in the soda. Mix all while frothing. Put on the greased oven slide with a teaspoon, bake brown in a moderate oven.

Anzac biscuits, named for the Australian and New Zealand Army Corps in the First World War, though it's unlikely they were ever eaten in the trenches.

from April to December 1915. It was at Gallipoli that the combined forces of Australia and New Zealand were given the name ANZAC – Australian and New Zealand Army Corps. The engagement at Gallipoli would come to be seen by many as the consolidating event of national identity.

SIX

Between World Wars, 1914–45

In 1914 Australia was a major supplier of wheat and meat to Britain. When the First World War broke out, the British government acted to guarantee supply would continue by protecting the sea lanes and prohibiting Australian meat, wheat and flour from being exported to countries other than Britain and her dominions. In 1915 Britain went further and agreed to purchase all Australia's export meat supply until the end of the war. In 1916 it agreed to buy the whole export wheat crop also.

At home, the prospect of shortages of these staples of the Australian table and other resources that would be diverted or prioritized for the war effort led to price hikes at shops and an overall rise in the cost of living. This was exacerbated as stock for overseas remained held up in Australia. The state premiers, who under the separation of powers could legislate on food prices, promised to enact controls. Only New South Wales did so. In July 1915 Ivy Brookes, a Liberal Party member, organized a Housewives' Co-operative Association 'to encourage co-operative buying and marketing of produce direct from the producer to the consumer'.[1] The venture was dropped in 1916. As food prices remained high, during August and September 1917 women took part in daily marches and occupations of the streets in Melbourne to demand the Commonwealth government release food in storage and punish those exploiting the shortages. The government did nothing. In July 1917 wharf labourers placed bans on loading wheat and flour for reshipment to Southeast Asia until prices dropped to pre-war levels. Again the government did nothing. In August 1917, Prime Minister William Morris Hughes referred the question of food prices, the impact of exports on commodities, and market manipulation by cartels to the Interstate Commission. But the commission had little power, and its reports, while conceding the impact on food shortages of produce locked in storage, denied any profiteering or conspiracy and did not produce any solutions.[2]

As the war ended, governments turned their minds to dealing with the return of the troops instead.

Soldier Settlements

'After the First World War,' writes the economist George Megalogenis,

> a series of epic policy blunders left the nation saddled with debts that would once again make Australia vulnerable to another global shock. The most symbolic of these mistakes was the soldier settlement scheme ... It might have yielded the fruits of diversity and creativity if politicians weren't so obsessed with the utopia of British agrarian identity for Australia.[3]

Soldier settlement schemes, developed in all states, were an attempt by governments to ensure a livelihood for returning servicemen and their families, in recognition of their service to the nation. But they also served to continue the process of breaking up the large pastoral holdings of the squatters, which had begun with the settlement Acts of the 1860s and 1870s, and to populate regional Australia, easing the increasing concentration of people in the urban capitals.

The schemes, writes historian Marilyn Lake,

> [were] predicated on a family production unit. Prohibited from generating and exploiting a (male) labouring class, these New World farmers were expected to use the labour of their families ... When a returned solider applied for the qualification certificate which would enable him to take up land, he was questioned not only about his own capital resources and experience, but also his wife's ... [inspectors] asked after the children's ages and whether they assisted on the farm and 'to what extent'. If waged labour was employed, the inspectors were asked to determine whether it was 'really necessary'.[4]

So it was with A. B. Facey and his wife Evelyn:

Soldier Settlement Memorial, Griffith, New South Wales.

> We were the first couple to be registered as man and wife under the Soldier's Settlement Scheme. The property was valued at the time at three thousand pounds and the limit on finance allowed by the Board for one soldier was two thousand pounds, so the Act was altered to allow the wife of a returned soldier to come in as a partner, and the allowed amount was four thousand pounds.[5]

Facey's property had 'approximately twelve hundred acres, a nice house, several horses and a number of badly neglected farm implements'. When they first arrived in July 1922 it was too late in the season to plant a crop, but by August they had 80 ha (200 ac) fenced in. He went to a sale at the property of another soldier-settler who had failed at wheat and sheep farming and bought the sheep. Within a year, he was seeing success: 'One lot of two hundred whethers that I had purchased for twenty-five shillings a head – they were very skinny and we kept them on good feed for six weeks – I sold to a butcher for two pounds and sixteen shillings each, not a bad deal for six weeks.'[6] In January 1924 he harvested his first crops of barley, oats and wheat. In February, fire destroyed their house. He built another, which absorbed all their savings. They had just found their feet again when in June of 1927 heavy winter rains destroyed the wheat crop, and the same happened in 1928. In 1930 they had success with 8,000 bags of wheat for sale. They were advised by their bank and the state Agricultural Department to store their wheat, on the expectation that the price would rise over 5 shillings a bushel. They were advanced a proportion of the prospective income. The wheat price did not recover, and they sold their wheat for 1 shilling and 7 pence the bushel. Then in 1931, with the collapse of the wool foreign market, they were dealt another blow, selling their wool for threepence halfpenny per pound of fleece. The final straw was an infestation of rabbits, who destroyed the crops and ate the acid-rich pasture of the sheep and cattle, needed for the stock to chew their cud. 'So these animals lay down and died in horrible agony . . . We lost all our cows . . . and eight hundred sheep within four months in spite of our hand-feeding oats and hay to them daily.'[7]

> My health broke and I had to go to hospital for one month in 1932 . . . When I returned home we were just about down and out . . . I made a special trip to the city late in 1932 to see the Minister for Agriculture and the manager of the Soldier's Settlement Scheme, and the manager of the Agricultural bank. I pointed out the hopelessness of trying to carry on unless we were supplied with enough rabbit-netting to put around our property to control the rabbit menace. But all to no avail. There were hundreds of soldier settlers leaving their properties and shifting to the city, or large country towns, as they were starved out.[8]

'One in three of the thirty-seven thousand soldiers who took up the offer of country living,' writes Megalogenis, 'eventually walked off the land.'

> The program would lose twenty-four million pounds by 1928 [more than $2 billion today]. Royal commission after royal commission documented the debacle. Among the most telling was the sharply worded report to the Tasmanian parliament in

Emphasizing British heritage was a none-too-subtle ploy to ensure a market for Australian produce.

> 1926. The soldiers made a rush for farms and the department had to work at flat speed . . . The fact is that every soldier who wanted a farm got it, where he was fit or not.[9]

Facey and his family left their farm at the end of 1933.

The Victorian government scheme to make dried fruit farmers out of returned soldiers had some success. In 1920–23 the Victorian government granted ex-servicemen seven hundred allotments at Red Cliffs, near Mildura. The scheme proved almost too successful. In 1923 production nearly doubled, leading to a drastic drop in prices from an average of £80 per tonne to £30 per tonne for dried fruit. Two strategies were used to increase consumption in the domestic market: the government put a duty of 6 pence per pound on all imported dried fruits; and the Australian Dried Fruits Association began promoting the health benefits of dried vine-fruits through free cookbooks.

Soldier settlements were also established after the Second World War, but with more success: they were mainly located in areas of good rainfall, with the added safeguard of reliable irrigation, and inexperienced soldiers had to spend two years in apprenticeship with an existing viable farmer.[10]

The Barossa Valley Germans

In Australia the First World War had an impact on a community that would play a significant role in Australian foodways – the Lutheran community in the Barossa Valley. In November 1838 two hundred Lutheran immigrants from Prussia landed in Adelaide. They were escaping religious persecution following the union of the Reformed Calvinist and Lutheran faiths in 1817, and the 1830 decree of King Friedrich Wilhelm III forbidding Lutherans from continuing to practise their faith. As more Lutherans emigrated, the pressure on the settlement grew. In 1842, on the basis of favourable reports of the Barossa Valley, about 60 km (35 mi.) from Adelaide, members of the Adelaide congregation set out to establish the settlement of Bethanien (now Bethany). By 1900 some 18,000 German migrants had arrived in South Australia, of which about two-thirds settled in the Barossa and the Adelaide Hills.[11] Here they began to grow wheat, barley, rye, maize and peas. Grape vines were planted at Bethany, but these initial plantings were for domestic consumption.

They also developed a unique cuisine fusing German and English traditions. Angela Heuzenroeder, who was born in the Barossa during the Second World War and returned to live there when she married, writes:

> Prussians had always been keen on fermented foods. Their baking of cake relied on fermented yeast cultures; the cheeses were fermented milk; the wine fermented; the beer, cucumbers,

> sauerkraut and metwurst were fermented. English people, on the other hand, had a taste for sweet jams and pickles. They were making good use of the sugar that came from the British colonies . . . the Prussians *did* use sugar in their food preparation and the English *did* make cheese, beer and wine. It is, rather, a question of emphasis. In the early twentieth century, many recipes cut or copied from English newspapers into notebooks which were otherwise written in German gave directions for making sauces, pickles and jams that were sweeter than much of the Prussian food had been.[12]

Over-cropping began to result in low yields in the 1860s and many Barossa settlers headed for newly opened lands in the Riverina district of New South Wales. Many of those who remained turned to viticulture and winemaking on a commercial scale. This was aided by the removal of tariffs between the states at Federation and the fact that the vines in South Australia had avoided the outbreak of phylloxera that devastated the eastern states. The first vines were varieties imported from Europe as well as South Africa, including grenache, mataro, hermitage, shiraz, black portugal and black morocco, madeira, verdelho, tokay, frontignac and rhine riesling. The early wines were heavy, sweet or fortified wines, especially the Portuguese styles of vintage and tawny ports.[13]

Barossa Valley vineyards, *c.* 1900.

The *Barossa Valley Cookery Book* was a way for Lutheran Germans to show support for Australian troops during the First World War. This is the cover of the 13th edition.

When the First World War broke out, anti-German sentiment was aimed at Australians of German heritage and their communities: some people with German heritage were interned; Lutheran schools in South Australia were closed; towns had their German names changed, and some families anglicized their German surnames, too. Food to be sold also underwent name changes. 'So *Berliner Pfannkuchen*,' Heuzenroeder writes, 'achieved respectability under the name Kitchener bun, in honour of the English general whose name was in everybody's newspapers.'[14] In 1917 the first edition of *The Barossa Cookery Book: 400 Tried Recipes* was produced in Tanunda, with proceeds to go to the South Australian Soldier's Fund. It was intended as statement of the patriotism of the community in the face of accusations of disloyalty. 'The book does its bit to show the flag,' writes Heuzenroeder, 'by offering recipes of a decidedly British flavour: dishes with names such as Exeter Stew, Dolly Varden Cakes and Thornton Pudding.'[15]

The communities survived and thrived, however. In 1935 three of the towns, including Hahndorf, had their names changed back to the original German ones. The Barossa Valley is now one of the premier wine regions of Australia with 120 wine producers, some of whom are now the sixth generation of descendants of the first Lutheran settlers. Wineries such as Chateau Tanunda, Leo Buring, Jacob's Creek, Orlando, Seppelt, Yalumba, Wolf Blass and Peter Lehmann are firmly entrenched in the market. In 1960 Max Schubert, Penfolds' first Chief Winemaker, produced his first Grange Hermitage, which would go on to garner awards both at home and internationally with each successive vintage. The Barossa now is equally famous for maintaining the traditions of the Prussian cooking of the first settlers, standing alone as a distinctive regional cuisine in the Australian food landscape with specialities like quark (*stinkerkaes* made from curdled milk), sauerkraut, wursts and sausages, pork-hock pudding and Streusel cakes. In 2012 the South Australian government passed the Character Preservation (Barossa Valley) Act with measures that guide the economic development of the region while preserving its special character.

Dining in High and Low

Sunday tea at the Australian novelist Hal Porter's childhood home in Melbourne was an elaborate affair:

> There is the Sunday tea-table: white damask glossily starched, and bearing, as the table-napkins stiff as cardboard do, a design of swans and bulrushes; the salad bowl, the cake-stands, jam dishes, pickle jars, sugar-castor and celery vase all of cut glass; the tiered electro-plated cruet; the silver trumpets of sweet peas; the butter knives, cake knives, jam spoons and Sunday bread-knife with mother-of-pearl handles, and silver-gilt blades and bowls engraved with florid scrolls and curly acanthus leaves . . . [16]

'The house,' Porter writes,

> contains also many indications of a lower middle-class lavishness Australians regard as bare necessities. In the meat-safe are a sirloin, pounds of rump steak and cutlets. In the pantry are a case of apples, a pineapple, peaches, oranges

Sugar Hits

Sugar-laden sweets or lollies are firmly ensconced as Australians' guilty pleasures. Many iconic Australian sweet snacks were first produced in the 1920s:

1921: Chocolatier Hoadley's launches the Violet Crumble, a chocolate-coated honeycomb bar in a distinctive purple wrapper.

1922: Sweetacres launches Minties, a jaw-sticking white mint toffee. It was advertised as the mint to turn to in embarrassing situations and its tag line – 'It's moments like these you need Minties' – became an Australian catchphrase.

1924: MacRobertson's launches Cherry Ripe, a thin bar of cherry jam and grated fresh coconut covered with chocolate.

1929: An April edition of the *Hobart Mercury* newspaper includes the first known reference to Fairy Bread: bread and butter sprinkled with tiny multicoloured balls of sugar icing called 'hundreds and thousands'.

1930: MacRobertson's launches Freddo Frog, a flat chocolate moulded to look like a frog.

1931: Sweetacres launches Jaffas, marble-sized balls of chocolate wrapped in a thin, hard orange-icing shell. Rolling Jaffas down aisles of cinemas would keep Australian children endlessly amused while waiting for the start of the picture.

Late 1930s: Sweetacres launches Fantales, a chewy caramel cube with film-star trivia on the wrapper.

and bananas. The shelves are lined with bottles of jam, with sauces, pickles, chutneys and jars of Rose's Marmalade.[17]

Porter's mother could buy these 'bare necessities' at the corner shop daily. She may have gone to a nearby butcher to buy the meat, though this would have to be done once or twice a week as she had a meat safe, not an icebox. Hawkers still brought food to her door regularly: 'The grocer, the fishmonger, the rabbit-oh,' Porter writes, 'the John Chinaman greengrocer and fruiterer, the iceman and the egg-woman appear once or twice weekly.'[18]

Or she could join other women spending the day in one of the arcades, chain stores or department stores that were well established in the cities by the start of the First World War. The arcade, a group of small purpose-built shops under substantial cover, had entered the shopping realm in 1853 when the Queen's Arcade opened in Melbourne. The Strand Arcade opened in Sydney in 1893 and by the end of the century there were two arcades in Adelaide – the Adelaide Arcade and the adjoining Gays Arcade. Cousins Thomas Moran and Frederick Cato had begun their grocery-store chain in 1882 and it became the dominant chain in the late nineteenth and early twentieth century. 'The chain store approach,' writes the historian Beverley Kingston, 'was geared to selling basic goods which were brought frequently and in quantity, articles which could be standardised, which required no selling and no advertising. In the chain stores there was no personal service, no home delivery, no credit, no pretence of exclusivity; there were no alterations, no special orders, no repairs.'[19]

For Myrtle Rose White and her husband, managing a small farm in the sandhill country near Lake Frome in South Australia, meals could not have been more different. Here food stores came in bulk twice a year:

> Flour and sugar by the ton; currants, raisins, dried fruits, baking powder, hops, sauces, jams, by the case; dried peas and beans by the bag, and compressed potatoes by the tin, when they did come. The stores came over the sandhills on pack-camel or string-teams as they are called.[20]

Carriage of a tin of Arnott's Milk Arrowroot Biscuits by 'swaying camels had acted as a mortar and pestle. The biscuits resembled nothing so much as fuller's earth; even the wrappings were reduced to infinitesimal scraps.'[21]

She began a vegetable plot:

> there were grape vines and citrus trees, with melons of all varieties – rock-melons, bouquet-melons, water-melons – to assuage our cravings for fruit. Hardy Northern Territory beans were planted to climb over and beautify the bush sheds . . . for one short season the vegetable garden flourished and multiplied, then the ground became impregnated with the minerals that were in the bore-water, and all growth withered and died.[22]

A selection of the iconic Australia confectionary launched in the 1920s.

And while Porter's mother had butchers from which she could get fresh meat, for White 'There is fresh beef for one day, and salt beef for twenty-nine . . . There were times in the later years at Noonameena, when I would have considered a lamb chop above rubies, cabbage food for the gods.'[23]

'What Shall I Prepare for Dinner?'

Porter's mother may also have kept up with the latest trends in home dining through the new magazines targeting middle-class housewives. In 1902 Fitchett Brothers Pty Ltd published the first edition of *New Idea: A Women's Home Journal for Australia*, its title changing in 1911 to *Everylady's Journal*, then back to *New Idea* in 1928, under which it continues. This was the first mass-circulation publication targeted at women in Australia. The magazine was the only one on the market until 1926, when the *Australian Woman's Mirror* began publication as an offshoot of the long-running *Bulletin* magazine, carrying poems and short stories written by women, as well as dress patterns, advertisements for clothes (including lingerie) and make-up, household tips, and advice from a woman solicitor on legal matters of concern particularly to women. It also published 'Proved Recipes'; those in its first edition show the continuation of British cake and dessert traditions: Fig Pudding; Baked Currant Pudding; Plain Pudding; Marguerite Pudding; Patmore Pudding; Baked Apple Sponge; Apple Batter; Ginger Sandwich; Cornflour Cake; Sponge Cake; Lamington Cakes; Pumpkin Scones; Short Cake; Mock Cream; and Lemon Syrup.[24]

The *Mirror* was very popular, with a circulation of 160,000 in the 1930s. But its dominant position was eclipsed in 1933 when the *Australian Women's Weekly* began production. The *Weekly* ran a competition for readers to contribute their 'Best Recipes' with a first prize of £5 and consolation prizes of 5 shillings each. In the 1 July edition, first prize went to Miss Mary Carr, Brimbl Road, Grenfell (in rural New South Wales) for her recipe for Ham and Apple Roast. Consolation prizes that week included recipes for Curry Puffs, and Escalopes of Veal and Macaroni.[25]

The latter two show that while the received wisdom in Australian food circles is that domestic food of this time rarely stepped away from

The Strand Arcade in Sydney, built 1890–92, was one of the first of the new-style shopping arcades.

Ham and Apple Roast

Miss Mary Carr

Take 1½ thick slices of ham, 1 lb of cooking apples, 4 ozs brown breadcrumbs, 2 onions, a little sage, 3 ozs of grated cheese. Arrange a layer of sliced ham in a baking dish (or a casserole from which the dish can be served). Sprinkle with brown breadcrumbs, a little chopped sage, and minced onion, and cover completely with a layer of sliced apples. Continue the layers till the dish is three-quarters full. Bake in a hot oven for half an hour. Beat two eggs with the grated cheese, spread over the top and return to the oven until the cheese is melted and the beaten egg is set.

the familiar, women were cooking across a more varied range and were getting kudos when they did. Opportunities were increasingly developing for women to share their skills and knowledge outside of their friendship and social networks. This began to change when books like the 1902 Presbyterian Church of NSW Women's Missionary Association *Cookery Book of Good and Tried Receipts* collected recipes from women in their congregations or charities and published them as shared practical knowledge as opposed to the knowledge of chefs or the emerging cookery experts teaching privately or in the domestic science colleges. It was a democratization of knowledge that would have a profound impact on the foodways of Australians. What's more, they were rewarded with modest amounts of money when their recipes were selected for publication.

Printing of community cookery books, which were produced to raise funds for particular causes like that of the Missionary Association, was costly. Often the cost was covered through advertising from local businesses, food manufacturers and makers of kitchenware and cooking ranges. The 1940 edition of the *Household Book*, for example, had advertisements from Dewar's (makers of Scotch whisky), Oliver J. Nilsen Radio and Electrical Engineers in Bourke Street, Melbourne, and Cornina 'The Superfine Cornflour' made by Parsons Bros.[26]

As new products hit the market, manufacturers also produced recipe books and pamphlets to introduce the product to housewives. The Edible Oils Industries of Australia in the mid-1930s published *What Shall I Cook*

Today? to promote copha, the shortening derived from copra, in which was included the recipe for 'Chocolate Crackles', now an Australian standard at children's parties and school and charity fund-raising stalls. It was a generous bit of cross-marketing, as the main substantial ingredient in the treat is Rice Bubbles, introduced by Kellogg's in 1929. The Electrical Association for Women published its *Sydney Cookery Book* in 1938. In its foreword Dr Frances McKay, president of the Advisory Council of the Association, wrote:

> How often some housewife or other has said: 'What shall I prepare for dinner?' It is with a view to answering this question and to help every housewife who has an electric range that Mrs McKenzie has devoted much care and thought to the preparation of this book. With the progress of knowledge of food and food values during the march of time, rule of thumb methods must be discarded, and the modern method of preparing food for consumption is ELECTRICAL COOKING.[27]

Advertisement for built-in electric kitchen, 1930s.

Cookery Book devotes a chapter to 'Refrigerator Recipes': Kelvinator-brand electric refrigerators had been available in Australia since 1926. The recipes are for cold puddings – caramel blancmange, flummery, parfaits, ices creams, cold drinks and jellies, and a range of salads. What McKay's foreword doesn't say is that this and other books of the time promoting 'electrical cooking' were aimed squarely at stealing some of the market that was still captured by gas cooking. Metters, a company established to manufacture fuel stoves in 1917 had launched its Early Kooka gas range. With its trademark drawing of a kookaburra, a much-loved Australian bird, with a worm in its beak, the range had become ubiquitous. Gas would continue its dominance until the 1950s.

One of the most important organizations through which women in rural areas came together for support, to take on activities to better their communities and to share knowledge, was the Country Women's Association established in 1922 in New South Wales and in all states and territories by 1936. The associations were formed to advocate for the needs of women and their families in rural Australia. As early as 1931 the associations began campaigning for labels that gave the date of packaging as well as for more nutritious processed foods, those for example using unpolished rice, wholemeal flour or less sugar in candied citrus peel.[28] The associations were entirely self-funded, raising money through membership fees and making and selling fabric and knitted clothing, napery, jams, pickles, cakes and scones. The associations produced local-branch and regional cookbooks of recipes collected from members, again an important way through which practical food knowledge was exchanged between women.

Aboriginal Labour: The Stolen Generation

While the cookery books described above and in Chapter Five of this history offer insights into the domestic lives of Australian women as home makers, what they don't tell is the stories of the thousands of Aboriginal women and girls forced into domestic service during these years. The immigrant supply of women as domestic servants fell under the extension of the White Australia policy, which excluded or limited immigration from more and more countries – Germany, Austria, Hungary, Bulgaria and Turkey in 1920, Malta in 1924 and Italy in the 1930s. At the same time Britain was increasingly reluctant to continue with assisted immigration schemes for its citizens as it sought to shore up its own population.

But there remained a pool to draw on: Aboriginal women and girls from reserves and missions – pejoratively called 'half castes' – forcibly removed from their families under the guise of protection. Between 1869 and 1911 every state and territory in Australia (except Tasmania) passed Aboriginal Protection legislation and established Protection Boards. The powers of the boards varied: some had more power in determining where Aboriginal people could live; some controlled the movement of Aboriginal people within the state. In reserves established under the boards, white managers had full control over the lives of the Aboriginal residents, including, in some cases, arranging marriages. All the boards had the power to remove children from their families and place them in the care of the state, on the ostensible grounds of preventing the children from neglect, and to ensure they received education they otherwise would not have had. The Boards could do this to 'half caste' children without any obligation to prove that they were subject to neglect.

Many of the young girls were boarded in institutions away from their families, trained to be domestic servants and then 'apprenticed' out to white households. Margaret Tucker was one such young girl who described her training at the Cootamundra Girls Home in the 1983 documentary *Lousy Little Sixpence*:

> When we were there at the training school we used to go round to the back of the homes and have a weep, two or three of us, for our home. We were supposed to know all about the stove and the cooking, but all the things that we cooked [in their own homes] ... was a damper, and mostly when we didn't have a stove it was in the ashes ... But after a couple of teachings she expected you to know ... before we'd realise we'd have a real hard smack on the face. I can remember a girl's mouth bleeding with the punishment that she had. We were scared stiff before we even went into the kitchen to learning the cooking ... I have the marks on my body right now from the beltings I had. I was only there about three months before they took me with another girl to Sydney.[29]

While the system was called an apprenticeship, it was more akin to indentured labour. The young Aboriginal girls were wards of the state. They were supposed to be paid at the same low rate as other state wards in service. However, few ever saw their pay, as Violet Shea, also forced into service, described:

> [The pay] was 1/6 a week. A shilling to a trust fund with the Aboriginal Protection Board, and sixpence a week pocket money for me but I never ever got that sixpence. Different people have said to me why didn't you ask for it, but you just didn't do those things, if I'd have asked for it she probably would have said oh I'm putting it away for you or something like that.[30]

Young boys who were taken away were 'apprenticed' out to farmers where again they were supposed to be trained in rural skills. Bill Reid said of his experience: 'The manager used to keep a tight rein on us. He wasn't a qualified teacher; couldn't teach above third class. Most of our time was spent working in the gardens or digging trenches, pit toilets, a lot of manual labour instead of being educated. The only thing I learned was how to work.'[31]

During their time in service the children were not permitted any contact with their families. They came to be known as the Stolen Generation. It was not until the 1960s that states repealed protection legislation. On 13 February 2008 Prime Minister Kevin Rudd delivered an unequivocal apology to them on behalf of successive Australian governments.

Radio Arrives

On a Sunday afternoon in 1930 listeners to radio station 2KY in Sydney first heard a song that would become one of Australia's most well known. It was an advertising jingle written by Albert Lenertz and Les Woods to promote Aeroplane Jelly crystals. The crystals had started their life in 1927 when their creator Bert Appleroth, a tram driver, made them in his bathtub and distributed them along his tram route. The jingle was first sung by three-year-old Jennifer Paykel, who was taken to the 2KY studio to perform it live on air.

The first radio licence in Australia was granted to Charles Maclurcan in 1921 for station 2CM, broadcasting from the Wentworth Hotel in Sydney, owned by the Maclurcan family. Charles was the son of the hotelier and cookbook writer Hannah Maclurcan. Disappointingly, the station only broadcast classical music concerts – no cookery content – and only on Sunday nights. The first commercial broadcaster was 2BD, also in Sydney, which began broadcasting in November 1923.

Businesses were quick to see the potential of the new medium for advertising, though the reach initially was not as extensive as print.

Vegemite on toast: an Australian breakfast tradition.

Appleroth and Lenertz recognized this, and their gamble paid off. In 1938 Aeroplane Jelly ran a competition to find a voice to re-record the jingle. Five-year-old Joy King beat two hundred other children and recorded the version that continues to be used in advertising the product today.

In 1922 the chemist Cyril Callister, employed by the Fred Walker Co., created a spread from brewer's yeast, which at that stage had the uninspiring name of 'Pure Vegetable Extract'. The company held a national competition to name the spread and Melbourne sisters Hilda and Laurel Armstrong won. Vegemite was on Australian grocery shelves on 25 October 1923. It would go on to be the most common, if not popular, spread in school lunches for generations. A jar of Vegemite was the first product to be electronically scanned at an Australian supermarket in 1984, and the one-billionth jar was bottled in 2004. Surprisingly, Vegemite had to wait until 1956 before it got its own radio jingle, the 'Happy Little Vegemites' song, written by Alan Weekes of advertising agency J. Walter Thompson in Sydney.

Dining Out Continental

When Hal Porter left home to take up art studies in the late 1920s he began 'shirking the roast lamb, mint sauce, three vegs, apple pie and custard restaurants' of Melbourne, for 'eating and drinking in foreign cafes . . . happy to be the one conspicuously blond Australian drinking ouzo or scented Metaxa brandy and eating vine-leaf-wrapped meat-balls at the Greek Club, or shrimps fried in batter at the Japanese *Hoi-Sin Café* [and] the *Chung Wah Café* in Heffernan Lane'.[32] He and his fellow art students were what the food historian Charmaine O'Brien calls 'a new generation of bohemians [and] cosmopolitan elite who were familiar with such food and service from travelling in Europe'.[33]

At the Café Florentino in 1929, Rinaldo Massoni installed the first espresso machine in Australia. In Sydney in 1930 the Russian immigrant Ivan Repin opened the Coffee Inn in King Street, a café offering 'Vienna Style' coffees with cream – fresh or whipped – and freshly ground beans roasted at another of his shops nearby. Repin's was also the café of choice for Hungarian refugees like Emery Barcs and his wife, '[because] they served two cups of coffee and a biscuit for sixpence, and because one could sit there in off-peak hours and talk as long as one liked'.[34] For lunch they would go to a Hungarian restaurant in the centre of Sydney where 'lunch only costs 1/6 [and] familiar odours of fried onion and goulash greeted us as we stepped into the doorway . . . [It] resembled a *bust resti* for the third-class passengers at a Hungarian provincial railway station.'[35]

For the less adventurous in the 1940s there were Cahills restaurants at various sites in the city. 'The one next door to the Hotel Australia was my choice,' recalls Margaret Fulton, doyenne of Australian cookery writers:

> Crumbed cutlets and other crumbed foods such as croquettes were much in demand. Many students worked their way through university in the kitchens at Cahills, gaining some extra-curricular knowledge by learning the fine art of crumbing. These crisp and golden-coated dishes enclosing tender lamb cutlets, or creamy melting centres of minced chicken, beef, or lamb were set off with a sauce to suit the dish. Very classy. For dessert, the highlight for young and old was a banana split or an ice-cream sundae served in a pressed glass dish. They were topped with crunchy, toasted nuts, fresh fruit, and sauces to die for. Chocolate fudge and caramel or butterscotch sauces were

first seen at Cahills. The caramel sauce became famous and was late sold in jars.[36]

The 'Six O'Clock Swill'

'There were seven or eight nightclubs [in Sydney in 1941],' Fulton remembers,

> where the fast livers could dance and drink till the early hours – but they had to order their liquor before six o'clock, pub closing time. Owing to the complicated liquor laws of those days, night clubs were not allowed to sell liquor, but if the patrons phoned before six o'clock the club could – at least theoretically – go out and buy liquor on the patrons' behalf and let them have it (usually at black market prices) when they arrived.[37]

Six o'clock closing was a victory for the Australian temperance movement. Early Closing Acts for shops in general had been introduced in a number of states in the early 1900s. The temperance movement seized on this and began campaigning for the same to apply to licensed hotels, which at the time were able to trade from five in the morning to eleven or half past eleven at night. In South Australia in 1925, 56 per cent of those eligible voted that all hotels be required to close at 6 p.m. Victoria, New South Wales and Tasmania followed in 1916 and Western Australia opted for 9 p.m. closing. Early closing led to what became known as the 'six o'clock swill': men would stop work at 5 p.m., head to the nearest bar and consume as much beer as they could before closing time. Queensland introduced 8 p.m. closing in 1923. In New South Wales in 1919 a referendum was held to determine whether to continue 6 p.m. closing as it had been introduced there as a wartime measure. It passed.

The temperance movement's victory was a pyrrhic one. 'The period after the World War,' notes the historian Ross Fitzgerald,

> did not see a great change in Australian beer and wine consumption despite the shorter hours available for pub drinking . . . Consumption of domestically brewed beer had risen towards the end of the nineteenth century but the introduction of six o'clock closing resulted in a reduction of the Commonwealth annual per capita consumption of beer

Let's Go to the Greek's

'If the Greeks were to move into agriculture,' wrote the Greek community historian Ioannis Kominos in 1916, 'through the various different means that the authorities in Australia offer, there is no doubt that they would become extremely rich and would quickly return to Greece, thus excluding any suspicion regarding the possibility that their stay in Australia would turn them into hostages of the country.' Happily for food in Australia, the Greeks did neither.

The first Greek immigrants to Australia arrived in the 1850s joining in the rush to the goldfields in New South Wales and Victoria. By the early 1900s their numbers were still small – not more than a few hundred – but they had already established themselves in the foodways of Australia. They had opened shops that stocked everything from fruit and vegetables to cake and confectionary. Grigorios Matorikos opened a small restaurant, the Athanaeum, in Melbourne in 1887, re-establishing it in 1893 with seating for four hundred and employing forty mainly Greek staff. Matorikos, like other Greeks at the time, was also an oyster-hawker, and opened an oyster saloon also at that time. Ioannis Kominos described these saloons as consisting of 'two or three floors, equipped, in some cases, with furnishings whose value varies between £1,000 and several thousand pounds, and in other cases, with furnishing whose value varies between £2,000 and £4,000'.

But it was the family-run Greek cafés which opened in the capital cities, and more importantly in rural towns, of which many Australians have fond memories. 'By the 1920s,' wrote O'Brien, 'the phrase "let's go to the Greeks" had come to mean having an inexpensive meal of chops or steak, eggs and chips (or some variation of) at one of the many Greek-run cafes.' Famed as much for their Art Deco interiors as their cheap meals, they imported soda fountains from

N. Andronicus Olympia Café, Allora, Queensland. The Greek café was an institution of many rural towns.

America and customers could sip milkshakes or spoon sundaes as they sat in booths and listened to the jukebox. 'It was the only place [those living in rural towns] could go out to dinner,' Effy Alexakis recalled, 'it was the only place to eat in the town except the pub.'[38]

> by less than a gallon for the years 1916–1930 . . . Seasoned temperance campaigners may have wished for a greater social transformation, but significant society-wide changes in patterns of alcohol consumption seem to reflect changing patterns of economic prosperity and decline.[39]

Weevils in the Flour

Poet and playwright Dorothy Hewett wrote the poem 'Where I Grew to Be a Man', from which the title for this section is taken, in the 1950s, based on the experiences of her friend Vera Deacon, who lived on Kooragang Island in the Hunter River at Newcastle. Newcastle was home to the steelworks of the Broken Hill Proprietary Co., which had been established in

1815 to mine silver and lead at Broken Hill in western New South Wales. When the Depression hit Australia, workers at the steel mills, like many others throughout all sectors of Australian industry, suffered severe hardship. Unemployment hit 30 per cent at its height. Margaret Fulton recalls the impact of food on her family and neighbours:

> Families were eating the cheapest food, dishes like tripe and onions, which most people hated but we loved it: it was the way Mother cooked the dish. Old mutton was the lot of many people, with bread and dripping a regular stand-by and bread and treacle for a treat. Fortunately for us, farmers who had been unable to pay Dad for the clothes he made [Fulton's father was a tailor] would bring in boxes of fresh produce as payment. So at least we had good food, even if it didn't pay the electricity bill or the rent.[40]

As unemployment worsened, governments took over the task of supplying food relief through coupons redeemable at charities, though it was barely adequate. Ina, living in Sydney and trying to manage a household where the breadwinner was now unemployed, recalls:

> You took a sugar bag, and you lined up – there'd be thousands of you – and you'd get a ticket . . . Depending on the size of your family you'd get food handed out to you. A tin of plum jam, a tin of condensed milk, a tin of syrup, three or four loaves of bread and a big hunk of meat cut just any way. That had to feed you and your family. There was no cheese or butter or eggs, nothing nourishing. No vegetables.[41]

Some suppliers took advantage of the coupon system; Wayne Bourne, unemployed and living in Adelaide during the Depression, recalled the beef riot there in January 1931:

> The Adelaide unemployed were being exploited by traders who had exclusive rights to supply food for the unemployed ration . . . Matthews was the butcher really triggered off the beef riot. He was supplying just the worst meat he could get from the abattoirs, the very cheapest stuff . . . Well the workers really knew what decent meat was and they wouldn't cop this rotten

> mutton they were getting. That triggered off the protest ... We decided to demand that beef be put on the rations ... Well we proceeded to march through Port Adelaide ... when we got to town, we all sort of milled around Victoria Square. But as the deputation came up to the great big Treasury doors, before we had time to knock, they swung open and the police were inside ... I think there was twelve arrested.[42]

Those who had food sometimes shared with those who did not. Tom Galvin lived in the self-deprecatingly named 'Happy Valley' – an unemployed people's camp at La Perouse in Sydney:

> Local fishermen would give us a hand-out especially when they got salmon, because their chance of selling it at the market were next to nil. Get tuppence a pound for it. We might help pull in the nets. The Chinese market gardens up the road could only sell their top production, and their cheapest grades they gave to us ... The Dairy Farmers' Co-operative donated sixteen gallons of milk a day to the camp.[43]

And so, writes the historian Wendy Lowenstein, 'there was still continuity in our society and this continuity with the past of wood stoves, night men and landlords who were open to pressure, of economy and ingenuity and household skills, of making-do, of hand-outs to travelling workers, all helped Australians to deal with the hardship.'[44] The last stanza of Hewitt's poem captures this, too:

> For dole bread is bitter bread ...
> But men grow strong as iron upon
> Black bread and sour.

Australians would need this strength in the war years to follow.

The Second World War

On 3 September 1939 Prime Minister Robert Gordon Menzies announced that Australia was at war with Germany. However, the impact on food at home was not fully felt until rationing was introduced in June 1942, beginning with tea and sugar, then butter (June 1934) and finally meat

(January 1943). The range of foods rationed was limited, but for a population that still ate large quantities of meat 'rationing meant that families had to stoically bear two beef-less days a week and eat sausages, offal, corned meats, bacon, ham, fish, or rabbits instead,' writes food historian Charmaine O'Brien. Cooking demonstrations to make the best use of basic items were run. The *Australian Women's Weekly* Winning Recipes for 23 May 1942 included recipes for mock potatoes and parsnip tea, both of which were judged by Olwen Francis, Food and Cookery Expert for the magazine, to be 'in touch with the times'.[45] In the 2 January 1943 edition of the *Weekly*, 'Two economy ideas, one for stale bread, one for potatoes are especially commended.'[46]

During 1937–45 Australia was also in the grip of severe drought. The wheat yield fell to its lowest levels since 1914. This, together with labour shortages and difficulties in importing goods, led to shortages in vegetables and fruit. The 'Dig for Victory' campaign was launched by Prime Minister John Curtin in January 1942, with Australians encouraged to grow their own vegetables in Victory Gardens and raise poultry. Gardening groups and collectives were formed, with money made from the sale of the excess produce often going to support the war effort. When Japan entered the Second World War in 1941, Australia was naturally called on to support the British army, and later the American forces, in Southeast Asia and the

Melbourne, Victoria, 1942: voluntary workers in the Victory Garden established in the grounds of WAAF House, Toorak.

Pacific. This further drained male labour, including in the farming sector. A national Australian Women's Land Army was formed in July 1942. The workforce was drawn from women in the cities, and while there was initial resistance on farms to this influx of unskilled labour they soon became an accepted part of farm life. The Army was never very large, peaking in December 1943 with 2,382 permanent members and 1,039 auxiliary members. It was disbanded in December 1945.

Women also swelled the factory workforce, with an additional 80,000 joining the labour force during the war. Many of them were in the rapidly expanding dehydrated vegetable industry, large amounts of which were produced for the Allied armed forces. In 1942 the Commonwealth government built 32 dehydration factories across all the major vegetable-growing areas in New South Wales, Victoria, South Australia and Tasmania.[47]

The most significant changes to Australian foodways during the Second World War, however, were a result of America's entry into the war in 1942. 'Virtually overnight,' writes the food-science historian Keith Farrer, 'the Australian food industry changed . . . especially the canners, faced [with] the manufacture of unfamiliar products to yet more unfamiliar specifications not only for the Australian and American forces, but for British, Dutch and Free French as well.'[48] Australian manufactures were still using old technology. By serendipitous chance, the Commonwealth Council of Scientific and Industrial Research had been established in 1936 and together with the United States Quartermaster Corps (USQMC)

Stale Bread Idea

A. Eshman, Sapphire, via Inverell New South Wales

Place scraps bread equal to a quarter-loaf in a muslin bag and soak in a bowl of cold water overnight. Remove and squeeze out all water with hands. Add to bread 2 large onions, and ½lb tomatoes peeled and chopped, with a little thyme, parsley and green garlic. Season with salt, pepper and mustard, add 2 eggs with enough milk to moisten and mix together. Drop small portions in boiling fat and fry till a light brown. Serve as a breakfast or luncheon dish or with dinner as a substitute for potatoes.

rapidly introduced new methods. 'What the Americans, especially had to offer,' writes Farrer, 'was to many Australian manufacturers a new technical approach to food processing and an unexpected emphasis on nutrition and quality control.'[49]

American influence wasn't limited to industrial advances. Coca-Cola and hamburgers came with the American troops on leave and based in Australia during the Second World War, and stayed, though the latter would be adopted as Australian with the addition of canned beetroot, and sometimes canned pineapple rings. J. J. Lynch began to supply canned and bottled orange juice – primarily for the American forces – and in time Australia's fruit juice industry emerged.[50] Margaret Fulton recalls eating at the Martha Washington, which 'served American-style salads which were eaten with a Splayd. This all-purpose eating instrument, a spoon with a forked end and a sharp cutting side . . . [was] very strange, we all thought.'[51] The 1943 invention of the Splayd is credited to Sydneysider William McArthur. It would become a standard wedding gift for many years.

SEVEN

Boundless Plains to Share, 1946–65

'For those who've come across the seas / We've boundless plains to share,' Scottish-born composer Peter Dodds McCormick had written in *Advance Australia Fair* in 1878. But as the preceding chapters in this history have detailed, in the years after Dodds's welcome government policy and public sentiment had been quite the opposite.

With the introduction of the White Australia policy, and then bans on immigration from countries with which Australia was at war, the welcome may had been well and truly withdrawn – with a few exceptions. British immigrants remained welcome. Under the 1925 Anglo-Italian Agreement between the British and Italian governments, Italian immigrants were accepted into Australia during the 1920s. Greeks migrated to Australia during the 1920s, fleeing the Greco-Turkish war of 1919–22. Immigration stopped with the outbreak of the Second World War. It became dangerous to undertake internal travel or sea journeys from countries from which Australia had drawn its migrants.

As the end of the war approached two population questions faced the federal government. First, in 1945 the National Health and Medical Research Council warned that Australian fertility had fallen below replacement level and that this would have an impact on the economic recovery of the nation. Second, Australian industry had surged during the war and labour was needed to maintain the development of this sector of the economy. It was in this context that the Labor government Immigration Minister Arthur Calwell uttered his now famous cry that Australia must 'Populate or Perish'.

In 1945 the Australian and British governments established the Assisted Passage Migration Scheme under which British subjects in any colony would pay £10 per adult for passage to Australia where they were

In 1956 a group of twenty young German migrants arrives under an assisted passage scheme sponsored by the Inter-governmental Commitee for European Migration.

committed to remain for two years. The immigrants under this scheme became known as '£10 Poms', 'pommie' being Australian slang for someone from England. About a quarter of the estimated 1 million who came to Australia under this scheme returned to Britain at the end of the two years, but many of them then re-immigrated to Australia.

Then, in 1947, Calwell took a bold step. A twelve-week tour of Europe convinced him that a large-scale intake of displaced persons from the camps across Europe would provide an immediate injection of much-needed labour. In the six years from 1947 to 1953 Australia received 170,000 refugees: 60,000 Poles, 24,000 Yugoslavians, 19,000 Latvians, 17,000 Ukrainians, 12,000 Hungarians, 10,000 Lithuanians, 10,000 Czechs and 9,000 Estonians.[1] A further 11,000 Jewish refugees were assisted through Australian Jewish charities. The Labor government also entered into immigration agreements with Malta (1948), the Netherlands (1951), Italy (1952), Germany (1952), and later Greece, Spain and Sweden, among other nations.[2] Calwell remained an ardent supporter of the White Australia policy, however, and no agreements were struck with any Asian country. Calwell called the immigrants 'New Australians', a designation that would continue until the end of the twentieth century.

Two groups of immigrants were to have major influences on Australian foodways: Jewish refugees from Central Europe and southern Italians.

Jewish Refugees

'The effect on Australia of this post-war immigration has been enormous,' wrote Donald Horne in *The Lucky Country*, his 1964 critique of Australia in the 1950s and 1960s: 'It has leavened the lump in Australia. It is doubtful if Australia would have got as far as it has in increased sophistication without the accelerated migration of the last two decades.'[3] One sign of this 'sophistication' was the broadening of choices for casual and formal dining out. Jewish refugees from Central Europe – Austria, Czechoslovakia, Hungary and Poland – played a significant part in this.

Eight Jewish convicts arrived with the First Fleet in 1788. Jewish free settlers began arriving in the 1820s. By 1901 there were an estimated 15,000 Jews in Australia. Most were British Jews. Polish, Russian and German Jews began migrating to Australia in following years. Between 1946 and 1954 more than 17,000 Jews arrived from Europe and Shanghai. A further 10,000 had arrived by 1961, including many following the Hungarian uprising of 1956. By 1961 there were 60,000 Jews living in Australia.[4]

As with other migrants, these refugees looked for familiar anchors in a socially alien setting. Finding places where one could eat familiar food and socialize with others from the same cultural, if not national, background was one of those anchors. For Jews wanting to continue kosher food practices, the need was even greater. Jewish migrants, both refugees and otherwise, established shops, cafés and restaurants to meet those needs.

Eighteen-year-old Tom Keleman escaped newly communist Hungary in March 1946 and spent the intervening years in displaced persons camps run by the United Nations Relief and Rehabilitation Administration in Austria and France. He arrived in Sydney in July 1947, the first boy sponsored by the Australian Jewish Welfare Guardian Society. On arrival in Australia, he lived with his guardians' family in Vaucluse, an eastern suburb of Sydney. Vaucluse and the bordering suburbs of Double Bay, Woollahra, Bellevue Hill and Bondi became the main Jewish enclave in Sydney. In the same year he began working for the Australian Jewish Welfare Society and studying accountancy at night.

> I would have my meals before or after class at the Hellenic Club in Elizabeth Street, where I often ate spaghetti bolognaise

> as it was inexpensive; or at one of the Silver Grills, a chain run by a Jewish musicologist in George Street where for two shillings and sixpence I could get lamb chops with chips and salad . . . I used to visit the Fiaker Austrian restaurant run by a refugee couple in Darlinghurst Road, Kings Cross, near the Fire Station. There one could eat real Wiener schnitzel and crumbed calf's liver, along with other Austrian delicacies . . . There was one other Continental restaurant in a side street of Macleay Street, which was run by a German Jewish family.[5]

In Melbourne, too, Jewish refugees were opening cafés and restaurants. Chef Stephanie Alexander remembers dining with her parents at 'The Topsy, a Hungarian restaurant in a small lane that ran of Little Collins Street, where I always ordered the schnitzel. I absolutely loved the chestnut Mont Blanc.'[6] In 1951 Georges and Mirka Mora migrated from France, where Georges had been a resistance fighter and Mirka had evaded transportation to Auschwitz by hiding in forests. They opened the Mirka Café in 1954 with a French menu. Later they opened Café Balzac and the Tolarno. Mirka was an accomplished painter, and the restaurants became social hubs for Melbourne artists and writers of the time looking for a less conservative life than post-war Australia offered, a life embodied in the Moras and one that their restaurants suggested.

To supply these restaurants with speciality meats, relishes, pickles and condiments, new butchers and delicatessens opened. In 1955 Tom Keleman bought a local delicatessen in Maroubra Beach, to the south of Vaucluse. Here he had a large clientele of Jewish refugees who had settled in Australia and a number of non-Jewish customers as well.

> I'd say about 70 per cent of my customers were Holocaust survivors, so I had to cater for continental goods from Europe – sausages, black bread, cucumbers, certain cuts of meat, frankfurts . . . I even sourced my black bread from a particular Latvian baker who only made two different kinds of sweet sour black bread. We also had fantastic European cheeses that were popular with Jews and non-Jews alike.[7]

Andrew Léderer and his wife Agnes also defected from Hungary and arrived in Sydney in 1957. Building on his experiences in his family's abattoir in Hungary, he began making special cuts of meat, smoked ham and salami. In 1985 Léderer launched his Primo brand of smallgoods, which became the leading meat and smallgoods provider in Australia and a major supplier for Coles supermarkets.

That bread could be anything but white was a revelation to the average Australian. In 1958 Tip Top Bakeries, established in 1949, became the first Australian bakery to offer sliced and wrapped bread nationwide. It was a white, soft, sweet, square loaf with a thin crust. This was a world away from what the European migrants were used to. Holocaust survivor Mendel Glick in 1960 began Glick's bakery in St Kilda where he began making boiled bagels, which became much sought after. He sold fresh-from-the-oven *challah*, a braided loaf used on the Sabbath and Rosh Hashanah. St Kilda was one of the centres of Melbourne's Jewish community.

But it was to the cafés serving coffee, cakes and simple meals that non-migrant Australians mostly headed. For Australians used to eating sponge cake fifty different ways and ever-replenished platters of scones and jam, the cakes of the middle European migrants were things of wonder. In 1934 Pearl Lavine, a Polish Jewish migrant, opened her Monaco Cake Shop in Melbourne selling *kooglhoupf*, a layer cake infused with chocolate, and *rugelach*, cream-cheese pastries filled with honey and nuts. Avram and Masha Zeleznikow ran Café Scheherazade in Acland Street, St Kilda,

A selection of smallgoods produced by Primo.

where they served cheese blintzes, tea with lemon, apple compote, almond torte, cabbage soup and borscht. In Sydney the Hungarian Berger family opened the Gelato Bar on Campbell Parade at Bondi Beach. Patrons could dine on matzah ball soup, goulash and borscht, and linger afterwards over coffee and cherry and sweet cheese strudel, Sacher torte or poppyseed cakes.

Many of these businesses also provided work for new immigrants while they reskilled, studied and saved enough money to establish their own businesses or put a deposit on one of the houses being rapidly constructed in the building boom that followed the war.

The Italians

By far the largest group of migrants after the war were Italians, with some 300,000 settling in Australia in 1941–61. As with Jews, Italians had a long history in Australia. A small number of Italians arrested and charged in Britain were transported to New South Wales in the late 1700s. Italians joined other migrants on the goldfields in the 1850s. The *First Australian Continental Cookery Book*, printed in 1937, was arguably the first major Italian cookbook published in Australia. The publisher – the Cosmopolitan Publishing Co. – was run by Italian migrants. Branded as fascists by the Australian Government, when Italy entered the Second World War, some of them were interned and the company was forced into liquidation.[8]

In 1891 several hundred Italians from Piedmont, Veneto and Sicily began working in the sugarcane industry in north Queensland and by the 1920s they were the largest group in the industry. In August 1935 they were among 2,000 sugarcane cutters and mill hands who downed tools in a nine-week strike demanding that the cane be burnt before cutting to prevent outbreaks of Weil's disease, a bacterial disease spread by rats in the cane fields that in some cases led to death. Around 6,000 Italians living in Australia were interned during the Second World War. Around 3,000 of them were taken from the cane fields in 1942 after the Japanese bombed Darwin, the capital of the Northern Territory, in fear that they would join any Japanese invasion of the north.[9] By 1944 about 4,000 had been freed to work in the Civil Aliens Corps, where many were returned to the cane fields.

When the soldier settlers' farms in the Murrumbidgee Irrigation Area failed, for lack of agricultural skills in the Australians who took up the

Sugarcane trains, Nambour, Queensland, *c.* 1910.

farms, migrants who had come from rural areas of Italy began to buy up the properties. In 1921 they owned 13 per cent of the farms around the town of Griffith. In 1940 they owned 23 per cent, and by 1954 they owned nearly half of the farms.[10] The Broadway Store, which opened in the mid-1930s, was one of the first 'continental' grocery stores selling olive oil, pasta and other imported food and household goods from Italy.

In the pre-war period most migrants came from the north of Italy, but 80 per cent of the post-war migrants came from the south. They were particularly eager to migrate, worried by the economic, social and political situation in Italy: the lost war, the displacement of a significant number of people, and the civil war between the Resistance and the Fascists in the Nazi-occupied north. Most of them were single men from the rural areas of Calabria, Sicily, Abruzzo and Campania, but they also included rural poor from Veneto and Friuli Venezia Giulia in the north. The agreements between Australia and Italy did not cover family reunion and young single women were included only from 1959.[11]

Some went north to join in the sugarcane industry working on the Italian-owned farms. Many became labourers on the Snowy Mountains Scheme. The scheme, begun in 1949, aimed to generate 1,720,000 kw of

The Ord River Irrigation Scheme: Expense with Little Return

In 1941 Kimberley Michael Durack, with help from his brother William Aiden Durack, established the Carlton Reach Research Station, an experimental farm for topical agriculture on their vast property in the Kimberley region of Western Australia, centred on the Ord River.

Between 1935 and 1942 a severe drought affected the Kimberley sheep and cattle pastoral industry. Proposals were made to build a dam on the Ord River to ensure adequate water during future droughts. The two projects came together in the Ord River Irrigation Scheme with the completion in 1963 of the Kununurra Diversion Dam across the Ord River. By 1966 thirty farms were operating, though they mostly produced cotton. In the early 1970s the caterpillar *Helicoverpa armigera* attacked the cotton crop. Heavy pesticide application was unsuccessful, leading to low yield that, together with a drop in world cotton prices, suspended the cotton industry in the area.

Experimentation with irrigation food crops continued, however: mango, citrus, watermelon, rockmelons, pumpkin, chickpeas, sandalwood and chia were planted. In 2017 the Australia Institute, an independently funded policy think-tank, published a report on the Scheme. Its conclusions were damning:

> Australian governments have been trying to develop northern Australia for a long time, with the latest policy papers and Northern Australian Infrastructure Facility

power by harnessing the water from the head of the Snowy River and its tributaries, which flow east to the sea from the Southern Alps, part of the Great Dividing Range in New South Wales and Victoria. Under the scheme, rainfall and snow melt were captured and diverted through huge tunnels to the western side of the range, generating electricity, with the bonus of channelling the water into rivers that feed the Murrumbidgee just the most recent in a long tradition of generally unsuccessful attempts to entice more people to the continent's north with the promise of jobs and prosperity. The Ord River Irrigation Scheme in the east Kimberley region of WA, near to the NT border, is one of the longest running, most expensive and best-known attempts to increase agricultural development in the north.

The report said that while over $2 billion had been spent on developing irrigation agriculture in the Ord region, only 250 people in the region were employed in the scheme and the irrigated area was just 1 per cent of all irrigated land in Australia. The scheme, however, continues.[12]

Ord River irrigation area.

Irrigation Area and the Murray and Lower Darling valleys. The Italian labourers, rural workers with few skills, were mostly involved in dangerous masonry work that formed the excavated tunnels. The scheme was completed in 1974; it now covers an area of approximately 8,000 sq. km (over 3,000 sq. mi.) and includes sixteen major dams, 145 km (90 mi.) of connecting tunnels and 80 km (50 mi.) of aqueducts.

Italians began to run cafés and restaurants, first for their fellow migrants but soon popular among non-migrant Australians. Stephanie Alexander recalls:

> We also went to The Latin or to Mario's, both very important restaurants. It was at The Latin I tasted my first bowl of handmade ravioli . . . I can also remember my first gelato at the Italian home-style restaurant Pellegrini's . . . Using a silver spatula the waiter pressed and pushed a wave of creamy zabaglione ice-cream up and over the edge of a silvery cup, following it with a scoop of snowy lemon gelato that chilled the teeth.[13]

Pellegrini's Espresso Bar was established in 1954 in Bourke Street, Melbourne, by Leo and Vildo Pellegrini. The brothers had worked at Florentino's, by then a well-established Italian restaurant run by Rinaldo Massoni since 1928. In 2014 Pellegrini's was inducted into The Age Good Café Guide Hall of Fame. It is listed as a heritage site by the National Trust of Australia.

In Sydney in 1956 Beppi and Norma Polese opened Beppi's. Beppi had begun his restaurant life working as an apprentice in the Albergo Dora in Milan in 1939, before moving to work in Venice at the Daniele and the Gritti Place in 1943. Opposed to the Fascists, he escaped to Austria where he was immediately held in a concentration camp. He escaped this too, spending the final years of the war on the run. At the end of the war he applied to come to Australia, arriving in 1952. Here he met and married Norma, whose family had migrated in 1929. Through his contacts he got a job as a waiter at Sydney's Romano's, a popular nightspot at the time named for its owners. This led to a stint running the family's second restaurant also called Romano's in Wagga Wagga, in the Riverina area in southern New South Wales. When that fell through he returned to Sydney, and in 1956 established Beppi's in a former Yugoslavian restaurant in Darlinghurst, an inner suburb of Sydney bordering the central business district. 'Gradually I changed the menu to an Italian one, calamari, artichokes, mussels . . . We used to use rice at the time, you couldn't find polenta. We made polenta in the beginning with semolina, the Roman way.'[14] The restaurant became a popular luncheon spot for the Food and Wine Society (founded in 1936) and its reputation spread. In 1963 Beppi's won Alitalia Airlines competition for the best Italian restaurant in Sydney.[15]

Galluzzo's fruit shop, opened in inner west Sydney in the 1930s, continues to serve local shoppers today.

Norma's mother supplied Beppi's with homegrown radicchio. Stefano Manfredi recalls his family also having difficulty sourcing familiar foods. One option was foraging:

> Mushroom season, we were out there, it's the wogs out there on the mountains picking mushrooms, and the Australians are at home wondering if they're going to be poisoned. So I can remember lots of trips along railway tracks picking wild fennel and wild chicory. When we got our first house in Sydney, without thinking, after the first rain, my mother gathered all the snails and put them in a cage and purged them and cooked them up. We had them with white wine and garlic and parsley, and they were great.[16]

There were Italians growing fruit and vegetables on market gardens on the outskirts of the capital cities, such as in the Hawkesbury area, into which the settlement of Sydney had first expanded in the 1880s when looking for soil and adequate water. They grew vegetables that were already staples in the Australian diet – potatoes, pumpkins, cabbages, peas and endless rows of tomatoes – and brought them to Sydney's wholesale market. Some also supplied their compatriots' fruit and vegetable shops that were soon

The 1952 Riot at Bonegilla

On arrival in Australia many refugees were housed for periods from a few weeks to several months in migrant receptions centres where they were given medical examinations, basic clothing, lessons in English and life in Australia, a stipend of £2 and five shillings a week and were interviewed for employment. By 1951 there were three centres across Australia and twenty holding centres for non-working dependants when pressure on numbers meant that it was difficult to keep families together in the existing centres.

Some 300,000 migrants from over fifty countries were housed at Bonegilla in northern Victoria between 1951 and 1970. It was an ex-army training camp that had been converted into a prison camp and then reopened as a migrant reception centre. Here they were housed in corrugated-iron huts and 1,600 tents and were managed by ex-military personnel.

Food was based on the Australian Army rations of the time and served in the former Mess Hall. Chef Stefano Manfredi was six years old when he arrived in Australia with his family and was housed at Bonegilla. He described the food at the Bonegilla Dinner held as part of the Fourteenth Symposium of Australian Gastronomy in 2005.

> So the diners would come into the kitchen, into the tray run area, get a tray and then get their food and come into one of three dining rooms . . . it was the smell of boiled mutton, and it was accompanied by pastel cubes of vegetables floating in bain marie water and, they were dished up for you, and there was gravy of course. And then for dessert we had junket and two fruits. And this would have been ok, but we had it day after day after day after day after day . . . What happened as a consequence of those meals that we had was that migrant families would get really sick and tired of eating in the mess hall and would then start to cook on their kerosene heaters

in their rooms and every now and then one of them would go up in flames. But it was a small price to pay.[17]

The unfamiliar, stodgy repetitive food became one of the grievances raised by 3,000 Italians in the camp in 1952. They also had for some time been unhappy that the work they had been promised had not eventuated. On 7 July a group of them demonstrated outside the main administration office complaining that the meat they were being given was too fatty to eat. Tensions escalated over the next days as the Italians insisted on meeting with the Italian Consul to air their grievances, which now included that their boots were beyond repair. Two meetings were held with the Consul who, fearing an all-out riot, negotiated with the Minister for Immigration for a settling of the employment issue. Within days, jobs were being found.

The food issue was also resolved, with Italian cooks appointed with supplies of fish, macaroni, spaghetti, salt, tomato puree, olive oil, garlic and coffee.

a familiar part of suburban shopping strips. Salvatore Galluzzo started a fruit shop in inner west Sydney in the 1930s that has continued in the same location until today. Margaret Fulton recalls shopping at De Luca's – 'the premier fruit and vegetable shop in Sydney' – in King Street in the 1950s.[18] When they grew vegetables for their own cuisine it was usually enough for their immediate family, with some spare to give away or barter with others. 'What we couldn't buy, or find, we grew,' recalled Steve Manfredi. 'And what we couldn't grow we swapped, with our Greek, Maltese and, later, Lebanese neighbours.'[19]

Eating 'Continental' at Home

In the immediate post-war years and into the mid-1950s most Australian home-cooking remained resolutely what it had been for the last 170-odd years. The author and food writer Marion Halligan's family dinners were typical:

Spaghetti Bolognese

'What seems obvious is that ordinary Australians themselves,' Donald Horne writes in *The Lucky Country*, 'have "assimilated" to Europeans more quickly and gently than most critics of ordinary Australians had allowed for.'[20]

Assimilation was the ideology that underpinned the origin countries of 'New Australians'. Europeans were seen as most likely to share Australian values and be able to integrate smoothly into Australian life. Donald Horne's observation turns this notion nicely on its head. It is part and parcel of his comment about the increased 'sophistication' he ascribed to immigration between the 1950s and 1960s.

Australians' love affair with spaghetti bolognese (or 'spag bol', as it affectionately became known) is arguably an example of this. This recipe, one of the first to have wide distribution, was published in the 9 July 1952 issue of the *Australian Women's Weekly*. It continues to be a favourite at the Australian home table.[21]

Quarter cup melted shortening, 1 clove garlic, ½ cup chopped onion, 1½lb. minced steak, 1lb. ripe tomatoes

> For meals we had lamb chops or cutlets, Sunday roasts that turned into cold meats or cottage pie or toad in the hole, stews, sausages, wonderful meat pies and steak and kidney puddings, brain patties, mighty chickens stuffed with a savoury bread and herb mixture, sometimes liver and bacon, rissoles, fish, the vegetables, three or four of them and the potatoes compulsory, always boiled except when roasted with the leg of lamb . . . There were beautiful puddings too, suet ones, golden syrup and spotted dog, or self-saucing chocolate, or graceful lemon meringue pies . . . or homelier apple and rhubarb . . .[22]

Halligan gives the *Australian Women's Weekly* in the mid-1950s the kudos for bringing about a change. '[It] created ambitions for tasty dishes . . . I remember as quite a young teenager helping make a meal for a family (or 1 16oz tin tomatoes), 1 cup water or stock, 1 teaspoon Worcestershire sauce, salt and pepper to taste, pinch of herbs, 1 lb. spaghetti, 1 cup grated cheese, butter or substitute, tomato slices.

Cook finely minced onion in melted shortening until lightly browned. Drain off surplus shortening, add steak. Wash and chop tomatoes, add to meat mixture with water or stock, sauce, salt and pepper, and herbs. Cover closely and simmer 1½ hours or until meat is tender. Cook spaghetti in boiling salted water, drain and fold into meat mixture. Turn into greased ovenware dish (suitable for serving). Top with a thick layer of coarsely grated cheese, dot generously with butter or substitute. Add tomato slices to garnish. Bake in a moderate oven until top is bubbly and brown. Serve piping hot. Sufficient for about 6 to 8 servings.

By the 1970s the dish had escaped the oven. The spaghetti was now served directly onto a plate, the meat and tomato sauce poured on, and Parmesan cheese grated over.

friend. I did Vichy carrots . . . they were cooked in butter and parsley in the oven and formed their own golden brown caramelly sauce.'[23] Certainly before 1954, dishes in the *Weekly* that stepped outside of the predictable, or minor variations on them, were few. There was the odd reader's prize-winning recipe that took small steps outside the norm. In the 16 June 1951 issue, Mrs R. Taylor won the £1 consolation prize in the 'Prize Recipes' section for her Monday Medley using leftover meat and 'creamed macaroni'.[24] In the 11 March 1953 issue, the £1 consolation prize went to Mrs T. M. Caulfield for her Egg and Spaghetti, which baked spaghetti or macaroni and tomatoes between layers of cheese and topped the dish off with poached eggs.[25]

Italian-influenced dishes like these were among the early 'continental' – meaning European – styles taken up. In the 9 March 1955 issue of the *Weekly* this trend got its imprimatur with a double-page spread, 'Continental Flavour . . . familiar favourites on the dining tables of Europe [which] are becoming increasingly popular here. The recipes are, for the most part, quite simple, and the ingredients are readily available.' The dishes, and the nationalities ascribed to them, included quiche Lorraine (France); apple strudel (Germany); beef Stroganoff (Russia); wiener schnitzel (Austria); Norwegian biscuits; chocolate mousse (France); and boiled potatoes with cottage cheese (Austria).[26]

There were other places to which the 'Housewives with a flair for high-style cooking' could look. In 1955 Maria Kozslik Donovan, a Hungarian who ran a cooking school in Melbourne and wrote a weekly Epicure's Corner in the *Age* newspaper, published *Continental Cookery in Australia*, which brought together recipes from across Europe: included were Ossobucco, Bouillabaisse, Hungarian Goulash, Lamb Paprikash, Transylvanian Sauerkraut, Sacher Torte and Malakoff Cake.[27] Commercial enterprises, too, were quick to take advantage of the trend. The Melbourne retailer James McEwan & Co. ran a series of continental cooking classes – French, Italian, Austrian, American and Chinese– to attract the shopper to their range of homewares.[28] Albright & Wilson Australia published the *Aerophos Recipe Book* to promote their phosphate-based raising ingredient, which was an essential part of self-raising flour and baking powder. In its seventh edition, in 1952, recipes included Pressure Cooked Salt Cod Spanish Style, Zakousi (a salad of picked herrings, apple and boiled potatoes with paprika mixed into the dressing) and Le Poulet Marengo.

Another way these new cuisines circulated was through what the anthropologist Ghassan Hage has called acts of everyday multiculturalism: food, ingredients and recipes shared between neighbours either piqued by curiosity – the scent of differently spiced meats on a barbecue – or as gestures of comfort for someone sick or old, and sometimes at 'welcome drinks' to a neighbourhood.

Wine

The continental dishes in the pages of the *Weekly* increasingly used wine. Harriet Goodwin was in advance of the trend when she published *How to Cook with Wine* in 1954. In her introduction she noted that more housewives were using wine in their cooking, which 'may be due to the influx over the past year or two years, of some many European nationalities into Australia which is already making its influence felt in food habits'.[29]

The wine industry had been progressing slowly and was still marginal to the Australian economy. 'Small but closely-knit circles of connoisseurs banded together,' writes the wine historian David Dunstan, 'to talk among themselves make contacts, and learn more in an environment where in the fifties and sixties prohibitionist influences still restricted the sale and distribution of wine.'[30] The Wine Society, founded in 1946 by the surgeon Gilbert Phillips, was one such direct-buying, member-run organization. Beefsteak and Burgundy Clubs were another: members would meet to dine on meals prepared by notable chefs, drink appropriate wines selected by one of the members acting as cellar master for the year, and purchase wines. Walter James began a wine column in the Melbourne *Age* newspaper in 1952. Also in 1952, Dan Murphy opened his first liquor store in Prahran, an inner suburb of Melbourne. Murphy's business would continue to grow until 1988, when he sold it to Woolworth's, who now operate the Dan Murphy's

Harriet Goodwin credited recent migrants for the increasing number of housewives who used wine in cooking.

Margaret Fulton

Margaret Fulton was the authority to whom Australian home cooks turned in the 1950s and 1960s. Fulton grew up in Glen Innes in New South Wales where her parents had migrated to when she was three years old.

At the age of eighteen, Fulton left for Sydney with plans to be a dress designer. After a short stint in a parachute factory she took up work with the Australian Gas Light Co., first as a clerk but soon giving cooking classes to the public in order to promote gas stoves. She left to take up a position with the Overseas Corporation, a manufacturer of aluminium cookware, where she became the resident home-economist, turning her hand this time to promoting pressure cookers.

It was in 1954 that her career as a cookery writer began on *Woman*, a weekly magazine. 'The editor was Elizabeth Riddell . . . She didn't ask could I write, but rather: "Can you make brown rolls, brown luncheon rolls?"' Within a year she moved on to be an account manager in the Australian office of multinational advertising company J. Walter Thompson. When the Australian government hired the company to boost the sugar industry through the promotion of eating jam, Fulton

liquor supermarket chain. In 1955 the Australian Wine Research Institute was established on the campus of the University of Adelaide.

Wine growing had continued in the Barossa Valley. In 1947 Colin Gramp of Orlando Wines and Bill Seppelt of Seppelt Wines organized a Thanksgiving Ball to celebrate the end of harvest and the end of the war. The event has continued as the biannual Barossa Vintage Festival. In 1956, as Australians were celebrating the Melbourne Olympic Games, Orlando Wines launched Barossa Pearl. 'Barossa Pearl helped change the drinking habits of the nation,' wrote Ross Fitzgerald and Trevor Jordan in their 2000 history of alcohol in Australia, 'and revolutionised the Australian wine industry . . . sparkling wines played a significant role in making wine accessible to the broader public, breaking down the barriers of mystique and price.'[31]

> thought of all the dishes that require or were improved by a dab of jam: Devonshire tea, scones fresh from the oven with clotted or thick cream and raspberry or strawberry jam; that Queen of Puddings which is an elaborate version of baked bread custard, having a creamy base topped with jam then a layer of meringue . . . [and] milkshakes flavoured with fruity jam.

She returned to the rebranded *Woman's Day*, where she continued to work for the next decade. During this time Fulton introduced home-cooks to an ever-broadening range of Continental and Asian cuisines.

In 1968 *The Margaret Fulton Cookbook* was published. 'Paul Hamlyn (the publisher), thought he was being optimistic with a first print run of thirty thousand for a first-time author. It quickly increased to forty, fifty, sixty thousand as orders poured in. It settled at a hundred thousand.'[32] Fulton would go on to write dozens of cookery books.

Fulton was awarded a Medal of the Order of Australia in 1983 for her services to journalism and cookery and in 1998 was added to the National Trust's list of 100 Australian Living Treasures.

In the 1960s, table wines began to overtake the market for fortified wines. In 1962 Len Evans began his 'Cellarmaster' column in *The Bulletin* magazine. Fitzgerald and Jordan said of him: 'Evans's relatively youthful outlook (he was then in his thirties) blew some of the cobwebs off a dust-laden subject.'[33] In 1965 Evans was appointed inaugural director of the Australian Wine Bureau, the first domestic promotional body for the wine industry.

From Chop Picnic to Barbecue

'For those imbued with the picnic spirit,' the *Australian Women's Weekly* announced in its March 1956 special feature, 'there's no finer way than a barbecue to share good food and fun. Most people enjoy eating outdoors,

The End of the Pub Ladies' Lounge

In all states and territories alcohol licensing laws had led to a glaring anomaly. Women could be barmaids, and women had been licensees of pubs – the Australian vernacular term for public drinking houses – since the earliest days of the colonies, but if they wanted to drink alcohol in a pub, they were relegated to the ladies' lounge, where men and women could drink together, or where women would drink while their male partner drank with his mates in the public bar. In some hotels women could only drink in the lounge if accompanied by a male. In others, women were not allowed to buy a drink themselves anywhere in the pub.

The public bar was an all-male preserve until the mid-1960s.

with a plate in one hand and a fork in the other, but, a few do not, so be tactful and don't include these among your guests.'[34]

Cooking meat on an open fire has a long history in Australia beginning with food of the First Peoples. Colonial accounts of Aboriginal foodways are full of descriptions of kangaroos, goannas, birds, fish and tubers being either cooked directly on the coals, buried in the coals or held above them on a stick. Early colonial cooking itself was an outdoors affair until the kitchen came indoors.

By 1967 all states and territories had repealed their six o'clock closing laws and 10 o'clock closing became the norm. The food and drink researcher Heather Hunwick sees this as one of the spurs to hotels changing their practices. 'The repeal of early closing laws forced pubs to accommodate more civilised drinking patterns, to create more women and family-friendly ambience.'

Merle Thornton and Rosalie Bogner did not wait for laws to change, however. On 31 March 1965 they chained themselves to the rail of the public bar in the Regatta Hotel in Brisbane and tried to buy a beer. Under the Queensland Liquor Act s58 publicans were prohibited from serving drinks in bars to drunks, Aboriginals, minors, lunatics – and women. The publican, who faced a fine of £10 to £20 if he served them, refused. The women were bought beers by male patrons. Police were called but soon left, wishing the women well.

'It is not that every woman would want to drink in a public bar, it is the injustice that she should be denied the choice,' Bogner said in an interview. Both women were critical of not only this injustice, but the raft of areas of law and culture where women were denied their rights. Their action is now seen as one of the defining moments of feminism in Australia.

Thornton went on to establish the Equal Opportunities for Women Association in April 1965 and introduced the teaching of Women's Studies in Australia in 1973. The Regatta Hotel now has a room named after her.[35]

In the late nineteenth and early twentieth century, expansion of the sheep industry led to the phenomenon of the 'chop picnic'. 'Even in the first half of the 19th century, chops were ubiquitous,' writes the food historian Barbara Santich, 'and in some seasons a pound of chops cost less than a pound of bread. Immigrants to the new colonies were enticed by the promise of feasts of mutton and beef.'[36] The chop picnic was a natural coming together of cheap meat and the popular pastime of the picnic. 'Like the early picnics,' Santich writes,

> it typically implied a foray into the bush and a small fire of fallen twigs and branches, the fire serving not only to boil the ubiquitous billy but also to cook chops impaled on sticks and eaten with the fingers. The chop picnic enjoyed a burst of popularity through the 1920s and 1930s, a period that coincided with a growing interest in bushwalking and hiking.[37]

By the 1950s barbecues were, as the *Weekly* pointed out, a common way of eating casually, particularly on celebratory occasions – birthdays, anniversaries or welcoming new neighbours, including 'New Australians' who would be confused by the invitation to 'bring a plate' and so turn up with no food – the expected 'plate' – to contribute. The *Weekly* followed the pattern set as early as 1948 by the *Australian Home Beautiful* and provided a step-by-step guide to building a brick barbecue. 'Do-it-yourself barbecues could be constructed at relatively little expense,' writes Santich, 'a 1960 design using concrete masonry blocks cost less than £3 10*s* in materials – a little more than ten pounds of rump steak.'[38]

In 1952 Malleys, which had been making iceboxes since 1884, released an essential piece of equipment for barbecues away from home – the Esky

By the 1950s a picnic barbecue was a common way of celebrating special occasions.

Steak Valerian

The *Weekly*'s feature on barbecues brought several trends together in the recipe for Steak Valerian – the continental, the barbecue and wine.

> Two pounds thick rump steak, 12 small button mushrooms (tinned or bottled mushrooms may be used), tomato sauce, chives, salt, pepper, one cup red wine.

Slit the steak to make a pocket. Brush inside of pocket with tomato sauce, fill with mushrooms and chopped chives, season with salt and pepper. Join pocket with small skewers or sew up with coarse thread. Soak the prepared meat in the wine for 1 hour, timing the preparation so the barbecue fire will be ready to cook the steak at the end of this period. Grill over glowing coals, turning once or twice. Note: Oysters may be substituted for mushrooms.

Auto Box, a portable insulated metal box to keep food and drink cool. The name was popularly shortened to 'esky', and this became the generic term for all subsequent models by Malleys, as well as other brands. By 1960 the company claimed that one in six households had an esky. As a bonus, an empty esky turned upright on its side could be used as the wicket for an impromptu game of cricket.

In 1965 Tom Angove of Angove's winery in Renmark, South Australia, invented another item that would become indispensable at barbecues: the wine cask, a plastic bag inside a cardboard box with an air-tight plastic tap at the bottom on one side. The wine cask had the added benefit that when empty you could remove the plastic bag, blow it up and use it as a picnic pillow.

Women as Consumers

From the earliest cookbooks and women's magazines, Australian women had been targeted as consumers of domestic cookery products. Those publications are full of pictures of women at stoves, iceboxes, holding packets of flour, sugar or baking powder. But 'the post-war boom period', writes foodways researcher Sian Supski in her study of the kitchen in 1950s Western Australia,

> heralded a new consumerism, for mass production required mass consumption and mass marketing; with steady employment and rising wages more money was available for 'discretionary purchases', namely household goods and services that were not basic requirements . . . For example, intense marketing and advertising programs made connections between labour saving devices, particularly electrical appliances in the kitchen, and women's identity as the 'glamorous hostess' proud to show her guests her new acquisitions.[39]

The 28 November 1956 issue of *Australian Women's Weekly* carries a two-page spread promoting kitchen appliances from Sunbeam, established in 1902. Featured in the promotion are the Automatic Frypan, which grills, bakes, stews, roasts and casseroles, with automatic heat control that 'removes all the guesswork'; the Mixmaster, which with 'just a flick of a switch whirls through all the mixing automatically – and at scientifically correct speeds'; the Cooker and Deep Fryer, which would bring 'new taste thrills', including 'delicious fish and chips' and 'Chinese meals'; and an Automatic Toaster that produced perfect toast quicker as it cooked both sides at once, could be left unattended and turned itself off. The lid of the Automatic Fry Pan is being lifted by a hand with perfectly manicured nails, suggesting Sian Supski's 'glamorous hostess' who has already prepared a meal with no fuss that is ready for her guests waiting at her dinner table. The body of the Mixmaster comes in 'four lovely colours, as well as white, to suit all kitchen colour schemes'.[40] The Automatic Fryer came with a recipe booklet with old favourites like Grilled Lamb Chops and Seasoned Roast Chicken, but also latched on to the continental and Chinese trends with inclusions like Kabobs, Swiss Fondue, Veal Maregno, Sweet and Sour Pork and Fish Chop Suey.[41] The frypan, in other words, was perfectly suited to the 'Housewives with a flair for high-style cooking and with that precious commodity, time' the *Weekly* had targeted in its 1955 feature 'Continental Flavours'.

The other appliance that made a significant difference to women's domestic workload was the refrigerator. That 28 November 1956 issue of the *Weekly* carried advertisements for two brands, one gas and one electric.

Westfield Plaza, Hornsby, opened in 1961, was one of the new mall-style shopping centres in Australian cities.

The electric Norge refrigerator is shown empty with a drawing of a woman, dressed as if for a cocktail with guests in a smart two-piece suit and black stilettoes. It details its storage elements: 'Full width Freezer chest, meat keeper and crisper drawers; Norge "Handidoors" carefully planned for efficient indoor storage; special butter, cheese and egg compartments.'[42] The Electrolux 'noiseless Gas refrigerator', on the other hand, is shown stuffed with food. On the door-less freezer shelf are cuts of meat and ice-cube trays; on the shelves inside are bottles of beer; milk bottles sit on a shelf on the inside of the door; there are also jellies, a salad in a bowl covered in the newly invented clingfilm, a tin of corned beef, jars of sauces and – inexplicably – two jars of peas, a roast fowl, a pack of Kraft Velveeta cheese spread and tomatoes and apples in the crisper.[43] Here again is a boon for the time-poor housewife: she no longer had to do daily or even weekly shopping, as she could now keep food fresh for longer. She could now do less-frequent shopping at one of the new mall-style shopping centres like the Chermside Drive-in Shopping Centre in Brisbane (opened 31 May 1957) or Westfield (opened at Blacktown, a western suburb of Sydney in 1959). She could self-serve more food items than she could ever have carried home by hand, drop them into a wire trolley and wheel them to her car in one of the mall's several-storeyed carparks and be home in no time at all.

But not all women could be, or wanted to be, the consumers the appliance makers targeted. 'Women engaged with the "new" consumer society in varying ways,' Supski writes.[44] Some migrant women in her study preferred to use traditional ways alongside of the labour-saving devices. For others, scarce household income had to be spent on basics. Sunbeam and others sought to capture this market, too, through easy payment plans, though these could become financial burdens instead through high interest rates that added considerably in the long run to the cost of the goods.

As 1964 drew to a close, manufacturers could not have imagined the new markets that would be open to them in the following decades, as the White Australia Policy was dismantled and Australia began its long road to becoming a multicultural nation.

EIGHT

Transformations, 1966–79

In January 1966 Robert Menzies, prime minister of Australia since 1949, retired, effectively ending Australia's post-Second World War era. Menzies was a supporter of the White Australia Policy, but it was under his government that steps first were taken that would hasten its abandonment. His government continued with the programme of accepting European refugees begun under Arthur Calwell. His immigration minister, Harold Holt, who would succeed him as prime minister, agreed to allow eight hundred non-European war refugees to remain in Australia, and in 1952 agreed that Japanese war brides of Australian and Allied servicemen could immigrate here. In 1957 non-Europeans with fifteen years residence in Australia could become citizens. In 1958 the dictation test introduced in the 1901 Immigration Restriction Act, under which immigration officers could deny an application for immigration on the basis that a person failed to be able to write fifty words in a European language of the officer's choice, was abolished.

Finally, in 1966, the Holt government enacted the Migration Act under which all potential immigrants were now subject to the same rules and restrictions surrounding visas and were eligible to become citizens of Australia after the same waiting period. People were to be selected based on what they might offer Australian society, rather than their race or nationality. However, the expectation remained that immigrants would integrate into Australian society: that they would adapt and suppress, if not surrender, their former social and cultural identity. It was the Whitlam government, elected in 1972, that would put the final nail in the coffin of White Australia. Its most prominent spokesperson for change was Al Grassby, Whitlam's Minister for Immigration, the son of Spanish and Irish parents, and the Member for the Riverina, the federal electorate in New

South Wales that generally follows the Murrumbidgee River and borders the electorate of Murray, which incorporates the Murrumbidgee Irrigation Area. In August 1973 Grassby delivered a paper to the Cairnmillar Institute's symposium 'Strategy 2000: Australia for Tomorrow' in Melbourne. The paper was titled *A Multi-cultural Society for the Future*. In it Grassby said:

> My vision of our society in the year 2,000 foreshadows a greatly increasing social complexity, in which the dynamic interaction between the diverse ethnic components will be producing new national initiatives, stimulating new artistic endeavours, and ensuring great strength in diversity . . . The various groups are constantly interacting and adjusting, slowly but steadily, to each other and to life in Australia, without losing – at least in the first generation – their essential ethnic character. In this situation, there is nothing threatening to Australia's future in the year 2,000.[1]

Australia now had a new framework within which to form relationships with its immigrants. This, together with increased travel by Australians into Asia and Europe, would fundamentally change Australian foodways forever.

'The Asianisation of the Australian Palate'

In her 1993 book *Goodbye Culinary Cringe*, the food journalist Cherry Ripe wrote:

> There are three separate phenomena in the 'public eating' arena that can be identified as part of the 'Asianisation of the Australian palate'. The most obvious of these three phenomena is the explosion of Asian, particularly Thai, restaurants in the early 1980s, and accelerating wildly in the late 1980s . . . The second is the inclusion of Asian dishes on menus of 'European' restaurants, for instance, on the menus of otherwise Italian-style bistros . . . such as Thai beef salad at Armstrong's in North Sydney, or the Thai-style vegetarian soup, and spring rolls with oyster chilli and garlic, at Darling Mills in Sydney's Glebe . . . Then the third, and most unusual of these three phenomenon is the extent to which Asian flavours, Asian techniques and Asian

> ingredients have been incorporated into individual dishes in Western or European restaurants, brasseries and bistros – not just on the same plate but in the same dish . . . This fusing of Asian and Western flavours is more widespread in Australia then in any other Western country.[2]

Before the 'Asianisation of the Australian plate', however, came the 'Asianization' of Australia itself. In 1950 the Colombo Plan was initiated at the Commonwealth Conference of Foreign Ministers meeting in Colombo, Ceylon (now Sri Lanka). The aim of the Plan was to build the technology and infrastructure of Asian Commonwealth member countries through partnerships with non-Asian members. The original signatories were Australia, Canada, Ceylon, New Zealand, Pakistan, the United Kingdom, Malaya and North Borneo. Australia's involvement in the Plan provided opportunities for Australians to interact with others from Asia countries. Australia, among other assistance, offered scholarships to students from signatory countries. By 1964 some 12,000 students from Asian countries had studied in Australia. Students had to return to their home country by the end of their studies, but some returned as skilled migrants. In 1962 Australia began its ten-year involvement in the Vietnam War, during which time Australian ground troops, air-force and naval personnel had tours of duty exposing them to Southeast Asian food – Vietnamese, Thai and Singaporean – and many of them looked for opportunities to continue this culinary engagement when they returned to Australia.

There had also been an 'Asianization' of the domestic table. The first Australian cookery book that set out to bring Chinese food into the Australian home was Roy Geechoun's 1948 *Cooking the Chinese Way.* Geechoun was the son of Chinese market-gardeners in the Victorian goldfields town of Bendigo. In his introduction to the sixth edition, in 1954, he writes that the recipes in the book 'are representative of the best and most popular Chinese dishes introduced to Europeans by Chinese away from their homeland'. He writes that the ingredients in the recipes are usually available wherever there is a Chinese community but also that 'The important thing to remember is whatever ingredients are available, we can cook them in the Chinese way.'[3] Clearly his intention is to encourage the home-cook to experiment, and it appears that many did: the book went through eight editions in ten years. The dishes ranged from what could be found in any Chinese restaurant in Australia at the time, like Chicken with

Pineapple Sweet and Sour, to more unusual dishes like Dried Squid with Vegetables and Stuffed Bitter Melon. Geechoun's book was quickly followed by Yep Yung Hee's 1951 *Chinese Recipes for Home Cooking*. Hee was also an Australian-born Chinese. The foreword to the book was penned by L. M. Wang, the Consul-General of the Republic of China. Wang, in what looks like pointed political messaging, wrote:

> It is sometimes said that the greatest aid to happy understanding between peoples is wining and dining together. Possibly this may be true also in the international sphere, and closer understanding may be attained by the gastronomic appeal which the correct preparation of food produces.[4]

By the mid-1960s Chinese food had well and truly crossed over into the home. 'As *Woman's Day* detected a growing interest in Chinese

Yep Yung Hee's cookery book was in its 15th printing in 1965, by which time Chinese food had become part of Australian home cooking.

cooking,' the food writer Margaret Fulton wrote, 'I was sent to Hong Kong several times to go to Chinese cooking schools . . . We brought out several Chinese pull-out cookbooks which were popular with our readers.'[5] The *Australian Gourmet Cook Book*, published in 1967 by *Australian Gourmet Magazine* (first published in 1966) had recipes for Ho Yau Nau Nok (beef in oyster sauce and Chinese rice wine) and fried bean sprouts with mushroom and pork.[6] Luba Winter contributed Roast Chicken Cantonese and Jean Harvey contributed Chinese Veal and Pineapple to the 1967 *Cookery Book* of the Melbourne Church of England Girls Grammar School.[7] Also in Melbourne in the 1960s there was interest enough for Elizabeth Chong to set up her Chinese cooking classes.

It was not only Chinese food (Cantonese mainly, strictly speaking – the introduction of other regional cuisines of China was yet to come) that was finding its way onto the plates of Australians from its Asian neighbours. In 1961 Maria Kozslik Donovan had published the Australian edition of *The Far Eastern Epicurean*, which included Indonesian, Malaysian, Singapore-Indian and Japanese dishes.[8] Curry in its British Raj clothing had been a constant in Australian cookbooks, but now recipes were being published that did away with the apples, dried fruits and lemon juice that had been used as substitutes for sharp, sweet Indian flavourings. Premade curry powders were still used, but the recipes demand individual spices as well. In 1963 the Festival of Asia Committee in Sydney published a slim booklet, *Cook Book*. Among the recipes from Ceylon are a chicken pilau that calls for cardamom, turmeric and cinnamon, a pork curry that calls for coriander and cinnamon, and a brinjal (aubergine) curry that calls for fenugreek.[9] Doris Ady published *Curries from the Sultan's Kitchen* in 1968 and assured her readers that ingredients like these – and others, such as tamarind sauce, frozen creamed coconut or garam masala, used in the Pakistani, Indian and Ceylonese recipes in her book – were readily available 'under several brand names, in many shops and delicatessens – also they are sold in bulk in a great many health food shops'.[10] While these books may only have reached audiences who were interested in a particular cuisines, *The Margaret Fulton Cookbook*, published in 1968, brought an expanded range of Asian cuisines to the notice of the 100,000 households that purchased it in its first year. 'I knew Australians were becoming interested in international foods,' Fulton later wrote, 'so I included Asian dishes such as Cantonese Roast Duck, Crab with Black Beans, Five-Spice Chicken, Chicken Biriani, and curries and sambols to go with them.'[11]

The Chiko Roll

While Australian's were experimenting in their kitchens with Chinese food or eating yet more Sweet and Sour Anything at the local Chinese restaurant, few knew that many of them held in their hands, on a regular basis, a snack food adapted from the Chinese table. It was the Chiko Roll, the creation of Frank McEnroe, an outdoor caterer who sold pies, pasties and hamburgers at country agricultural shows in New South Wales. Like his other products it was designed to be eaten piping hot without plate or cutlery, so one could hold it and eat it while walking and viewing the new farm equipment or the prize-winning merino sheep.

It was basically a very big, very fat, deep-fried spring roll. Despite sounding like it had chicken in it, there was none. The filling was primarily cabbage and barley, along with carrots, green beans, beef, beef tallow, wheat cereal, celery and onion. All of this was diced and extruded into a tube of egg and flour pastry and cooked as it moved along the production line. It was then deep fried and frozen (one of the first products to be quick frozen) and distributed. When purchased, it was deep fried again to reheat the roll.

At the time of McEnroe's death in 1979, some 40 million were sold annually in Australia.

The chiko roll, adapted from Chinese fried spring rolls, is still a favourite snack.

The Asianization of the Australian domestic table was firmly achieved when in 1976 Charmaine Solomon, Margaret Fulton's protégée at *Woman's Day*, published *The Complete Asian Cookbook*. Solomon was a Sri Lankan who emigrated with her family in 1959. She had worked as a journalist at the *Ceylon Daily News* and had edited the women's pages and contributed recipes. In 1964 she came second in the *Woman's Day* 'Butter White Wings Bake Off', catching the attention of Fulton who asked her to join the magazine as a food writer. The book was well-timed to capture the enthusiasm for a wider range of Asian cuisines from young Australians who in the late 1960s and early 1970s took the 'hippie trail' overland from Asia to Europe, travelling through Bali, Thailand, India, Nepal, Pakistan, Afghanistan, Iran and Turkey. In her introduction to the book, Solomon extolled the virtues of the wok:

> If I had to choose one cooking pan to be marooned on a desert island with, I'd choose a wok. It would cope with any kind of food that happened to be available. In it you can boil, braise, fry and steam, and while you can do all these things in pans you already possess, the wok is almost indispensable for the stir-frying technique that many Asian dishes call for. Because of its rounded shape and high, flaring sides you can toss with abandon and stir fry ingredients without their leaping over the sides; and because the wok is made of thin iron you get the quick, high heat necessary to much Asian cooking.[12]

Her enthusiasm for the wok was contagious. 'We returned home from our travels,' wrote the food historian John Newton, 'and began eating – and drinking – out, partly to rediscover the food and wine we had encountered. And for the home, thanks largely to Charmaine Solomon's million-copy-selling *The Complete Asian Cookbook*, we bought woks in their thousands.'[13]

Asianization also led to more Australians eating rice. The first person to grow rice in Australia was Jō Takasuka who arrived in Melbourne in 1905. Within a short time he had moved to Nyah, on the Murray River near Swan Hill in northwest Victoria, where he sowed his first crop. He grew small amounts for commercial sale. Rice production began on a large scale when a cooperative of growers built a rice mill in Leeton in the Murrumbidgee Irrigation Area. In 1955 they launched Sunwhite rice,

Malu Bola Cutlis

In her introduction to *The Complete Asian Cookbook* Charmaine Solomon, like others before her, is sensitive to the need to encourage the Australian domestic cook to experiment with less familiar dishes by assuring them that both the ingredients and techniques were within their comfort zone. 'Not all Asian food is exotic or wildly unusual . . . Many of the ingredients will be familiar to anyone who knows their way around a kitchen,' she wrote. Her recipe for Malu Bola Cutlis was a good example, a crumbed fish cutlet (cutlis) that entered Sri Lankan cuisine via British colonial cooking (and was spiced up along the way). Her recipe was a variation on the recipe below familiar to Sri Lankan cooks.

425 g tinned tuna
500 g potatoes, boiled
1 tablespoon finely chopped onion
1 large or two small eggs, beaten
1 cup fresh white breadcrumbs
salt and pepper
1 teaspoon of curry powder
1 teaspoon finely chopped dill
1 dessertspoon Worcestershire sauce
dry breadcrumbs
vegetable oil enough to shallow fry the fish balls

the product that would dominate the Australian rice market for the next decades. Margaret Fulton wrote:

> When the Australian Rice Marketing Board got going, we worked in with them. Cooking rice had not been one of Australian cooks' strong points. The old formula had been eight cups of water to one cup of rice, and when the rice was cooked you rinsed it under a running tap. Voila! You had each grain separate, but at what cost – it was tasteless. We introduced the absorption method of cooking one cup of rice in two cups of water . . . Not only have our rice cooking skills improved,

Drain the fish and flake it well. Mash the potatoes well.

Mix the tuna, potatoes, onion, eggs, fresh breadcrumbs, curry powder, a pinch of salt and a little ground pepper, dill, Worcestershire sauce and mix well. Take small amounts of the mixture and roll it into balls about the size of a golf ball.

Roll each ball in the dry breadcrumbs as you make them and set them aside on some kitchen paper or baking paper. Leave them for an hour or so.

Heat the oil until quite hot in a frying pan. Test the heat by putting one of the fish balls into the pan. If it sizzles the oil is at the right heat. If not, remove the fish ball and wait a minute or two and try again. When the oil is hot, put a few of the fish balls in the oil, but don't put in so many that they crowd the pan: this will end up steaming the fish balls and not frying them. Let the fish balls brown nicely on the bottom, gently turn them over till browned all over. As they are made put them on kitchen paper to drain off excess oil.

> but rice-growers have introduced more user-friendly varieties. Today we choose our rice for the dish – jasmine for South-East Asian food, basmati for pilaus and Indian dishes, arborio rice for risotto, white short-grain rice for puddings, calasparra for Spanish paella, sushi rice for Japanese sushi, Thai black rice for coco nut dessert, and brown rice with the bran layer still intact, the choice of the health enthusiasts, for their dishes.[14]

Solomon's book included a section on Vietnamese dishes, a cuisine that was to become increasingly familiar as the 1970s drew to a close. In 1961 and 1962 Ngo Dinh Diem, leader of the government in South Vietnam, repeatedly requested assistance from the United States and its allies in the war it was conducting against the North Vietnamese and internal insurrection. The Menzies government despatched thirty military advisers to the country in July–August 1962, beginning Australia's involvement in the war. By the time the government of Gough Whitlam ended Australia's involvement in 1973, some 60,000 Australians, including ground troops and air-force and navy personnel had served in the war. When the war ended in April 1975, Whitlam resisted calls from the then Leader of the Opposition in parliament, Malcolm Fraser, and diplomatic pressure from the United States, to accept refugees from South Vietnam. Whitlam was dismissed from office in November 1975 and subsequently lost the federal election. Fraser became prime minister and promptly changed the policy. A former Minister for Defence, he told the political historian George Megalogenis that he felt all along that Australia 'had a very particular obligation – ethical, moral – to people from Vietnam'.[15] More than 80,000 Vietnamese migrated to Australia in the next decade, many of them refugees.

Many Vietnamese were initially housed in the Cabramatta Migrant Hostel, in western Sydney, and settled in the area when they left the hostel. Here they became market gardeners, opened restaurants and bakeries making the French-influenced breads and buns that were part of South Vietnamese cuisine. In Melbourne they lived in the inner suburbs of Footscray, Springvale and Richmond. 'With the end of the Vietnam War in 1975,' chef Stephanie Alexander recalled,

Australian rice farmer Rod Smith examining his rice crop near Griffith, in the Murrumbidgee Irrigation Area of New South Wales.

Vietnamese refugees found a niche with small bakeries.

> Melbourne's Victoria Street was about to be transformed. Within two or three years shining roast ducks, soy-dipped chickens and bubbly-skinned roast pork hung from hooks in the windows of small restaurants, mountains of unknown green vegetables were stacked outside the rapidly proliferating fresh food stores, and hitherto unavailable items such as fresh lemongrass, kaffir lime leaves, bundles of fresh coriander, and dried noodles of bewildering variety filed the colourful shelves.[16]

The two foods that came to define Vietnamese cuisine in Australia were phò and banh mi. Phò is a soup of a bone broth and rice noodles, flavoured with star anise, cinnamon and clove, and lightly poached cuts of meat, chicken or offal, to which the diner then adds their choice of fresh Vietnamese mint, bean sprouts, spring onions, fresh red chilli and whatever soy sauce, sesame oil, fish sauce or hoisin sauce they desire. Banh mi – generally known as a Vietnamese pork roll – is a buttered, crisply crusted baguette filled with any or all of pressed pork, barbecued pork, pâté, coriander, shallots, chopped red chilli, grated carrot, thinly sliced cucumber and fish sauce.

À La Française

French cuisine had been a mark of fine dining in Australia since the late 1880s. So entrenched was this reification of French cuisine that the 1901 Federation banquet in Sydney followed the format for service down to the naming of dishes: Potage – Tortue Claire (turtle soup); Poissons

– Saumon Sauce Ravigote, Blanchailles (whitebait); Entrees – Vol au Vent à la Toulouse, Cotellet's de Agneau aux Champignon (lamb cutlets); Reléves – Dinde Farcie à la Perigourd (turkey stuffed with truffles), Jambon d' York, Asperges Glacés; Rôti – Perdreaux, Grives (roast partridge and thrush); Entremets – Charlotte Russe, Gelèe au Marasquin, Gateau St Honore, Pouding aux Armandes, Gelèe au Dantzie, Gateau à la Diplomat, Patisserie Francaise, Crème Glace de Passion, Eau Glace aux Pêches; Pailles au Parmesan.[17]

Over the decades, French, or French-influenced, dishes also made their way into popular cookery books. In *Something Different for Dinner by Australian Hostesses*, compiled in 1936 by Barbara Knox, Mrs W. D. Merewether contributed Fish à la Provençale and Mrs Julian Simpson contributed Poulet à la Crème.[18] John D. Porter's 1949 *The Chef Suggests*, while promising 'strange and exciting dishes and delicacies for the table', is virtually entirely composed of instructions for French dishes such as Frogs' Legs à la Poulette, Cabillaud à la Bretonne (cod with mushrooms) and Gelée Benedictine.[19]

In 1952 Ted Maloney and Deke Coleman published *Oh, for a French Wife!*. Maloney was a director of the Australian branch of American advertising behemoth J. Walter Thompson, where Margaret Fulton began working as an account manager in 1955. 'Ted was greatly influenced by Louise Coleman,' she recalled, 'and the wives of French wool buyers, businessmen and consular officials who had formed a little community in Sydney. Being a lover of good food, he cooked up an idea with Deke to get four of these French wives to submit recipes and menus which would form the climax to a book about French food and cooking.'[20] Coleman contributed a short introduction to each section 'On the Chemistry and Philosophy of Cooking'. They are curious short-form pieces built around situations he claims to have encountered which allow him to comment on some aspect of cooking. For example, a conversation with a barman about shaking or stirring a Martini turns into a discussion on the importance of air in some dishes. Maloney wrote the recipes, including writing up the meals the 'French wives' were invited to cook for him and Coleman.[21]

In 1973 the October edition of *Le nouveau guide Gault-Millau*, the magazine of the French gastronomers Henri Gault and Christian Millau, heralded the start of nouvelle cuisine, a break from the haute cuisine of Auguste Escoffier that had dominated French restaurant fare since 1890. The new style was to be simpler, using the freshest ingredients and newest techniques, replacing the heavy sauces of haute cuisine with seasonings of fresh herbs, high-quality butter, lemon juice and vinegar, and chefs were to invent new combinations of ingredients. Tony and Gay Bilson had opened Tony's Bon Gout in Elizabeth Street, Sydney, with a menu heavily based on Escoffier's *Ma Cuisine*. 'A three course lunch', Gay recalled in her 2004 book *Plenty*, 'might be watercress soup, braised oxtail and pears poached in red wine . . . [it] owed everything to French culinary tradition (though it was more personal, more individual than French cooking).'[22] In 1974 the Bilsons travelled across France where they met the chefs central to nouvelle cuisine: Paul Bocuse, Alain Chapel, Roger Vergé and the brothers Jean and Pierre Troisgros. They returned converts to the new style, introduced it on their menu and continued to refine it when they opened Berowra Waters Inn. 'In France, *nouvelle cuisine* became a manifesto in Henri Gault's hands,' Gay wrote. 'In Australian cities, particularly Melbourne and Sydney, the ides of the new French cooking acted as a catalyst and gave us the freedom to see that we were cooking Australian food, not French food, because it was our produce and we were doing it here.'[23]Another convert was Patric Juillet, who had owned a string of French-influenced restaurants in Sydney since 1971 and opened his nouvelle-inspired Le Café Nouveau in 1977.

French restaurants had also been making their mark in Melbourne. In 1956 Melbourne hosted the Olympic Games, and to save the athletes and officials from the proposed diet of 'Nothing but Australian Food' the Melbourne hotelier Tom Carlyon was sent to Europe to select fifty chefs, who were brought to Australia as assisted migrants to cook in the Olympic Village. Most of the chefs returned to Europe at the end of the Games, but Swiss-trained Hermann Schneider stayed. In 1958 he became chef at Antonio's where he perfected his French techniques and revolutionized service, bringing the food fully plated from the kitchen without having waiters fussily spooning sauces and garnishes at the table. In 1961 he opened Two Faces, which would set the standard for fine dining over the next decade.

One chef who bucked the nouvelle trend was Mogens Bay Esbensen. Classically trained in the Escoffier tradition, he refused to simplify his dishes in the restaurants he ran in Sydney from 1976 – Hyatt Kingsgate, the Pavilion on the Park, and finally Butler's. It was here that he took that third step which Cherry Ripe identified in the Asianization of the Australian palate. Esbensen had worked at the Rama Hotel, Bangkok, before migrating to Australia. Now he began to introduce Thai flavours into his dishes, marinading Moreton Bay bug tails (*Thenus orientalis*, the flathead lobster) in lemongrass, chilli, lime juice and fish sauce, cooking with Thai aubergines and tropical fruit. He was moving Australian dining towards what would in the next decades be called Modern Australian.

'The Dining Out Boom'

'The dining out boom is probably the biggest thing which has happened to Australia recently outside uranium shares,' wrote journalist Margaret Jones in the *Sydney Morning Herald* on 5 September 1970. 'Even in the dark reaches of suburbia, restaurants are proliferating like mushrooms . . . packed to the doors with newly born gourmets trying out exotica like raw lamb pounded in a mortar with garlic and oil.'[24] By her reckoning, the number of licensed restaurants had risen from 99 in 1950 to 551 in 1970, of which 349 were in the Sydney metropolitan area.

From 1960 household disposable income per capita increased on average about 2 per cent each year. The average weekly earnings for a male wage earner increased by 10 per cent in 1970 and 11 per cent the next year. This did not mean that everyone could afford to eat at the fine-dining end of the restaurant spectrum. 'One of the main charges now being made against restaurants is that they are pricing themselves out of existence,' Jones wrote, 'except for the fortunate lunchers and diners on expense accounts.' Jones identifies two causes for high prices: increased labour cost and mark-ups on the wine being sold by restaurants. On the latter she quotes Mr A. Critchley, chief executive officer of the Wine and Brandy Producer's Association of New South Wales: 'Sometimes it goes as high as 300 per cent. How can you justify this when the only preparation needed is the chilling of white wine?' Ameliorating this were changes to alcohol licensing laws across all states that allowed customers to bring their own alcohol to restaurants that remained unlicensed. The food journalist Stephen Downes wrote: 'In 1965 [in Victoria] a new Licensing Act initiated a wholesale change in the numbers of Victorians who ate out, the way they did it, and how important it became in their lives. Indeed, in tandem with an increase in disposable income, the new regulations turned eating out into a popular Melbourne pastime.'[25]

Margaret Jones identified two other factors in the dining out boom: 'small, migrant-run restaurants in the inner suburbs', and registered licensed clubs. The latter had been established throughout Australia over several decades to provide premises and low-cost meals and drinks to their members. In New South Wales in 1969, there were 1,444 clubs ranging across lawn-bowling clubs, football clubs, golf clubs and workers' clubs.[26] The clubs had a significant boost to their custom when in 1956 the New South Wales government became the first in Australia to legalize poker machines in clubs. By the 1990s other states had approved this move into registered clubs and public hotels, a move that would become a battleground in the early years of the twenty-first century from those who decried their local pub being turned into a mini-casino. Hotels had also taken advantage of the extension of their hours, including being able to trade on Sundays, expanding weekend dining options.

Critchley's comment about high mark-ups on white wine mark the beginning of a change in Australian wine preferences from red wine to white wine. 'Ultimately,' write Ross Fitzgerald and Trevor Jordan in their history of alcohol in Australia, 'the increased interest in red wine, prompted by a newly formed minority, would be overtaken by a white wine boom in the 1970s that finally delivered the hoi polloi to the industry . . . at a time when more beer than ever was being consumed, the "drink now" styles of white wine were more attractive to those who had no interest in cellaring a wine until it was drinkable.'[27]

However, they note that there was more to it than this:

> A study completed in 1985, found that the newly emerged meaning and social role of white wine, as opposed to red wine or other types of alcoholic drinks, was the main reason for the increase in its popularity. The study confirmed that, at the time, beer was seen as a predominantly masculine beverage. Women felt uncomfortable about beer drinking by other women, but sometimes also by men, because of its heavy masculine and sometimes 'ocker' [slang for an Australian who speaks and acts in a rough and uncultivated manner and uses a broad Australian accent – can be used either affectionately or pejoratively, as it is meant here] identity. Men also reported that seeing women drinking beer was off-putting as it made her appear unfeminine . . . people associated red wine with 'high' culture. Red wine was known to be more variable in quality than white wine and therefore to select a good red wine required expert knowledge. The corollary was that white wine came to be seen by the general public as much more accessible.[28]

This observation sits well with the popularity of the wine bar in the 1970s. These were typically one large room with a counter, tables and chairs, often with entertainment, serving platters of cheese, cabanossi (a thin, dry-smoked sausage, similar to a mild salami) and pickles, seen as 'an alternative, more sophisticated venue . . . where young men and women could socialise together in an atmosphere more accepting of and respectful to women . . . Yet by the end of the twentieth century with the proliferation of restaurants and cafes the wine bar as such had virtually died out to be replaced by the private bar which often served food on the side.'[29]

The 1970s also saw new wine regions established. At Margaret River, 300 km (185 mi.) south of Perth in Western Australia, in around 1851, Elijah Dawson planted 1.2 ha (3 ac) of commercial vineyard at Vasse. Giacomo Meleri established a vineyard at Yallingup in 1920 and produced wines for the next thirty years. But it wasn't until Tom Cullity planted Vasse Felix in 1967 that the region began to fulfil its potential. In quick succession came Moss Wood (1969), Cape Mentelle (1970), Cullen (1971), Sandalford (1972), Leeuwin Estate, Woodlands and Wright's (all three established in 1973). The combination of boutique wineries, surfing beaches, national parks and Mediterranean climate proved highly attractive commercially and the region soon became a food and wine destination. On the other side of the continent, at the nation's capital, Canberra, the entomologist Edgar Riek planted vines at Lake George in the early 1970s. In the following decade John Kirk established Clonakilla (1971), Ken and Judith Helm established Helm Wines (1973) and Sue and Dave Carpenter established Lark Hill Winery (1978). The Canberra region gained a reputation for cold-climate wines.

Between 1966 and 1976 the per capita consumption of beer increased from 24.2 gallons to 30.2 gallons, and consumption of wine from 1.3 gallons to 2.9 gallons.[30] The increasing number of licensed places to drink alcohol, particularly at night, led to concerns about the high rate of motor vehicle accidents involving intoxicated drivers. By the mid-1970s all states had passed laws with harsher penalties for drink-driving offences, setting a legal blood-alcohol concentration for drivers at 0.08 per cent across Australia, except for Victoria where it was 0.05. (The blood-alcohol concentration is the amount in grams of alcohol in every 100 ml of blood.) In 1969 New South Wales was the first state to begin a breathalyser system whereby drivers suspected of drink-driving or being involved in an accident could have their blood-alcohol level read. Victoria began random breath testing in 1976 and by 1988 similar legislation had been passed in all states and territories. In 1990 all states and territories adopted 0.05 as the standard, and by 2018, the drink-driving death toll had dropped from 44 per cent before the introduction of roadside breath testing to 30 per cent nationally, with some cities below 20 per cent.

Fast Feeding

There was one other dining-out trend that Jones noted. 'The most successful single venture in the restaurant trade,' she wrote' 'and one which provides a thoughtful pointer to the future, is the *Cahills' Brass Rail* chain of restaurant wine-bars ... The *Cahills'* credo is that Sydney diners do not want to linger over meals, European style, but that they like to eat quickly (and well).' Apart from one outlet in Melbourne, Cahill's was an exclusively Sydney phenomenon. Where the desire to eat quickly, if not well, was satisfied nationally was in the fast-food franchises that were emerging at the time Jones wrote. The first Kentucky Fried Chicken outlet opened in the outer western Sydney suburb of Guildford in April 1968. Pizza Hut opened in 1970 in Belfield and McDonald's first outlet was in Yagoona in 1971. Burger King could not use that brand name in Australia as it had been trademarked by a hamburger shop in Adelaide; it rebranded as Hungry Jack's and opened in the suburb of Innaloo in Perth, Western Australia, in 1971. The first Australian-owned fast-food chain, Red Rooster, opened in 1972, also in Perth. These outlets were not by any means designed for lingering in, a feature emphasized with their drive-through service where the whole transaction from ordering food to getting it could be done without leaving one's car. To add to the convenience the meal could be eaten sitting in the car in the parking lot that was an essential part of the layout. Take-away food was not in itself a new phenomenon: buying fish and chips or ordering take-away Chinese were well-established food practices. The impact of these newer fast foods, heavy with saturated fats, on the health of Australians, particularly children, would become clearer in the next decades with consequent concern for how much 'junk food' was an integral part of Australian families' diet.

The new foods also provided one solution to an increasing emphasis on getting meals prepared quickly. The fast food outlets' answer was to buy the meal already prepared: a bucket of Kentucky Fried Chicken, plus a family-sized serving of fried potato chips, a tub of brown gravy, and later a serving of sweetened coleslaw was a quick way to have a family dinner without the drudge of cleaning pans, crockery and cutlery afterwards.

Frozen food provided another solution: Birds Eye had been growing vegetables in Australia specifically for its quick-freeze process since 1949, and its frozen peas were an early success. The range of frozen vegetables grew, and other manufacturers were quick to follow. The main selling point for them was their freshness, as there was little chance for spoilage having been quick-frozen soon after picking, transported in a refrigerated container, put directly into the refrigerated cabinets in the supermarket, and then, hopefully, rapidly transported to the freezer compartment of a home refrigerator. The other selling point was that they were then quick to cook, needing only a few minutes in boiling water to take the chill off and cook through. So ubiquitous had they become that the 13 August 1975 issue of the *Australian Women's Weekly* had a two-page feature article on 'How to glamorise Quick Frozen Vegetables'. Recipes included Spinach Balls (chopped spinach mixed with cottage cheese, Parmesan and egg rolled into balls and deep-fried), Chinese Green Peas (peas and ginger simmered in stock) and Parmesan Crumbed Cauliflower (cauliflower pieces dipped in egg, Parmesan and breadcrumbs and deep fried).[31]

Canning technology also had improved after the Second World War, with increasing mechanization driving smaller canneries out of business.[32] Heinz and Campbell's battled it out for dominance of the canned soup trade, the latter promoting their product as 'just like home-made minus the work'. Kia Ora was an early entry into canning whole meals, like its 'Delicatessen style' beef and pork frankfurter, and its SpaghettiOs targeted

Bill Burgess of Fourwinds' Glass House Mountains standing next to a trailerload of pineapples ready to pack for the Golden Circle cannery, *c.* 1950.

at the mum who wanted to give her children something quick – 'circles of spaghetti even the small fry can handle – you can eat it with a spoon'. Others soon followed: Edgell produced canned fruit pie fillings, promoting them as '30-second pies' – the catch being that the cook had to make or buy the pastry and roll it out and shape it in the pie case, which of course took more than 30 seconds. Fruit-canning technology also made the pitting, peeling, coring and slicing a foolproof, fully automated enterprise. One company and its product dominated the market, however. Golden Circle, a cooperative established in 1947 in Brisbane, Queensland, became the largest fruit canner of them all, and its canned pineapple would become an Australian food icon, gracing everything from pizzas and hamburgers to cakes.

Powdered cake mixes had been available for some time, but both White Wings and Betty Sydney went one better, bringing out powdered pavlova bases. The big winner in the powdered food stakes was French onion soup, in its incarnation as the popular party dish French onion dip. The humourist Richard Glover was painfully accurate in his description of the dish: 'The recipe is simple: take a bucket of sour cream and throw in a sachet of French Onion Soup Mix. Add some chopped hard-boiled egg if you want to impress.'[33]

Eating Our Greens

In the 18 February issue of the *Australian Women's Weekly*, readers may have been slightly taken aback by a two-page advertisement headed 'Break the monotony of meat meat meat.'[34] It was a bold move by the Sanitarium company whose usual copy in the *Weekly* focused on how healthy were its high protein meat substitutes in a can – Soyameat, Vegeburger and Nutolene.

Vegetarianism has a 120-year history in Australia. The first Vegetarian Society of Australia was founded in Melbourne in February 1886 and branches in other states soon followed. The Society's manifesto said that its object was to 'induce habits of abstinence from the flesh of animals (fish, flesh and fowl) as food'.[35] The Society claimed that chemical analysis showed vegetables had all the elements necessary for health and strength, and that 'consumption of animal food promotes diseases and unhappiness amongst mankind . . . [and] makes men ferocious and quarrelsome, and tends to keep up the love of war'.[36] It was also critical of the treatment of animals being brought to the Melbourne slaughter yards.

The first fully vegetarian restaurant was the Thistle Company's Luncheon room in Melbourne in 1885. The premises also served as the offices of the Vegetarian Society of Australia. The Society and its branches lasted until the First World War when numbers dwindled, perhaps in part under the onslaught of attacks on them from *The Bulletin* magazine, which was outraged on its readers' behalf that anyone should be threatening the Australian meat industry, or criticizing the treatment of animals at the slaughtering yards, as vegetarians were openly doing. In its issue of 21 November 1912, the magazine carried an attack on the recent Melbourne convention of the Women's Christian Temperance Union through a scurrilous poem: 'The Accursed Meat' by one Silas Snell.

> Cold tongue, and fish, and pickled feet,
> These gnaw the morals out of us.
> 'Tis tripe and such infernal meat
> Should raise the Rechabitish cuss.
> Were there no pork there'd be no port;
> No chicken, no champagne. In short,
> The Butcher Fiend is grim and swart![37]

Reportedly, the convention had said that 'It was being recognised more and more that flesh food was more impure than vegetarian food.

Advertisement for Weet-Bix in the *Australian Women's Weekly*.

Sanitarium's Weet-Bix competed with Kellogg's for the children's breakfast-cereal market.

The person who never ate meat had never been known to be a drunkard, and a drunkard had never been known to be a vegetarian.'

The earliest written material in Australia promoting vegetarianism was by the spiritualist William Henry Terry in his self-published magazine *The Harbinger of Light*. Australian members of the Theosophical Society, established by the spiritualist Helena Blavatsky in 1875, promoted vegetarianism and animal welfare. However, arguably it was the Seventh-day Adventist church that had the strongest influence on vegetarianism, lasting until the late 1960s and early 1970s. The church began when Ellen White, her son and five other members of an American congregation arrived in Melbourne in 1891. White converted to a largely vegetable diet because she, like the Women's Christian Temperance Union, believed that eating meat inflamed the passions and led to violence. Members of the Adventist congregation gave lectures to branches of the Temperance Union.

In 1898 the American Adventist Edward Halsey was sent to Australia to establish a factory to produce non-dairy milks, peanut butter (the first produced in Australia) and breakfast cereals. The first batch of Granola left the factory on 27 January 1898. The Sanitarium Food Co. would soon be the largest manufacturer of vegetarian products, selling them through Adventist shops in the capital cities and larger regional towns. Weet-Bix would become its flagship breakfast cereal in Australia. The only competitor was F. G. Roberts, who in 1936 made the first Australian soy products. That company, like Sanitarium, continues and now includes gluten-free products in its range.

The Great Aussie Pie

'We love football, meat pies, kangaroos and Holden cars,' blared Australian television sets in 1976. The General Motors Holden jingle, sung by a chorus of heavily Australian-accented male voices, was intercut with images of the beach, sporting events, the Australian flag, marsupials and Holden cars. True, it merely exchanged Australian images and words for the original in an American Chevrolet commercial. But the meat pie's claim to icon status was now unassailable.

Pies have been an ubiquitous part of Australian convenience food since the earliest days of the Sydney colony. Piemen wandered the streets with hot pies on trays, in baskets and handcarts. William Francis King, in the 1840s, earned the title of 'The Flying Pieman', as he raced on foot between selling pies at Circular Quay to people boarding the steamer to Parramatta and meeting them 30 km (nearly 20 mi.) upriver as they disembarked, to sell any that remained.

In the 1870s a pie cart in Adelaide had the market-grabbing idea of taking a pie and turning it upside down into a plate of thick pea soup. In 2003 the pie floater, as it came

The classic Australian combination: a meat pie with tomato sauce.

Harry's Café de Wheels.

to be called, was recognized as a South Australian Heritage Icon by the National Trust of South Australia.

In 1891 George and Charlotte Sargent opened a bakery in Paddington, an inner suburb of Sydney, and began selling pies at a penny each. In 1912 they opened a shop in Melbourne and were soon catering for the new Parliament House. It is now one of the largest pie manufacturers, having taken over its main competitor Big Ben.

Perhaps the most famous pie cart in Australia is Harry's Café de Wheels. It started to trade when Harry Edwards set up a caravan near the front gates of the naval dockyard at Woolloomooloo, the bay next to Sydney Cove, site of the first colonial settlement. It was the late 1930s and Harry captured the wartime trade of servicemen and their sweethearts looking for a quick snack before the ships sailed. The city council regulations were that mobile food vans had to move a minimum of 30 cm (12 in.) a day. Harry did that just that, and 'Harry's' became 'Harry's Café de Wheels'.

Joan Haddon's 1972 *The Australian Book of Health Food Cookery* was an early popular publication catering to the growing interest in non-meat-based diets.

The current Australian Vegetarian Society was established in 1948 in Sydney, and initially was a base for the emerging naturopathy and alternative health practitioners. These practitioners began to open 'health food' shops in competition with those run by the Adventists. The latter closed their enterprises in 1980, by which time, however, Sanitarium cereals, milk alternatives and meat substitutes were on the shelves of the supermarkets. In 1976 the Victorian Vegan Society was formed, and the national Society followed in 1977.

Two other influences during the 1970s continued the growth of vegetarianism in Australia. The first was the establishment in Australia of Ananda Marga and the International Society for Krishna Consciousness, commonly called the Hare Krishnas – both Hindu-based religious groups that promote vegetarianism. The Hare Krishnas started a food service for the homeless and impoverished that continues today. The other influence was what is generally called the counterculture, which arose in the United States in the late 1960s and was entrenched in Australia by the mid-1970s. The big public event that symbolized its emergence in Australia was the Aquarius Arts Festival in the New South Wales north-coast town of Nimbin. But its precursors were two magazines: *Earth Garden*, first published in 1972, and *Grass Roots*, first published in May 1973. Both promoted vegetarianism, though not exclusively, animal welfare – being critical of the emerging factory farming of poultry in particular – and organic fruit, grain and vegetable growing in both the home garden and on farms.

'Many youngsters interested in vegetarian foods are gradually changing the food habits of their families,' said the 17 September 1975 issue of the *Australian Women's Weekly*. 'For non-vegetarians, an occasional vegetarian meal will be a healthy and pleasant change in the menu.' The article delineated four types of non-meat practice: vegan, being exclusively vegetable-, fruit- and cereal-based; lacto-vegetarians, who excluded eggs; lacto-ovo-vegetarians, those who included eggs; and ovo-vegetarians, who ate eggs but did not use dairy products. Recipes in its 'Cooking the Vegetarian Way' feature included Nutmeat loaf, spinach and spaghetti casserole, aubergine (eggplant) in batter, and brown rice salad. Vegetarianism had crossed over into the mainstream.[38]

The list of variations on vegetarianism would come to challenge restaurants and cafés as the dining-out boom continued through the 1980s with the emergence of the 'foodie'.

Aboriginal Labour: The Wave Hill Walk-off

In 1966 Vincent Lingiari, a Gurindji man, led a walk-off of two hundred Aboriginal workers on the Wave Hill cattle station in the Northern Territory. Established in 1883 by the Buchanan family, the property was bought in 1914 by the Union Cold Storage Co., one of the British Vestey Group. There was a long history of complaints about the conditions of the Indigenous workers, both stockmen and domestic servants, including an inquiry in the 1930s that was critical of Vestey. Aboriginal workers on cattle stations were excluded from the Cattle Station Industry (Northern Territory) Award, meaning that they could be paid at whatever rate of pay and in whatever way their employers chose. Aboriginal workers were

Prime Minister Gough Whitlam pours soil into the hands of Vincent Lingiari to signify the handing back of Wave Hill station, 1975.

generally paid less than non-Aboriginal workers, and on some stations wages were reduced by the imputed cost of their food and accommodation. Government benefits paid to Aboriginal people on stations were also often paid directly into pastoral companies' accounts, making them dependant on the manager's largesse as to when and how much they had in hand. In 1965 the Northern Australian Workers' Union successfully applied to the Commonwealth Conciliation and Arbitration Commission to delete the words 'excluding Indigenous workers' from the award, so that they would not be exempt from its provisions. This was the basis on which the Wave Hill workers took action.

The Gurindji set up camp at Wattie Creek on their traditional lands. As the walk-off continued, their demands broadened into a claim for possession of the land, the first claim by an Aboriginal group in Australia. The Gurindji wanted to reclaim their millennia-long ownership of the land, ownership that had been disregarded as pastoral lands were sold and leased. The walk-off continued for nine years until 1976 when the Commonwealth passed the Aboriginal Land Rights (Northern Territory) Act 1976. This act gave Aboriginal Australians freehold title to traditional lands in the Northern Territory and, significantly, the power to negotiate over development, including pastoral and mining works on those lands, and the kind and amount of compensation they could receive for loss of their land.

It would take until 1992 for the High Court of Australia to finally overturn the doctrine of *terra nullius*. In 1982 Meriam man Eddie Koiki Mabo and four others began a High Court case challenging the Australian legal system's assumption that Indigenous Australians had no concept of ownership before the arrival of the British in 1788, and that the declaration by the British of sovereignty of all land in the colony to the Crown, abolishing any rights that may have existed previously. The case ran for ten years culminating in the 1992 High Court ruling that 'native title' or Indigenous ownership of land could still exist where there was a continuing relationship with the land, and where the Crown (the government) had not sold it. This finally repealed the doctrine of *terra nullius* under which Australia had been colonized. The judgement led to the Australian Government passing the Native Title Act in 1993.[39]

NINE

Foodie Nation, 1980–99

During the last two decades of the twentieth century food became something of a national obsession, and the 'foodie' was its public face. The origin of the term is generally attributed to Gael Greene, writing in *New York Magazine* in 1980, but arguably it was with the publication of *The Official Foodie Handbook* by Ann Barr and Paul Levy in 1985 that the term became established.[1] 'What is new about an interest in food?' they asked. 'Everyone knows some older person who was called a "gourmet" before the term "Foodie" arrived . . . But Foodies are new, children of the consumer boom . . . Foodies are the ones talking about food in any gathering – salivating over restaurants, recipes, radicchio . . . Food is the staple diet of social intercourse now.'[1] While their intent was satirical, the term 'foodie' soon became adopted by the very people they set out to satirize.

To support a foodie culture, Barr and Levy wrote, several things were necessary: high-class shops, fast transport to bring fresh produce from the land, enlightened, 'well-paid eater-outers' to support the whole expensive edifice, and lower-paid workers to make the food.[2] As Australia moved out of the late 1970s and into the early 1980s, it met these pre-conditions. The energy and mining booms of the late 1970s and early 1980s provided a sufficient pool of 'well-paid eater-outers'. 'High-class shops', both restaurants and providores, were establishing themselves. The hospitality industry in Australia was and is a low-paid and casualized sector. And it was at this time that a class of journalist arose to enlighten the eater-outer. This chapter begins by looking at the shaping of Australian foodie culture.

Guiding Dining

Writing about where one has dined and the quality of the food and wine has a long history in Australia: the writer Marcus Clarke in a series of articles in Melbourne's *The Age* in 1879; Will Bede Dalley Junior in the short-lived magazine *The Triad* over 1927–8; and Oscar Mendelsohn in the magazine *Focus* in 1947–8, to name a few.[3] In 1966 Ted Maloney, co-author of the 1950s recipe book *Oh, for a French Wife!*, and Johnny Walker, a restaurateur and wine merchant, and founder in 1939 of the Wine and Food Society in Sydney, began a column in the *Sun Herald*, a Sydney newspaper, called 'Your Guide to Good Living'. 'Their columns,' writes the food historian Alison Vincent, 'were an odd combination of culinary anecdotes and recipes, tales of their own food adventures and the amazing restaurants they dined in. Consequently, their articles read more like what today would be called "advertorial".'[4] These, however, were not intended as guides for the prospective diner: their audience was the gourmet of Barr and Levy.

The first stand-alone restaurant guides as such were television chef Graham Kerr's two pocket-book-sized editions: the 1968 *Guide to Good Eating in Sydney*, and the 1969 *Guide* for Melbourne. His guides were not extensive – 150 'eating establishments' for Sydney and 73 for Melbourne. They did not provide descriptions of the food or the dining experience and did not use a rating system.[5] Kerr left for Canada in 1969 and no further editions of the guides were published.

By the middle of the 1970s restaurant reviewing had become a regular feature in major newspapers: Eric Page for *The Herald* (Melbourne) from 1970; Richard Beckett writing under the pseudonym Sam Orr for the *Nation Review* from 1971; Leo Schofield, first in the *Sunday Australian* in 1971 and then the *Sunday Telegraph* (Sydney) from the following year; and Peter Smark in *The Age* from June 1975. Schofield (1975) and Smark (1977) published the next iteration of restaurant guides in Sydney and Melbourne respectively. In 1980, *The Age* newspaper in Melbourne published its first *Good Food Guide*, edited by Claude Forell and Rita Erlich, and in 1984 the first *Sydney Morning Herald Good Food Guide* was published, edited by Schofield. Both these guides continued to be published annually from that time. In contrast to Kerr's, these guides provided short descriptions of two or three signature dishes from each restaurant, the ambience and dining experience as a whole. By the early 1990s they were both rating restaurants and awarding 'chef's hats' to those ranking highest.

'There is no doubt that the reviewers had an enormous influence on what we ate, how we ate it and how we used restaurants,' writes the food historian John Newton:

> The critics heralded the new age of restaurants as entertainment and taught us that there is more to the restaurant than sitting at a table and ordering a meal. They taught us rules. The restaurant is one of the most complex and difficult of our public spaces, and it was the restaurant critic who guided the trainee restaurant-users of the 1970s through its nuances of manners, behaviour and conduct. And Australians took their advice seriously.[6]

As *The Age* and *Sydney Morning Herald* guides increasingly focused on the 'high-class shops', *Cheap Eats* guides were published in the late 1980s by both, reviewing casual dining, cafés, bars and other options for feeding and watering the foodie. This democratization was furthered in 1992 when the Special Broadcasting Service, Australia's multicultural and multilingual broadcaster, published its first *Eating Guide.* Edited by journalists Joanna Savill and Maeve O'Meara it focused on the rapidly expanding range of restaurants owned by immigrants and their second- and third-generation families. These restaurants rarely were reviewed in the *Good Food Guides,* which focused on the fine-dining end of the market

It was not only through restaurant reviews that foodies were enlightened. Kerr had included in his guides a 'Short Glossary of Continental Terms' – bearnaise, hollandaise and au poivre, for example – indicative of the trend to 'continental' dishes in the recipe sections of women's magazines. Also included in each guide were brief sections on Australian wines and cheeses. The *Epicurean* and *Australian Gourmet Magazine*, both first published in 1966, had articles about gourmet foods and international cuisines, wine and recipes. As interest grew from readers and advertisers, the newspapers, too, began expanding their coverage of all matters related to food and wine, including profiles on emerging chefs, producers and vignerons, trends in wining and dining, and industry news. In 1988 Tasmania was the first state to hold a food festival: 'Tasting Tasmania'. In 1998 the *Sydney Morning Herald* sponsored Sydney's first 'Good Food Month'. The festival included a night noodle market, special events at restaurants, panels of national and international speakers, cooking demonstrations and other food- and wine-related activities.

The highly paid eater-outer was also being enlightened on wine. The vigneron and wine judge James Halliday was a regular contributor to *Epicurean* and published *James Halliday's Australian Wine Guide* in 1986, and continued to publish guides to Australian and New Zealand wines over the next decades. In 1992 Andrew Wood began *Divine* magazine with content roughly 50/50 between food and wine. Each issue of the quarterly publication featured a food product or trend and a wine style. Wood and his wine critics reported also on vertical tastings of wines in particular wineries, and held an annual State of Origin competition between wines from different areas of Australia, the name being a play on the title of the annual rugby league football match between New South Wales and Queensland.

Television and the Rise of the Celebrity Chef

While there had been experimental and demonstration broadcasts of television since 1929 in Australia, the first licenses for public broadcasting were issued in 1956. In the same year Will Koeppen arrived in Australia from Berlin to be the Executive Chef of Melbourne's Chevron Hotel. Within a year Koeppen became the first chef appearing on the new medium. *The Chef Presents* screened between 1957 and 1959 on the commercial station HSV-7, beginning with just 5 minutes wedged before the 7 p.m. news, and expanding to 15 minutes in the afternoon before *Every Woman's Theatre*, a half-hour drama series. Koeppen went on to open The Cuckoo restaurant in the Dandenong Ranges with his wife. His mysterious disappearance in 1976 remains a suspected homicide 'cold case'.

There was a six-year hiatus before the next television chef appeared. Graham Kerr was a self-taught cook, crediting the beginning of his career as the Specialty Catering Officer in the British Army in the 1950s. He first appeared as a television chef in New Zealand. In 1965 he was inveigled by Harry M. Miller, an Australian entertainment manager and entrepreneur, to present a half-hour cooking show, *Entertaining with Kerr*, on the recently established Network TEN. Kerr cooked while impeccably dressed in suit and tie, wine glass in hand, from which he would generously 'slosh' wine into whatever he was cooking, arguably single-handedly popularizing the practice. *Graham Kerr's Studio Kitchen* can lay claim to the first cookery book tie-in to a television programme. It brought together recipes Kerr had published in the programme guide magazine *TV Week*. Kerr left Australia for Canada in 1969 to embark on a new series, *The Galloping Gourmet*, which also screened in Australia in 1969–71.

Graham Kerr, the first Australian television celebrity chef, in a characteristic pose with a glass of red wine.

Where Kerr had presented with a Savile Row panache, his successor in the national-television-chef spot was the flamboyant Bernard King. King's career famously began with a lunch he hosted for actress Vivien Leigh. Maureen Kistle, presenter of ABC television's *A Woman's World*, was also at the lunch and asked King to show his skills on the programme. King went on to host a daily segment on Network TEN's *Good Morning Australia*, and then his own show *King's Kitchen*, which aired from 1972 to 1983. King was the first television chef to promote sponsor-supplied products on his show.

Continuing the line of television chefs during this period were Peter Russell-Clarke and Ian Parmenter. Russell-Clarke hosted a five-minute show called *Come and Get It*, airing nine hundred episodes on the ABC network for nine years during the 1980s. Russell-Clarke was as well-known for the programme as for his popularizing of the Australian welcome 'G'day'. Ian Parmenter, like King and Russell-Clarke before him, was a self-taught cook. He was a journalist who joined the ABC network in 1974 and began presenting *Consuming Passions* in 1992. In 1995 Parmenter was awarded the Presenters Award at the Festival de la Tele Gourmande in France, and *Consuming Passions* was awarded the Lucien Barriere Grand Prix. The programme aired until 2001 and was sold on to fifteen countries.

The men did not have it all their way, however. Ghanaian Dorinda Hafner responded to racism against her children in a primary school in Adelaide by beginning a cultural food programme in the 1980s. The programme was successful and Hafner soon was catering Cuisine Africaine private dinner parties. She then successfully approached the Special Broadcasting Service for a television programme, *A Taste of Africa*. The service was established by the Commonwealth Government in 1977 to provide radio and television content in languages other than English. Hafner's programme was syndicated in 48 countries. Elizabeth Chong began her time as a television chef with short segments on the Network TEN breakfast programme *Good Morning Australia* and went on to host and cook on her *Tiny Delights* series, which combined travels around China with in-studio cooking demonstrations of Chinese regional dishes.

Women were also members of the permanent and guest presenters on *Gardening Australia*, produced by the Australian Broadcasting Commission. Beginning in 1990, and hosted by Peter Cundall, the programme was directed at the backyard vegetable and fruit gardener, continuing the tradition of gardening columns in print media but with the advantage that now gardeners could see how to do what they were being advised to do.

Food Consumption Trends

What were other factors shaping what Australians were eating over the 1980s and 1990s? In 2000 the Australian Bureau of Statistics published its report on Apparent Consumption of Foodstuffs 1997–8 and 1998–9. The findings compared the apparent consumption of foodstuffs in the penultimate year of each decade from 1938 to 1939. The method for determining the rates of consumption used information relating to the supply and utilization of foodstuffs. This means the data are an approximate estimate of foodstuffs *available* for consumption by persons in Australia, after allowing for other uses and losses.[7]

There was a 30 per cent reduction in consumption overall of meat and meat products between 1938–9 and 1998–9. Beef and veal consumption dropped with rationing during the Second World War. It rose again until 1978–9, after which it dropped dramatically to 38 per cent. Mutton had fallen steadily. Lamb rose to a high of 66 per cent and fell back to almost half of that by 1998–9. Pork had steadily increased. Poultry was separately measured and data was available only in 1968–9 onwards and this showed a steady increase. The consumption of eggs and egg products showed a drop of around 43 per cent. Butter showed a 78 per cent reduction over the period.

Why the changes? By the 1970s 'animal fats had been identified as "saturated"', writes food historian Barbara Santich,

> and more likely to promote the accumulation of dangerous cholesterol and other fatty substances in the blood. This negative association was to tarnish the image of meat – and in Australia 'meat' meant red meat: beef, mutton and lamb. Experts advised Australians to eat less of these, substituting the supposedly 'better', and less fatty, white meats – fish, chicken, veal, turkey. Other animal products, such as eggs and dairy foods were demoted in a similarly cavalier fashion.[8]

Spearheading the war on saturated fat was the National Heart Foundation, established in 1959. At the time, coronary heart disease alone accounted for one in every three deaths in Australia. The foundation's objective was to 'reduce premature death and invalidation from all forms of heart disease in Australia'.[9] In 1974 the foundation endorsed the independently published book *Polyunsaturated Cookery*, its director Ralph Reader writing in the introduction:

> *Polyunsaturated Cookery* is not a diet book, but a cookbook. It aims to show that you needn't give up the pleasures of good food to reduce your risk of heart disease. Basically all you need to do is cut down a little on fatty foods as a whole, at the same time substituting those rich in polyunsaturated fat for some of those which are high in started fat and cholesterol.[10]

The book sold 100,000 copies in four years. In 1989 the foundation went further and began its 'Tick Program'. The programme encouraged food manufacturers to submit their products to get a 'Tick' logo, which they could affix to the labelling. The pay-off was that the consumers in turn were encouraged to choose foods that had the Tick. Foods were eligible if they complied with prescribed standards for saturated fats and salt and had acceptable amounts of cholesterol, dietary fibre and added sugar. 'At August 1992,' wrote Santich, 'the list of approved products included 800 fresh and processed foods, ranging from such obvious choices as fresh vegetables, fresh fruit and fresh fish, to certain brands of frozen chips, fish fingers, sausages, frozen dinners, meat pies, cheeses and modified icecreams'.[11] The foundation stopped the programme in 2018. 'Now that Nutrient Information Panels are mandatory,' the foundation said, 'and front-of-pack labelling is firmly established on the food agenda, the Heart Foundation can retire the Tick to focus on its next innovations that will improve the cardiovascular health of all Australians.'[12]

Table margarine consumption increased fourfold between 1968–9 and 1988–9. The production of table margarine had been subject to quotas since 1940 through pressure from the dairy industry who saw it as a competitor to butter. In 1963 Marrickville Margarine introduced the first Australian polyunsaturated margarine: Miracle. Many of the recipes in *Polyunsaturated Cookery* specify using polyunsaturated margarine. It was not the only publication to do so. In 1971 Stork margarine had partnered with publishing house Paul Hamlyn on *The Family Cookbook* in which the eponymous brand was an essential ingredient in the majority of recipes.[13] In 1976 the quota on margarine was lifted and this, together with the push from the Heart Foundation, is a likely factor in the rise in consumption. Recipes in *Australian Women's Weekly* in the 1980s and early 1990s, however, continued to call for butter or oil. Olive oil was initially specified only for Italians dishes, but by 1995 it had begun to cross over to other dishes also, notably salads and barbecued meat. Promoted as a healthier alternative, imports of olive oil tripled between 1886 and 1999, from 7,000 tonnes to 23,000 tonnes. Olive-oil production in Australia also grew rapidly.

What did these shifts mean for the total consumption of oils and fats? The Bureau figures show a small increase in overall consumption between 1938–9 and 1998–9, at just 7 per cent. However, this figure masks a significant intervention by the Bureau. In its figures pre-1975–6, the total oils and fats per person included 2 kg (4 lb) for vegetable oils and fat, to represent fats and oils consumed in processed and cooked foods. The Bureau reviewed this and used a figure of 10 kg (20 lb) per person from that time. That is, the Bureau had factored in a fivefold increase in fats and oils consumed in processed and cooked foods after 1975–6. This is reflected in the substantial increase in the total consumption between 1968–9

Despite health warnings, Australians were not about to give up on eating sheep.

and 1978–9 of 50 per cent. This increase happened when five fast-food franchises were established across Australia: Kentucky Fried Chicken (1968), Pizza Hut (1970), McDonald's (1971), Hungry Jack's (a franchise of Burger King; 1971) and Red Rooster (1972). The companies pitched their products not just as casual, occasional meals like pies, sausage rolls or hamburgers; they promoted them as healthy alternatives to home-cooked meals. In the 3 January 1979 issue of *Australian Women's Weekly*, Kentucky Fried Chicken had a two-page advertisement showing three generations of an Australian family – plus the family dog – sitting together on the white-painted timber deck of the family home, one of the young girls in the family holding aloft a crumbed drumstick, the signature red-and-white-striped takeaway container prominently displayed. The accompanying text encourages the view that crumbed fried chicken is a healthy accompaniment to family get-togethers.[14] By 1998–9 total fat consumption in Australia had fallen 14 per cent from the 1978–9 peak, which may indicate that concerns raised by dieticians about the fat content in fast food were being heard and acted on.

The Australian Bureau of Statistics report showed that while there had been modest growth in consumption of seafood (including crustacea and molluscs) until 1968–9, it was over the next decades that consumption had the biggest rise. Three factors may explain this dramatic increase in seafood consumption.

The first was messaging that positioned fish as a healthy alternative to meat; the second was support from state governments for the development of commercial fishing. 'Until the 1940s,' writes Anna Clark in her 2017 history of fishing in Australia, 'commercial fishing was pretty rudimentary along the entire logistics chain from the small boats that worked the inland and coastal waters to the storage, transport and warehousing of their catch.'[15] Fish stocks were high but catches were low. The

As early as the 1970s, the Australian dairy industry, concerned at the rising market share of margarine for cooking, sought to win back home cooks.

Commonwealth and state governments began to see this as a lost economic opportunity. From the 1940s they intervened to develop the industry, subsidizing canners and transport infrastructure, establishing fishing co-operatives, and funding research and development.[16] The third factor was the influx of migrants from the Mediterranean, Italy in particular, who arguably were responsible for the increased consumption of crustaceans and molluscs – squid (calamari) and pippies (vongole) heading the list.

Consumption of refined cane sugar fell by 72 per cent between 1938–9 and 1988–9 (figures were not available for 1998–9), with the biggest fall of 41 per cent in the period 1978–9 and 1988–9. CSR, established in 1855 as the Colonial Sugar Refinery Co. and virtually the monopoly producer of sugar in Australia, continued to promote refined sugar. In the 1970s it had promoted sugar as a quick energy boost for children. During the 1980s the pitch shifted. Worried that consumption of sugar was being linked to weight gain, the sugar industry fought back arguing that people could continue to eat sugar as long as they also ate a variety of food in moderation and exercised. But over those same six decades, the amount of sugar being consumed via manufactured foods doubled. The 22 per cent rise between 1968–9 and 1988–9 parallels the rise in grain breakfast foods over those decades – 42 per cent. Some of these foods came in for criticism as containing added sugar, so much so that advertisements for particular brands prominently stated that they contained no added sugar.

'Modern Australian'

In the 1994 edition of the *Good Food Guide to Eating Well In and Around Sydney*, the editors, William Fraser and Helen Greenwood, introduced a new category of dining out: 'A new way of eating has sprung up . . . more often than not it will offer interesting food, fusing ethnic styles with the bistro approach to create another version of modern Australian cuisine.'[17] Once released into conversations through the *Guide* and other writing on food in Australia, the term 'modern Australian' became a catch-all for a number of observable trends that were changing what Australians ate when they dined out.

Cherry Ripe identified the increasing use of Asian ingredients across cuisines:

> The one thing we do – from Perth to Port Douglas, Adelaide to Darwin – which is substantially different from the rest of

> the (Western) world is the degree of incorporation of Asian ingredients into our food. Whether it's the local Greek deli turning out a chicken salad snow peas, bean sprouts, ginger, soy sauce and sesame oil, or recipes in *Vogue Entertaining* for Asian noodle with lobster and green pawpaw, flavoured with kaffir lime, lemongrass and laksa (Vietnamese hot mint or *rau ram*) leaves, it is our singular point of difference.[18]

Writing in the introduction of their catalogue of *Landmarks of Australian Gastronomy*, Barbara Santich, Graham Pont and Paul Wilkins also point this way: '[The emerging character of Australian gastronomy] can be discerned in the confluence of still vital native traditions, a rich European inheritance and diverse Asian influences, as a wine-drinking culture gradually absorbs and integrates with the alimentary traditions of Asia and at the same time is modified by the challenge to utilise unfamiliar indigenous resources.'[19] Chefs Mogens Bay Esbensen, Cheong Liew, Tetsuya Wakuda and Neil Perry are variously credited as bringing about the marriage of Asian ingredients with classically French techniques.

In *Looking for Flavour*, Santich broadens her scope, emphasizing quality of the ingredients: 'Modern Australian ... is an enthusiastic romp through the world's favourite recipes. Its bywords are "fresh" and "seasonal", with lots of colour, lots of salads, lots of fresh vegetable and herb flavours plus a health dash of sweet chilli, bold and undisciplined (in the sense of being free of disciplinary shackles).'[20] By 1997 the new editors of the *Good Food Guide*, Terry Durack and Jill Dupleix, had abandoned any attempt to pin the term down: 'More and more, Sydney dining has a Pacific flavour, in its freshness and sunny attitude. "Modern Australian" has come to mean simply Australian.'[21]

The incorporation of Asian ingredients and techniques and an emphasis on freshness were well suited to the dietary advice of the time. In a move that would have gladdened the heart of Philip Muskett, who urged its adoption in his 1893 book *The Art of Living in Australia*, the 'Mediterranean diet' became popular. Not a 'diet' in the sense of a strict regimen of limited foods and quantities, it emphasized fish, poultry, whole grains, nuts and olive oil. 'The diet of the Mediterranean region,' wrote Charmaine O'Brien in her history of dining in Melbourne,

> with Italy often held up as the poster child, was touted as the ideal one. Meat and three vegetables were still on the menu, but

In 1966 the Sydney Fish Market relocated to Blackwattle Bay, Pyrmont. It is the largest of its kind in the Southern Hemisphere.

> now the vegetables were chargrilled or incorporated into a wide variety of salads or stir-frys. Spaghetti Bolognese once a week had been replaced by penne, rigatoni, fettucine and tagliatelle, bathed in a variety of sauces and served several times a week.[22]

The shift to healthier eating was also aided by the entry into dining at home and dining out of other cuisines that were less based in heavy dairy sauces, red meat and butter. As in the past, some of these cuisines – Lebanese, Sri Lankan and Iranian, among others – were introduced via new groups of refugees. In June 1989 Prime Minister Bob Hawke granted visa extensions to all Chinese students in Australia in the wake of the Tiananmen Square massacre. About 42,000 Chinese people took up the offer and were later given permanent residency. Many of the students came from regions of China other than Canton, the source of most Chinese immigration to Australia until then. As permanent residents they were able to bring their families to Australia also. Regional Chinese restaurants sprang up and soon Australians were eating across the breadth of Chinese cuisines. Thai people had been migrating to Australia since the 1970s, but numbers increased in the 1980s. David Thompson would take Thai food upmarket first with Darley Street Thai and then at Sailor's Thai, both in Sydney. As happened with Asian ingredients, chefs like Greg Malouf in Melbourne and George Haddad and Anne Ripper in Hobart began to fuse their Lebanese culinary traditions with those of Europe. Later, Christine Manfield would do the same for Indian cuisines.

The new cuisines were also popularized through the television series *The Food Lover's Guide to Australia*. The programme was developed and hosted by Joanna Savill and Maeve O'Meara for the Special Broadcasting Service. The half-hour documentary-style programme broke the mould of television cooking shows up to that time which had usually been five- to ten-minute fillers between other programmes or short segments in longer entertainment programmes. In keeping with the multicultural charter of the Service, the programme showcased the cuisines of immigrants and refugees in both their home kitchens and their restaurants, and the cuisines were shown in their wider cultural contexts.

More than Emu on the Menu

Kangaroo meat for human consumption was legalized in South Australia in 1980. This was well-timed to take advantage of the health warnings about eating too much fatty meat. Kangaroo is a notably lean meat, low in saturated fats and high in protein. Over 1993–4, suppliers invoked the Constitutional guarantee of freedom of trade between states to successfully push for its legalization across Australia. By 2019 kangaroo meat was being sold in supermarkets and appearing on the menus of restaurants, though its move into the domestic kitchen was still tentative.

Interest in native foods had stayed at the fringes of public Australian eating since colonization. Early colonial cookbooks carried recipes for dishes of game – kangaroo, wallaby, wild fowl and parrots mainly; riverine and ocean fish (barramundi and Murray river cod prominently), crustaceans and molluscs: and fruits suitable for making jam – lilly pilly (*Syzygium smithii*) and quandong (*Santalum acuminatum*). In 1965 a group of women in Gippsland, Victoria, published *Is Emu on the Menu? Historical Homesteads and Recipes of Gippsland*.[23] Despite its provocative title the book only included recipes for Braised Leg of Emu, Parrot Pie, Kangaroo Tail Stew and Birdsville Track Damper: most of the recipes stayed firmly in the traditions of English cooking, with the occasional French or Middle European recipe.

Native foods began to take their place in Australian cuisine more decisively during the 1980s. In 1988 Army Major Les Hiddins featured in a popular television series, *The Bush Tucker Man*. In 1987, Hiddins had received a Defence Fellowship to research survival in northern Australia, which resulted in him being the principal author of the Australian Army's military survival manual. During the research Hiddins was introduced to the Kakadu plum (*Terminalia ferdinandiana*) by unacknowledged Aboriginal informants. This sparked his interest and he leveraged it into two series of the television programme focused on native food in the north of Australia, including plants and fruit.

The first fine-dining chef to incorporate native foods in his menu was Raymond Kersh, who with his sister Jennice opened Edna's Table in the central business district of Sydney in 1981. While Kersh had cooked native meats before, he acknowledges a visit to his brother's cattle station at Balgo in the Kimberley area of Western Australia and his engagement with the Kukatha people there as the source of his introduction to native plants and their 'strong distinctive flavours'.[24] They were followed by Jean-Paul Bruneteau, who opened Rowntrees with his business partner Jennifer Dowling on Sydney's north shore in 1984. Bruneteau's interest was stimulated by a short stay in New Zealand where he saw women picking wild greens, which led him to research native foods in Australia. In 1991 he opened Riberries in 1991, in the inner-Sydney suburb of Surry Hills, winning a coveted 'hat' in the 1996 *Sydney Morning Herald Good Food Guide*.[25] What was significant here was that these chefs were using native plant matter – lilly pilly/riberries, wattleseed, warrigal greens/native spinach, leaves of the lemon myrtle (*Backhousia citriodora*), mountain pepperberry (*Tasmannia lanceolate*), Illawarra plum (*Podocarpus elatus*), Kakadu plum – and so broadened the definition of native food/bush tucker to encompass more than just meat or fish.

In 1990 Vic Cherikoff presented a paper at the Fourth Symposium of Australian Gastronomy that put two challenges before the chefs, academics and foodies gathered there. Cherikoff, a researcher with degrees in biology and biochemistry, had begun working in 1983 with the University of Sydney's Human Nutrition Unit. The unit was collecting wild foods in the field and analysing them for their nutrient value, publishing papers and passing on the results to government and non-government bodies working to improve the health of Indigenous people. In his paper, Cherikoff said:

> I believe that the present decade will be a landmark in gastronomy, as we experience a concerted move to integrate elements of traditional Aboriginal cuisine into that of contemporary Australia . . . Contemporary Australian cuisine is most often described as consisting of fresh seasonal ingredients, produced

> locally and used simply. According to this definition, however, some 'Australian' dishes are difficult to distinguish from those of Europe and even Asia. I maintain that only a cuisine utilising indigenous produce can be truly Australian.[26]

To demonstrate the first of these challenges, he and Jean-Paul Bruneteau presented a Bush Food Buffet as one of the Symposium meals. But Australian diners were not yet ready to take up the challenge. The Kersh's described their experience to food historian John Newton:

> Putting the ingredients on the menu 'scared the living daylights out of the customers,' Jennice said. It was, Raymond now admits, 'the worst move we ever made. Before, we were using it and people were eating it unaware' . . . 'The resistance and judgement on what we were doing absolutely blew us away,' Jennice said. 'We couldn't believe it. It hurt. And we talked about it and said – what must it feel [like] to be Aboriginal?'[27]

While over the next decade more chefs would incorporate native foods into their menus, it would not be until the next millennium that they were fully embraced in high dining or made the transition to the domestic table.

Alcohol Consumption

The Australian Bureau of Statistics report showed that beer consumption increased by 150 per cent in 1938–9 to 1978–9, then fell 15 per cent by 1988–9. The overall consumption of beer and wine combined shows a fall of nearly 25 per cent between 1978–9 and 1998–9. This corresponds to the period over which random breath testing was introduced across Australia.

Over these same decades the two biggest supermarket chains also moved into the liquor trade. Coles led the way when in 1971 it began to sell alcohol through its Coles New World outlet in Warrnambool in Victoria. Then in 1981 it ramped up this side of its business, buying the 54-store-strong Claude Fay Cellars and the fourteen-store Liquorland chain. Woolworths was slow to follow Coles, which was unusual for the duopoly that historically expanded lockstep with each other. Woolworths took over the long-established Dan Murphy's chain in 1998 and Vintage Cellars in 2001 and began leading the retail liquor market. The outlets for

Kangaroo meat has gone from pet food to gourmet product.

both Coles and Woolworths were often located next to, or very close to, their supermarkets, making it more convenient for the consumer who until then had had to go out of their way to one of the standalone liquor cellars, or a hotel with a 'bottle shop' attached.

Wine tastes were changing. 'Consumers were turning away from sweet wines, with dry white wines accounting for two-thirds of sales,' wrote Ross Fitzgerald and Trevor Jordan.[28] 'The preference for white wines of the chardonnay grape is now widespread,' said wine writer Max Lake in 1990. 'After the success of my book on cabernet in 1977, there was a request for a companion volume on chardonnay. There was a manageable number of about forty wines when the project began; but, by the time the work seemed to be reaching a definitive stage, there were hundreds!'[29] 'The sweetness gap', Fitzgerald and Jordan note, 'was taken up by wine coolers: refrigerated carbonated blends of white wine and fruit juices with lower levels of alcohol, marketed mainly to young women.'[30] Wine casks accounted for over 67 per cent of sales.

Australian Gastronomy Begins

In 1979 Graham Pont, a lecturer in General Studies at the University of New South Wales, delivered the first programme of what would later become known as food studies. He began teaching it as an elective subject in 1979, naming it after Reay Tannahill's book *Food in History*. 'When *The Philosopher in the Kitchen* came out in its second edition, I changed the name of my course to "Gastronomy", but had to add a long and quite forgettable subtitle to pacify the critics on the Board of Studies in General Education,' he said. 'I made Brillat-Savarin the textbook of the world's first undergraduate course in Gastronomy, later adding the *Deipnosophists* of Athenaeus, Muskett's *Art of Living in Australia*, and Michael Symon's *One Continuous Picnic*.' The course continued until 1988.

Arguably, though, it was Michael Symons who birthed gastronomy in Australia. Symons's 1982 book *One Continuous Picnic: A History of Eating in Australia* was the first comprehensive history of foodways in Australia. Symons begins the book with the most often quoted of the aphorism of the eighteenth-century French gastronomer Jean-Anthelme Brillat-Savarin in *The Physiology of Taste*: 'Tell me what you eat, and I shall tell you what you are.' Symons sought to understand 'why Australian society seemed culturally impoverished' and, following Brillat-Savarin, 'formed the conviction that a study of eating reveals Australia's uniqueness.'[31] The crux of Symons's view, which he acknowledges was influenced by a year's stay in Tuscany, was that Australian history, at least the two hundred years of post-colonization history, was a 'History without peasants'. The impact of this, Symons wrote, was that Australian cuisine, and, following Brillat-Savarin's aphorism, Australian society, was imbued with 'the persistent temporariness of our industrial society, its lack of links with the land'.[32] Symon's view has been challenged but the book's place as a history of Australian foodways to that point stands the test of time.

Symons's book was significant in stimulating the birth of gastronomy in Australia. Gastronomy, broadly, is the study of food and culture and good eating. Two years after his first publication, Symons, together with food historian Barbara Santich, chef Gay Bilson and the academic Graham Pont, brought together a group of fifty people at the First Symposium of Australian Gastronomy, the theme of which, suitably, was 'The Upstart Cuisine'. The participants were a mixture of academics, chefs, food writers and others who simply had an interest in food: its production, distribution, cultural and social meanings and practices. The symposium continues to be convened on average every eighteen months, rotating among the eastern states, hosted by a small core group of previous symposiasts.

In 2003 Santich and Lyn Martin developed and administered the first Australian Masters in Gastronomy, a partnership between the University of Adelaide, at which they both were lecturers, and Le Cordon Bleu Australia. After the partnership ended in 2010 the University of Adelaide introduced a new, albeit short-lived, Graduate Program in Food Studies, complementing its courses in food writing.

By 2019 degrees in gastronomy and food studies more generally at masters, diploma and certificate level were being offered by a number of academic institutions such as the William Angliss Institute, a college of Technical and Further Education, and Deakin University.

Other colleges of Technical and Further Education administered a range of course in hospitality and cookery which included units of study on food systems. Some universities, for example the Western Sydney University, included units in hospitality management in Business Studies degree courses.

Changes in the Agricultural Sector

What was happening at the production end of the food system in Australia? By the 1980s Australia's agricultural sector was undergoing significant changes. In trade, Britain's entry into the European Economic Community in 1973 impacted heavily on Australia's largest export market for agricultural products. In 1947 Britain had imported one-third of all Australian exports including 80 per cent of all beef and 90 per cent of all butter. The number of dairy cattle in Australia fell from 4 million to just 2.5 million by 1988. Butter exports dropped from 79,000 tonnes in 1973 to a low of 7,000 tonnes in 1981–2 and had only risen back to 40,000 tonnes in 1988. The fresh fruit industry was also affected. Between 1975 and 1990, Australia's annual apple exports fell from about 86,000 to 27,000 tonnes. The market for Australian beef also shifted from Britain to America and Japan, which exposed it to fluctuations in the market which led to price falls in the mid-1970s. Prices only began recovering at the end of the decade. By the mid-1990s the rural sector's contribution to total exports had dropped from around 75 per cent in the early 1950s to 28 per cent. Mining, manufacturing, service industries and construction had outstripped agriculture in relative importance to the economy, and this would remain the situation in the decades ahead. Interestingly, given Australia's

Bushfoods Buffet

Fourth Symposium of Australian Gastronomy (1990)
Presented by Vic Cherikoff, Jean-Paul Bruneteau and Jenny Dowling

Grubs and Riberry
A relative of the desert witjuti grub served with riberry from NSW
York Ham with Illawarra Plum Sauce
Wood smoked kangaroo served with the blue Illawarra plum
Smoked Roo with Rosella Chutney
Kangaroo smoked with eucalyptus leaves and served with wild hibiscus chutney
Peppered Water Buffalo
Northern buffalo spiced with the native Dorrigo pepper
Wild Green Salad
With warrigal greens, water lily stem, macadamia nuts, lemon aspen and assorted salad greens
Samphire Salad
The mangrove saltbush
Burrawang Bread
Made from the treated nut of the prehistoric burrawang served with King Island butter
Stewed Quandong
The native peach from the outback
Wattle Pavlova
A traditional dish but using seeds from an edible wattle

hundred-year-long fear of Asia, it was due to members of the Association of Southeast Asian Nations – including China, Korea and Japan – that new markets developed for dairy and apples. Likewise, in 1990–91 and 1996–7, the trade in live cattle, particularly to the Philippines and Indonesia, expanded enormously.[33] On the positive side, new regional and bi-national trade agreements were opening possibilities for some agricultural product export industries as tariffs in partner countries were lowered,

In the 1930s the Australian Wine Industry produced a booklet encouraging immigration by wine growers in Europe.

for example safflower (*Carthamus tinctorius*) whose seed is used to make cooking oil.

Changes that would have significant impacts in the early years of the coming millennium were also happening in production and distribution of agricultural goods within Australia. The small family farm was in decline as a result of low returns, rising input costs, growing farm indebtedness, high interest levels and falling land values. Taking their place were 'Big Food and Big Ag' companies: local and multinational food and beverage companies that had grown through mergers and takeovers to wield increasingly concentrated market power. These companies were vertically integrated, providing the farmer with all the inputs from proprietary seeds to machinery, agrochemicals and fertilizers, through to transporting produce to markets. In 1996–7, about one-tenth of farm businesses were responsible for almost half of farm-business turnover. Elders-IXL was one of the three largest in Australia. By the late 1980s it had an estimated turnover of $1,200 million per year and a chain of seven hundred country branches. It was the largest provider of farm inputs, handling 40 per cent of livestock auctions and 60 per cent of live sheep exports. The company also provided finance and insurance services and managed rural property sales.[34] In the 1980s and 1990s Australia entered into more global, regional and bilateral trade agreements under which protection through tariffs was further wound back. The supermarket duopoly of Coles and Woolworths began to purchase fresh fruit and vegetables directly from growers who could guarantee large volumes over a long period, sacrificing quality and variety in the process.

The impacts of nearly a century of over-stocking and poor cultivation practices began to be clear: soil degradation, land clearance and salinity being of particular concern. Irrigated cotton farming was on the rise competing for precious water particularly in the upper areas of the Murray–Darling Basin. Chemical control of pests, while effective, was leading to the development of insect and microbial resistance that was combated through increasing use of chemical agents, leading to concerns about chemical residue in vegetables and fruit and destruction of fish and birdlife. In 1986 Bovine spongiform encephalopathy was first identified in Britain as a major problem traced to the practice of feeding cattle on

Farmers' markets, like this one in inner Sydney, bring growers and consumers together directly, focusing on local, seasonal organic products.

animal-protein supplements, allowing infected animal products to be ingested. No cases were ever recorded in Australia, largely due to the strict biosecurity practices and quarantine regulations, but the possibility of a similar disease occurring was concerning.

Government and consumer-led responses to the impacts of these changes on foodways in Australia began in the late 1980s and 1990s. In 1989 the Hawke Commonwealth government instituted the Landcare programme to fund projects aimed at addressing loss of vegetation, soil degradation, water quality and flows, fire regimes, and pest eradication. The National Standard for Organic and Bio-Dynamic was first implemented in 1992 as the Australian Export Standard for products labelled organic or biodynamic. In 1995 the first farmers' market began trading at French's Forest on Sydney's North Shore, bringing growers and consumers together directly and concentrating on trading in organic and locally grown food. Also in 1995, the first Australian Slow Food convivium was set up in the Barossa Valley, South Australia, by the farmer and producer Maggie Beer. In 1996 the Australian City Farms and Community Gardens Network began.

The impact of these changes and countermeasures would shape the future history of food in the first decades of the new millennium.

TEN

Millennium Reckonings, 2000–2020

The new millennium began with southwest Australia, the nation's major food bowl, in the grip of a drought brought on by a particularly severe El Niño effect. Australia was just recovering from the drought when the global financial crisis hit in 2008. When this happened, wrote the economist David Alexander, Australia was 'in rude financial health: debt-free, growing strongly with significant assets and running surplus budgets'. It was these, along with favourable terms of trade, Alexander wrote, that 'guaranteed that Australia would survive the crisis in very good shape'.[1] In its submission to the 2009 House of Representatives inquiry into the impact of the crisis, the Department of Agriculture, Fisheries and Forestry said:

> For agricultural export earnings as a whole, the adverse impact of the global financial crisis is expected to be less substantial than for other sectors, such as mining, at this stage. While there has been downward pressure on some agricultural prices, such as wool and dairy products, the demand for grains, beef and sheep meat appears to have been largely maintained. In addition, the Australian exchange rate has declined significantly since mid-2008. A lower Australian exchange rate against the U.S. dollar, if sustained, is expected to provide support for farm export earnings, although it can also place some upward pressure on the cost of imported farm inputs.[2]

It was with the confidence of having weathered two storms that Australia proceeded into the second decade of the millennium. The word 'reckoning' in the title of this chapter means both a summation and coming to account. The chapter sums up where the various aspects of foodways in Australia come to at the end of the second decade of the millennium. The chapter, and this history, ends with describing the damaging effects of some important past foodways and the efforts being taken to recover from them.

Trends

Trends that emerged at the end of the last decade continued into the new millennium. New immigrants added to the range of cuisines available. Increased South Asian immigration created a market for more regionally inflected dining, such as Nepalese, South Indian, Afghani, Pakistani and Chindian (Chinese-Indian). Similarly, 'Middle Eastern' as a category diversified into Turkish, Lebanese, Iraqi and Iranian. Refugees and migrants from African nations brought their cuisines to the table – Somali and Ethiopian being prominent. Even the meat pie's emblematic status came under challenge from the kebab roll (spiced slices of meat formed into a cone around a metal skewer and cooked as a vertical rotisserie, the meat then thinly sliced and rolled up in flat bread with salad) and Portuguese grilled chicken (a whole chicken butterflied flat and cooked over coals).

Allergies and diseases related to food became widespread. Restaurants, cafés, growers and manufacturers were often playing catch-up, broadening their menus to keep their customers. MSG, a flavour enhancer in Chinese food, had long been popularly associated with asthma and headaches. Food Standards Australia New Zealand (FSANZ) reviewed the safety of MSG in 2003 and concluded that there was no convincing evidence for any health effect from ingesting it. As a food additive, however, MSG must be identified when labelling a product. Some Chinese restaurants turned to promoting themselves as MSG free. Peanuts, commonly associated with potentially life-threatening allergic responses, were the next ingredient that was either avoided when cooking or highlighted with warnings that a particular dish or snack bar may contain traces of the nut. For some this became avoiding all nuts. As with Chinese restaurants and MSG, Southeast Asian restaurants began to make it clear on menus which dishes contained peanuts. Gluten was shown to be the cause of coeliac disease and providing gluten-free options became expected. Soy-, oat- and nut-based drinks (almond and macadamia mainly) provided alternatives to milk for the lactose intolerant.

In 2016 the market research company Roy Morgan reported findings that between 2012 and 2016 the number of Australian adults who said that their diet was all or almost all vegetarian had risen from 9.7 per cent to 11.2 per cent.[3] No comparable research has been done on the number of Australians whose diet is vegan, but market research shows that it is increasingly a choice people are making. Restaurants and cafés are responding by providing no meat options. IBISWorld in 2019 reported on research which found that the range of products and sales of vegan-friendly foods had risen dramatically over the past five years, but red-meat sales had plateaued. The reasons for this included environmental and health concerns and the cost of red meat.[4] Gluten-based alternatives were increasingly appearing on grocery shelves, often sold as 'vegan (insert the name of a meat product: mince, sausages, schnitzel, and so on)'. There was growing interest in plant-based alternatives to meat. The fast-food outlets Hungry Jack's and Nando's added plant-based burgers to their menus. In mid-2019, the Commonwealth Scientific and Industrial Research Organisation in

Hungry Jack's Rebel Whopper combines a plant-based patty with vegan cheese and all the usual burger trimmings.

partnership with the private companies Main Sequence Ventures and Jack Cowin's Competitive Foods Australia launched venture v2food to develop a range of wholly Australian meat alternatives including products made from legumes with added fibre and nutrients.[5]

In good news for shoppers, the dominance of the grocery supermarket share by the Woolworths and Coles duopoly was challenged. Their market shares had fallen in 2017 to 35.7 per cent and 33.2 per cent respectively. Competition came from German company Aldi, with 13.2 per cent and rapidly growing, and Independent Grocers of Australia (IGA) – a chain owned by the Australian company Metcash, with each store, however, independently owned – which had 9.3 per cent of the market.[6] At the end of 2019, IGA began an advertising campaign against the vertical integration of Woolworths and Coles. Its campaign purported to show small-scale producers being able to get their product onto shelves through directly contracting with their local IGA proprietor.

Animal Cruelty

The other reason people were choosing to become vegan was growing concern for animal cruelty. Two issues were at the forefront here: battery cages for layer hens and live export of cattle.

There are three system for egg production in Australia: battery cages, barn and free range. Around two-thirds of layer hens in Australia are in battery cages. Battery cages are made of wire, and house four to six hens, each bird having about an A4 paper-sized area in which it lives its entire life. The Australian Royal Society for the Prevention of Cruelty to Animals says that there is overwhelming evidence that 'the needs of layer hens can't be met in battery cages.' They cannot walk, fly, stretch, perch, nest or take dust baths. Physical problems include feather loss, foot problems, brittle bones and weak muscles, and they have no escape from aggression, feather pecking and cannibalism.[7] Egg-farmers who use such cages say they have the lowest biosecurity risk of the three systems, have low incidence of disease and require less antibiotics than free-range layer hens, which are more exposed to pathogens.

Under the barn system, hens are housed in large sheds that allow them some freedom to engage in usual hen behaviours. The sheds can be very large, holding tens of thousands of birds. Under the current system, eggs labelled for sale as cage-free are laid in barns, in the majority of cases. In free-range systems, hens are not confined in cages or sheds.

Despite the evidence of physical and mental damage to caged layers, the Council of State and Territory Agriculture Ministers in 2000 agreed that cages would continue to be used for the foreseeable future. It proposed that the floor space per hen should be increased from 450 sq. cm. to 550 sq. cm. (70–85 sq. in.), and this has become law in all states subsequently.

Live export of cattle was established early in Australia, when cattle were exported in small numbers from the colony of New South Wales to New Caledonia, Russia, Japan and India.[8] The trade remained small until the mid-1970s when markets were opened for Australian live sheep export to the Middle East. Australia was well placed to meet the demand, with a ready supply of good quality, disease-free stock. This was followed in the next decade by demand from the Philippines and Indonesia. In 1985 the Senate Select Committee on Animal Welfare conducted an inquiry into the treatment of sheep for live export. In its report, the Committee concluded that if a decision on the future of the trade were made on animal welfare grounds alone, there was enough evidence to stop the trade. However, it accepted that the trade was of significant enough economic value to Australia for the trade to continue with some animal welfare improvements. The Committee recommended that no sheep under two years old should be exported live. It also called for long-term solutions, including working with markets to gain acceptance for substituting refrigerated meat for live export.[9]

Scrutiny of the trade abated. The environmental historian Nancy Cushing argues that this was because the process from pastoral property through to loading onto ships passed through public spaces – cattle yards, rail and road freight carriers, and feedlots – and so was open to public scrutiny. What happened once the animals were on board ship, however, was hidden.[10] This changed when in 2018 the Nine Network current-affairs programme *60 Minutes* aired footage secretly shot by a crew member of a ship taking live sheep to the Middle East. Sheep were in cages stacked 10 storeys high, unable to move and subjected to extremely hot conditions. The ship's log noted that 880 sheep died in one day from heat stress.[11] Other reports highlighted the fate of the animals on landing in foreign markets. In 2003 a shipload of 58,000 sheep was rejected by Saudi Arabian authorities because they claimed that 6 per cent were infected with 'scabby mouth', the result of viral infection when the skin of the mouth suffers abrasions. An inquiry by the Australian government led to recommendations for more stringent quarantine monitoring.

In 2019 the live export company Emanuel Exports was charged over the death from apparent heat stress of 2,400 sheep bound for the Middle

East. A three-month moratorium on live export to the Middle East was placed while the government inquired into what further could be done via regulation. As a result, shipments to the Middle East must now submit a heat-stress management plan, have lower stocking densities and collect on-deck temperature data, which has to be forwarded to the Australian Department of Agriculture.

Halal Food and Islamophobia

In April 2017 Senator Pauline Hanson, leader of the One Nation party, took to Facebook to urge the public not to buy Easter eggs from companies that manufactured halal-certified chocolate, including Cadbury, Australia's largest chocolate manufacturer. Halal is an Arabic word meaning lawful or permitted. In Islam, as a rule, all food and food-manufacturing practices are halal unless specifically prohibited in the Qu'ran. Food or practices that are *haram* (prohibited) or *mashbooh* (questionable) can be cleansed and so become halal. Meat and meat products where the animal from which they are derived was not slaughtered in the manner prescribed by Islam are haram. Australia has had halal certification since 1974. The Australian Federation of Islamic Councils certifies and trains Islamic slaughtermen for the meat and poultry industry.

Hanson called for a boycott because she believed that fees paid for halal certification were being used to covertly fund the Islamization of Australia. She was not alone in her views. In 2014 anti-Islam groups campaigned against Australian companies with halal certification arguing both that certification increased the price of halal food to all consumers and that funds were being channelled to Islamic terrorist groups. As a result some companies stopped producing halal products, including Kellogg's.

In May 2015 the Australian Senate commenced an inquiry into 'third-party certification of food'. One of the terms of reference was to examine Australian food certification schemes, and certifiers, including those related to halal foods. It found no evidence that fees charged for halal certification were being used to fund terrorism or organized crime in Australia. It also found that certification did not increase the cost of food and that halal certification had the benefit of allowing certified Australian companies to access large international markets.

Australia's live cattle and sheep export trade is mainly to Islamic countries and has been opposed by animal rights activists on the basis of the

Halal certification in Australia began in 1974 to meet the needs of Muslim migrants and also exports to Muslim-majority countries.

conditions under which the animals are transported and the cruelty of halal slaughtering practices. Animal slaughtering in Australia mandates stunning the animal before killing. Where animals are being slaughtered for the Muslim market in Australia a 'reversible stun' process is used, under which the animal is sufficiently stunned to let it bleed out before it regains consciousness. Halal practices in other countries vary, but stunning prior to slaughter is not usually the case. In 2011 the Australian Broadcasting Commission current affairs programme *Four Corners* showed disturbing images of cattle being slaughtered in Indonesian abattoirs. The trade was temporarily suspended until the Indonesian government addressed the standard of butchering. Indonesia remains Australia's largest market for live cattle. The regulatory system was tightened. An exporter under the regulatory framework is responsible for the health and welfare of Australian livestock and must comply with the Australian Standards for the Export of Livestock and the Exporter Supply Chain Assurance Scheme.

The Internet, Social Media and Disruptive Technologies

Cookery shows on television came under challenge as people turned more and more to the Internet for information. Cookery sites grew exponentially; anyone with some knowledge of how to cook could build a website and post written instructions, with each step accompanied either by highly styled photographs or by an embedded video. Or you could skip the written form entirely and just post videos to YouTube. Many of the sites and videos were developed by women not formally recognized as chefs, continuing the creation of spaces where women could share knowledge and get recognition from peers for their skills.

Television fought back by applying successful existing programme formats to cooking. *MasterChef* (2009) and *My Kitchen Rules* (2010) turned cooking into a competitive sport with elements of reality television. Individuals in the former and teams in the latter took on challenges to demonstrate their food knowledge, cooking and presentation skills. Former food critic Matthew Evans charted his transition to *Gourmet Farmer* in Tasmania, combining practical information on growing garden produce and raising fowls, pigs and dairy cattle, while demonstrating recipes using his farm produce. *MasterChef* winner Adam Liaw combined food and travelogue. The Special Broadcasting Service in 2018 set up an entire separate channel to screen multicultural and multilingual food programmes 24 hours a day.

Social media transformed restaurant reviewing. No longer was it necessary to have any industry- or media-based credibility to pass judgement of the quality of the food, wine and ambience. Taking pictures of your meal and then posting them on Instagram or Facebook became part of dining out. With the advent of such sites as Zomato and Urbanspoon, anyone could now post an online review, and did. Where media food critics were scrupulous about refusing financial inducement to write a favourable review, some social media 'influencers' (those who claim to have followers in the tens of thousands) tried to blackmail restaurants into providing them with a free meal and wine with the threat of posting a bad review. The practice was abetted by some public relations companies who would make such an offer to 'influencers' when the company took on a new client restaurant, or an existing one made changes to their menu or design.

As of 30 June 2018 there were nearly 27 million mobile phone (cell phone) subscribers in Australia.[12] The first phone-app meal ordering and delivery platform in Australia was Menulog, launched in 2006. Since that time the industry has grown by 72 per cent with three new services starting up: Deliveroo, Uber Eats and Foodora. In 2018 the business models of these platforms, and of the gig economy generally, came under scrutiny through an unfair dismissal application brought by a worker against Foodora before the Fair Work Commission. Whether people working in the gig economy are employees or independent contractors is fundamental to determining their rights and obligations across a number of areas of their employment, including tax, superannuation and the conditions under which they can be dismissed. In this case, the Fair Work Commission ruled that the individual was an employee and upheld his argument that he had been unfairly dismissed. Foodora went into voluntary administration in 2016. No cases have been brought against the other three online delivery services to test the nature of the contracts under which their workers are hired.

Food Insecurity among Indigenous Australians

Food insecurity among Indigenous Australians is one of the areas where the damaging effects of past practices have become recognized. In 2018 a cross-disciplinary research team was asked by the Gkuthaarn and Kukatj people of the Gulf of Carpentaria in northwest Queensland to undertake research on a group of remains that had been unearthed at Conwell Flat on the outskirts of Normanton. The remains, dated to the 1890s, were those of young people aged between seven and fifteen years. The research found evidence of dental hypoplasia, a defect of tooth enamel that occurs as teeth are developing, a condition that is a sign of chronic nutritional stress. There is no evidence of the condition in pre-colonization Indigenous populations. The researchers concluded that the condition was a result of a shift from a diet low in starchy processed food and absent of refined sugar to 'reliance on a carbohydrate-rich, European diet, including processed flour and sugar'.[13]

The remains were found in an area where Aboriginal Australians had come in to live on pastoral stations, subsisting on rations – white flour and white sugar were staples – supplemented by what they could hunt or gather. Chapter Two of this book detailed the impact of displacement of peoples from their traditional lands. In Chapter Four, the practice of rationing and its impact was described. Limited access to fresh fruit and vegetables and healthier processed food continued into the era of canned and frozen foods, which often were the only stock available in remote rural communities and reserves.

In 2018, 125 years after these children died, diet-related chronic diseases such as cardiovascular disease, type 2 diabetes and chronic kidney disease were found to be responsible for at least 75 per cent of the mortality gap between Indigenous Australians and other Australians.[14]

Recognizing this situation, in December 2007 the Council of Australian Governments (COAG) agreed to a partnership between all levels of government to work with Indigenous communities to address inequalities in health outcomes for Indigenous Australians. The primary targets were to close the seventeen-year gap in life expectancy between Indigenous and non-Indigenous Australians, within a generation, and to halve the mortality rate of Indigenous children within ten years. The national 'Closing the Gap' strategy of 2008 was a framework for measuring, monitoring and reporting on their joint efforts to achieve specific targets. One of these was that 90 per cent of Aboriginal and Torres Strait Islander families by 2018 would be able to access a standard healthy food basket for a cost of less than 25 per cent of their available income.[15] However, by 2018, this goal had been dropped from the framework. The strategy's Healthy Lives target was now simply to close the gap in life expectancy by 2031.

A 2019 report on progress said that this target was not on track. This report identified that endocrine disorders, mainly diabetes, accounted for 9 per cent of Indigenous mortality. The report did identify progress, however, in improving nutrition in remote communities, highlighting two programmes. There were more than one hundred shops operating under the Northern Territory Community Stores Licensing Scheme, making healthy food and drinks more accessible for local residents. The Commonwealth-owned company Outback Stores manages 37 remote community stores in the Northern Territory, Western Australia and South Australia. In 2017–18 Outback Stores-managed businesses sold 430 tonnes of fresh fruit and vegetables. Seven and a half tonnes less sugar was consumed from sugary drinks in these communities with the stores.[16]

The Bush Tucker Industry

One of the recommendations for Aboriginal and Torres Strait Islander better health from the health agency Diabetes Australia is 'Have plenty of bush tucker.'[17] Ironically, it is non-Indigenous Australians who are the bulk of the market for the well-established bush food/native tucker industry. The beginnings of the industry stretch back to 1989 when Denis and Marilyn Ryan converted a dairy farm on the North Coast of New South Wales into the Valley of the Mist organic native foods enterprise, growing finger limes (*Citrus australasica*), lilly pilly, Davidson plum (*Davidsonia*), lemon myrtle (*Backhousia citriodora*), aniseed myrtle (*Syzygium anisatum*) and macadamia nuts. 'When I started out,' Denis Ryan told food historian

John Newton, 'they said, what are you going to do? And I said, I'm going to grow native foods, and they said, you've got rocks in your head. You growing blackfella food, who's going to eat that?'[18]

By 2012 the naysayers had been proved wrong. Driven in the main by their increasing incorporation in menus of fine-dining chefs, native foods have carved out a niche in Australian cuisine. This was stimulated by two events. During the first Western Australia Gourmet Escape, held in November 2012 – a showcase for the food and wine of the Margaret River region in southwest Western Australia – Wardandi man Josh Whiteland of Koomal Dreaming introduced a veritable who's who of international and Australian chefs to the native food of the region. Among them was the Adelaide chef Jock Zonfrillo, who was already making a name for himself with his modern takes on native foods at his Orana restaurant, and Peter Gilmore, owner/chef at Quay, one of the most 'hatted' restaurants in Sydney. Also among the chefs there was René Redzepi, owner/chef of the Danish restaurant Noma, famed for his use of native Danish ingredients. So impressed was Redzepi that in 2013 he invited Whiteland to speak at his annual MAD food symposium, and followed this with his 'Australia on a Plate' event in 2016, where he and his staff flew to Australia and foraged and hunted with Indigenous people to produce Noma-styled Australian dishes.

Coincidentally in 2012 the Commonwealth Rural Industries Research and Development Corporation carried out a stocktake of the native food industry. Overall, it found that while production across twelve priority products averaged just 8 tonnes, 'the gross value of production at the "farm gate" was between $15 million and $25 million and value adding may increase this estimate by up to 500 per cent.' Lemon myrtle was the industry's marquee product, with an estimated annual production between 575 tonnes and 1,100 tonnes. The stocktake also found that most species were being sourced from cultivated supplies, though wild harvesting remained the major source of supple for mountain pepper, bush tomato (*Solanum centrale*) and Kakadu plum. Production variability was an issue, but producers said that their forecast supply through to 2016 was stable with modest increases. While producers were typically small, some had scaled up through linking with mainstream processors and retailers and were growing a range of crops.[19]

However, in 2018 Bushfood Sensations, an alliance of businesses that promote Indigenous Australian food, surveyed more than 120 people in the industry and found that only 1 per cent of the industry's produce and

Exploiting Migrant Labour

Seasonal workers are brought into Australia for farm work under two visa categories. The Seasonal Worker Programme, which brings in people from nine Pacific Island nations (Fiji, Kiribati, Nauru, Papua New Guinea, Samoa, Solomon Islands, Tonga, Tuvalu and Vanuatu) and Timor-Leste to pick fruit for up to nine months after which they must return home. They can then come back for further nine-month terms. In 2016–17 over 6,000 people came to Australia under the programme. Employers have to be approved by the Commonwealth government and must abide by Australian labour law and be paid according to an appropriate industrial award. In the 88-day scheme, travellers in Australia aged between 18 and 31 and from nineteen countries (including many European countries, Korea and Japan) can extend their one-year holiday visa for a second year if they work on a farm. Others may be in Australia on a Temporary Skills Shortage visa, under which employers can bring in workers where they cannot find suitably skilled Australian citizens.

In 2016 the Commonwealth parliament held an inquiry into the Seasonal Worker Programme to assess its success and recommend on any necessary legislative or regulatory changes. The inquiry heard submissions from several sources of exploitative practices by a small number of employers in the programme. The allegations included paying less than a living

dollar value is generated by Indigenous people. This is changing, through non-Indigenous businesses partnering with Indigenous communities and also with Indigenous communities setting up their own businesses. Mike and Gayle Quarmby began the food company Outback Pride in 1998 to supply restaurants with native produce. They worked with fifteen Indigenous communities in South Australia and the Northern Territory, providing training in native food horticulture and sourcing their products from the communities. Plants were grown at the Reedy Creek Nursery and were DNA fingerprinted to protect them from being patented by non-Indigenous growers. In 2018 the company was sold to the Indigenous wage, excessive deductions from wages for board and lodging, substandard living conditions, long hours with excessive overtime, and lack of access to health care. Many also questioned the labour-hire companies' practices in the home countries from which workers were drawn. The Australian government representatives said that five approved employers had been suspended in 2016–17 and one had been expelled for serious non-compliance. No organization or department called for suspending the programme. The inquiry supported the recommendation of the Senate Education and Employment References Committee calling for more stringent regulations on labour hire companies including a public register of the companies and greater emphasis on their compliance with all workplace laws and the licensing overseas sub-contractors.

It is not only workers in Australia whose working conditions have come under scrutiny. In 2019 Australia's Modern Slavery Act commenced. Forcibly detained adults and children work in industries from which Australia imports food products, including fishing and cocoa. Under the Act Australian businesses and other organizations with a consolidated revenue of $100 million are required to report annually on the risks of modern slavery in their operations and supply chains, the action they have taken to assess and address those risks, and the effectiveness of their response. Smaller businesses can report voluntarily.

enterprise Bushlolly. Mayi Harvests (Milari Aboriginal Corporation) is a wholly Indigenous-owned and managed business in Broome on the north coast of Western Australia that specializes in wild harvesting of foods on traditional family lands in the Ngumbari and Jabirr-Jabirr country. In 2012 the Aboriginal community of Warruwi on the Goulburn Islands began a trepang industry that had its first successful harvest in 2015, destined again for the Asian market.

Indigenous organizations have also established successful pastoral businesses. In 1999 Mungalla Station in Allingham, Queensland, which had been a cattle ranch since 1882, was handed back to the Nywaigi people. The station is now managed by the Mungalla Aboriginal Business Corporation, which continues to raise cattle while incorporating cultural and eco-tourism, and provides long-term employment, education and training for the community. National Indigenous Pastoral Enterprises is the agribusiness arm of the Indigenous Land Corporation, which manages fourteen cattle stations in northern Australia. It runs more than 90,000 head of brahman and brahman-cross cattle across more than 2 million ha (nearly 5 million ac). The Corporation also operates one of the largest live-export cattle depots near Broome in Western Australia, a cattle and buffalo abattoir at Gunbalanya in the Northern Territory, and a sheep operation on Bruny Island, on Tasmania's southeastern coast. Around 65 per cent of sales in 2018 were to live-export markets, mostly Indonesia and Vietnam. In 2016 the Corporation began an exchange training programme with the Indonesian cattle industry.

2007 Northern Territory Emergency Response

In June 2007 the Commonwealth government put in place the Northern Territory Emergency Response (commonly called 'the Intervention'). This was a set of actions intended to curb alleged sexual abuse of children in Aboriginal communities in the Northern Territory. The breadth of actions taken under it were perceived to go well beyond responses to the allegations, encompassing compulsory acquisition of Aboriginal land, suspension of the Racial Discrimination Act and abolishing a government-funded employment programme. There was no consultation with Indigenous people prior to implementing the intervention.

One of the measures taken was the introduction of the Basics Card as a means of compulsory income management. In the case of Aboriginal Australians who are in receipt of government social-security payments of an income-support nature, the governmental social-security agency diverts a proportion of the value of that payment to the smart card, which may only be used for certain designated items. Between 50 per cent and 80 per cent of a payment can only be accessed

The Obesity Epidemic: Tackling it in Schools

In 2017 the Australian Institute of Health and Welfare reported that 25 per cent of children and adolescents between two and seventeen years old were overweight or obese.[20] Schools were identified by the Institute as obesogenic environments, that is, environments that promote obesity. Since the 1950s Commonwealth and State governments have from time to time run programmes aimed at providing nutritious food and drink in schools.

In 1937 the Advisory Council on Nutrition of the National Health and Medical Research Centre called for a school milk programme with these two aims, but nothing came of it at that time. A free school-milk scheme began in New South Wales in 1941, with another running concurrently in Victoria. In other states voluntary organizations provided milk to individual schools, the cost sometimes discounted by milk providers or the state government. Then, in July 1950, the Commonwealth instituted

through using the Basics Card at government approved food outlets. The intention is to prohibit spending income-support money on alcohol, gambling and discretionary ('junk') food.

A 2010 study by the Menzies School of Health on the impact of compulsory income management found no significant changes in consumption patterns on alcohol, cigarettes, soft drinks, or fresh fruit and vegetables. In 2014 the Australian Council of Social Services reviewed studies evaluating the effectiveness of compulsory income management generally. It concluded that there was no evidence that the practice resulted in widespread or long-term benefits. Schemes are poorly targeted, not cost-effective (achieving poor outcomes for the money spent), result in strong negative subjective experiences, damage financial-management skills and discourage vulnerable people from seeking assistance. The scheme has also been criticized as a new form of rationing and a return to colonial era controls on Aboriginal Australians.

Notwithstanding the research findings, the scheme was extended until June 2020.

a scheme to provide up to half a pint a day of free milk to an estimated 1 million children in creches, nurseries, and private and public schools across Australia.[21] In 1973 the Whitlam government stopped the scheme following a review which found that the scheme had not resulted in children drinking any more milk than previously, and that there was no evidence of a calcium or protein deficiency in Australian school children.[22]

In 1941 the Opportunity Clubs for Boys and Girls, a welfare organization providing recreation activities for children from disadvantaged backgrounds in Victoria, conducted a six-month experiment with school children in Collingwood in Melbourne to promote the health benefits of the Oslo lunch. The lunch, pioneered in Norway in 1932, had drawn the attention of Dr John Dale, the Health Officer of the City of Melbourne, but he was unable to get support from the Victorian state government. The Opportunity Clubs organization decided to investigate the health claims of the lunch. 'The meal consisted of 3 slices of wholemeal bread with a good spread of butter and cheese, half-pint of milk, half-an-ounce of weatharts [a commercial wheat-germ preparation] with the addition of an orange or half and [sic] apple.'[23] The researchers gave fifty children the Oslo lunch with the other children acting as a control group. 'The average increases for all Oslo groups,' the report on the research noted, 'when compared with the average increases for the control group, show that those on the Oslo lunch gained in weight by 2½ times as much as the control group children.'[24] A study was also run with the Camperdown School and Camperdown Children's Playground in Sydney in the same year. 'And again,' writes historian Barbara Santich, 'the Oslo lunchers showed a weight gain ... compared with the control group whose bought lunch typically consisted of a saveloy and threepenceworth of lollies, or six penny-meringues, or broken biscuits.'[25] Despite the success of the studies, neither the Victorian nor New South Wales government took up the scheme. 'No doubt cost was a prohibiting factor, but it is also probable that school lunches were considered a maternal rather than a state obligation.'[26]

In 2014 the Commonwealth Department of Health published *Guidelines for Healthy Foods and Drinks Supplied in School Canteens* based on the 2013 Australian Dietary Guidelines. The guidelines promote servings of food from five 'food groups': vegetables of 'different colours' and legumes and beans; fruit; grain foods, with a preference for wholegrain or grain products high in fibre; lean meats; tofu, nuts, seeds; and dairy products with reduced fat. They stress limiting the intake of foods high in saturated fats, including cakes, pastries, processed meats, commercial burgers, pies, fried foods and chips. The *Guidelines* also detail the recommended size and number of servings for each of the food groups, and uses a colour coding to suggest foods that should always be on the canteen menu (green), selected carefully (orange – with portion size identified as an issue) and not recommended for the canteen menu (red – foods with excess energy, measured in kilojoules, and those high in saturated fats).[27]

School canteens have, until recently, been independently run by each school and staffed by volunteers, usually the parents of students. Decisions about what food and drink to stock have varied over the years with what is popular, easy to portion-control, easy for children to handle (sandwiches, pies, sausage rolls or wraps, for example) and what can be sold at an effective mark-up – enough to cover canteen costs other than food and drink. What is on offer will also reflect pressure brought from parents for what they understand of the latest advice on healthy eating. In recent years, schools increasingly have been outsourcing the management and stocking of canteens to food enterprises, which in some cases also supply other institutions, such as prisons and nursing homes. Hence the guidelines are only that: they are not enforceable.

A different approach has been championed by the chef Stephanie Alexander. She had become concerned about the rising level of childhood obesity in Australia and what she was reading and hearing about children's eating habits. Taking inspiration from the Edible Schoolyard project run by California chef Alice Waters in 1995, Alexander began a kitchen garden programme with primary-school students in Collingwood, Victoria. Every student in grades 3 (8–9 years old) to 6 (11–12 years old) would have hands-on work in the garden and a purpose-built kitchen for preparing food and eating it. Classroom teachers would accompany the children in these activities and would develop complementary curricula on foodways. In 2004 the Victorian government took the programme on and offered grants for four years to forty schools. In 2007 the Australian government began supporting the programme nationally by funding infrastructure for up to 190 schools for four years. Alexander subsequently set up the Stephanie Alexander Kitchen Garden Foundation to provide educational resources and professional development for educators interested in school-kitchen gardens.

The obesity epidemic is also ascribed to high ingestion of sugar, particularly in sugary drinks, and saturated fat through over-consumption of fast food. While the guidelines for canteens, if implemented, may lead to less intake of these at school, consumption of these in the home remains

Native produce has completed the transition from ignored and disparaged to household essentials. Pictured are macadamia nuts, mountain pepper berries and salt mixed with dried lemon myrtle leaf.

concerning. In the Australian Bureau of Statistics data household expenditure on average per week in 2015–16 on fast food and takeaway (excluding coffee and frozen foods) ranked seventh in the list of the items of highest expenditure, above electricity and mobile phone expenditure. This had not changed significantly since the 2009–10 data.[28] In 2017 the World Health Organization recommended governments help combat the health effects of excessive consumption of sugar by a sugar tax on sweetened drinks. The Australian Medical Association has voiced support for this. However, the Australian government has rejected the suggestion. In June 2018 the Australian Beverages Council announced a pledge that will see the non-alcoholic beverage industry commit to a 20 per cent reduction in sugar across the industry's portfolio by 2025.

The battle is now being taken to supermarkets and advertising agencies. A 2019 study found that 'junk food' – including chocolate, crisps, confectionery, ice cream and high-sugar breakfast cereals – were twice as likely to be discounted and on special offer as healthier foods.[29] Also in 2019, the Obesity Policy Coalition reported on their research on the content of 779 food advertisements across 21 sites in Melbourne. The research showed that almost two-thirds of food ads within a 750 m (2,460 ft) radius

Smoked Eel Patties

Mark Olive

Indigenous chefs and catering businesses are also using and promoting bush foods. Mark Olive, a Bundjalung man from northern New South Wales, is the most prominent Indigenous chef working in Australia. He became a celebrity television chef first through a segment on *Message Stick*, a programme of Aboriginal and Torres Strait Islander contemporary life-style and culture produced by the Australian Broadcasting Commission since 1990. So popular was the segment that Olive soon had his own half-hour series, *The Outback Café*. In 2018 he became one of three judges on *The Chef's Line*, a Special Broadcasting Service competitive cooking programme similar to the more mainstream *MasterChef*.

1 smoked eel
1 cooked sweet potato
1 tsp lemon myrtle
2 dstspns chopped desert lime
1 egg, separated
1 tsp mountain pepper
1 handful chopped dill
2 tsps cornflour

Skin and debone the eel and break the meat up into a bowl. Add the cooked sweet potato and mash together. Add lemon myrtle, desert lime, egg yolk, mountain pepper, dill and cornflour, mix thoroughly. Roll the mix into small balls and flatten out to form patties, then dust with a little cornflour. Heat a frying pan with a little oil and fry off the patties until golden brown, remove from pan and drain on greaseproof paper.[30]

of schools were for unhealthy 'junk' foods, and that nearly two-thirds of advertisements on Victorian public transport also promoted unhealthy foods. The Coalition called on the Victorian government to remove this kind of advertising from state-owned facilities.[31]

Alcohol, Men and Violence

Wine sales by Australian winemakers continued to grow strongly in the 2000s in both domestic and export markets. Total sales value increased 8 per cent to more than $5.6 billion. Some 86 per cent of the year's sales growth came from red and rose wines.[32] In 2018 the Australian government announced a $50 million Export and Regional Wine Support Package focusing on sales to the United States and China. In June 2019, the Package was credited with resulting in $1.2 billion in exports of wine to China and $432 million to the United States.[33]

Domestically, wine sales increasingly were being driven by the Coles and Woolworths supermarket duopoly. In 2018 the Woolworths Group had 62 per cent of the market share and the Coles Group had 26 per cent of alcohol sales.[34] Both were vertically integrated through purchasing bottling, packaging, storage, filtration and testing facilities. They also began to sell low-priced alcohol with brand names suggesting that they were a premium product, though the wine and beer were in fact their own private-label and generally low-quality products.

The 1990s had seen the rise of boutique wine producers. In the 2000s it was the turn of beer brewers. Home-brewing has a history in Australia from the early days of the Sydney colony. Now, young would-be brewers latched on to the zeitgeist for small producers of 'artisanal', 'hand-crafted' foods made from high-quality ingredients. Microbreweries soon became ubiquitous in capital cities across Australia, with Mountain Goat, Little Creatures and Young Henrys leading the field. Responding to dietary issues some began producing beer with low carbohydrate content or that were gluten free.

Amid this growth, government and public attention turned to violence by men when intoxicated. The issue hit the headlines nationally when two young men were assaulted in separate incidents in The Rocks, a harbourside entertainment precinct near the central business district of Sydney. Each was struck by a single blow to the head, knocking them to the pavement and both subsequently died of their injuries. The New South Wales Parliament passed the Liquor Amendment Act 2014, which amended the Liquor Act 2007 and the Liquor Regulations 2008, giving the minister in charge of those Acts the right to declare areas as prescribed precincts, ones in which specific conditions were put on licensed premises that did not apply outside those precincts. This was based on the success of existing regulations in the central business district of Newcastle, north of Sydney, in response to alcohol-related violence by young men there. That licensing legislation reduced trading hours in hotels and nightclubs in the central business district to 3 a.m., and a lockout prevented patrons entering licensed venues after 1 a.m. Assault rates dropped almost immediately. In Sydney a new entertainment precinct was gazetted covering the existing late-night entertainment areas of the central business district and Kings Cross (historically, Sydney's 'red-light' district).

The alcohol industry argues that lockout laws simply shift the problem of violence to areas that are not subject to them. Some residents and businesses in the latter areas agree. Data from a report from the NSW Bureau of Crime Statistics and Research released in April 2015 showed a 26 per cent reduction in assaults in the lockout area, and a 32 per cent reduction in assaults in Kings Cross.[35] In a March 2017 report, however, areas adjacent to the lockout precinct showed a 12 per cent increase in assaults, with a 17 per cent increase in 'easy-to-reach' areas.[36] The laws have also been seen as damaging to the night-time economy, particularly in areas where live music is performed in clubs and hotels by entertainers, live music premises and young people wanting to enjoy music and drink responsibly. A 2019 poll of attitudes and behaviour in relation to alcohol by the Foundation for Alcohol Research and Education found that 85 per cent of Australians believe that pubs, clubs and bars should close at 3 a.m. or earlier.[37] In 2019 the New South Wales government instituted a review of the regulation of the legislation resulting in the winding back of the area covered by the law to only the Kings Cross area.

The Foundation's study also found that 56 per cent of those polled supported banning alcohol advertising at sports grounds.[38] Linking alcohol and sport has a long history in Australia. In the early twentieth century, poster advertising in hotels often featured images of men playing football, tennis and lawn bowls with a tagline that tied the image to popular brands of beer. Towards the end of the century brewers began to strengthen links between beer drinking and sports with advertisements streaming during live coverage of matches of the two main football codes. Advertising alcohol on commercial television is restricted to between 8.30 p.m. and 5 a.m., with an additional three hours, 12 noon to 3 p.m., on weekdays, in an effort to prevent children under eighteen years (the legal age for buying alcohol or drinking in a licensed venue) being exposed to messages that encourage drinking. However, such advertising is allowed during sports programmes on public holidays and weekends (starting from 6 p.m. on Friday). This means that children and adolescents who watch these programmes are in fact exposed to alcohol advertising regardless. Despite calls from the Royal Australasian College of Physicians, some prominent sportsmen and support from the public to ban alcohol advertising during televised sport, the rules remain.

The Revival of Coffee

'Australia has been described as the world's "coffee capital",' wrote Emma Felton in 2019, 'and its coffee shop culture has been exported across the globe from New York to London to Singapore, inserting its signature flat white on coffee menus.'[39]

The First Fleet brought coffee plants with them, and by the 1880s coffee was growing in the warmer parts of the east coast. In the late 1800s the temperance movement in Australia built 'coffee palaces', which served as board and food alternatives to public houses. There were more than fifty in Melbourne by 1888. The banking crisis of 1893 and the subsequent depression in Australia in the mid-1890s, however, saw many proprietors become bankrupt. Others bought more profitable liquor licenses. The coffee growing industry also had collapsed by 1926.

But Australians continued to drink imported coffee. In 1907 Emmanouil and Kosmas Andronikos established Andronicus Brothers, Indent Agents & Importers to supply the growing number of Greek cafés with speciality goods including coffee roasted on the brothers' premises. They were soon supplying the general public. Coffee drinking got its first boost during the Second World War when three roasting machines had to be shipped to keep pace with the demand for coffee from U.S. servicemen stationed in Australia. Hard on their heels came post-war Italian and Jewish migrants and

The flat white, arguably the most popular coffee in Australia.

European café culture. In 1984 the first imported Gaggia espresso machine gave baristas the tool to produce a frothed milk topping dusted with chocolate for cappuccinos which won favour with the new wave of coffee drinkers.

The rise in coffee consumption over the past thirty years has been unstoppable, with coffee displacing tea as the national non-alcoholic refreshment. Australian Bureau of Statistics food consumption data for 2011–12 showed that 46 per cent of Australians drink coffee while 38 per cent drink tea. Coffee drinking is big business. In 2018–19 industry revenue was $9.9 billion. There were 20,781 cafés and coffee shops employing 142,044 people. By the 2011 census 22,000 identified their profession as barista.[40]

The style of coffee Australians drink has diversified, like other food and drink, to take account of dietary and health concerns. Decaffeinated was the first step in this direction, followed by replacing dairy milk with soy and nut equivalents. Coffee has also had its artisan moment, with small roasters focusing on single-origin, ethically grown and harvested beans.[41]

The other area of growing concern is alcohol-related domestic violence. According to the Australian Institute of Criminology, 44 per cent of all intimate partner homicides are alcohol-related.[42] In 2016 the Centre for Alcohol Policy Research published the results of a study looking at the rates of police-recorded assaults in New South Wales during the annual State of Origin football game. The study found there was an increase of 40.7 per cent in domestic assaults for State of Origin nights compared with non-State of Origin nights. The researchers said that the findings are likely to reflect increases in social activities (parties, or going to bars) and alcohol consumption.[43] These findings have added to the call to ban alcohol advertising at sports events or in relation to them.

The Emptying Ocean

Overfishing in Australia has a long history. By 1880 the situation had become so bad in the New South Wales colony that a Royal Commission into New South Wales fisheries was conducted. It found that a significant problem was the use of 'stalling': the practice of netting off-tidal flats, trapping everything when the water retreated. While the fishers collected the larger fish, small fish and spawn were also caught but left to rot. The inquiry recommended introducing a minimum size of mesh so that the fish can swim through, prohibiting netting across the full width of creeks and inlets, and closing off areas to fishing at times to allow replenishment of stock.[44]

The measures proved futile as new technologies increased vessels' capacity to take catches from the open sea. By the late 1920s tiger flathead stocks south of Sydney had collapsed under a decade of ocean trawl-fishing. In the 1970s and 1980s it was southern bluefin tuna (mainly in the Great Australian Bight) and orange roughy (around Tasmania and west to southern Western Australia) stocks that fell to disastrous levels. Marine parks and national regulations on catch sizes, fishing zones and seasons, and again limiting the mesh size of nets, were put in place.

However, in 2005, 24 out of 83 fish stocks assessed in Australian government-managed fisheries were overfished.[45] This time the Australian government embarked on the 'Securing our Fishing Future' package of measures. The package consisted of a $220 million structural adjustment component and new management measures, to be introduced by the Australian Fisheries Management Authority, to halt overfishing and give overfished stocks a chance to recover. Up to $149 million was made available to buy back fishing concessions within and across commercial

Australian-managed fisheries. A further $50 million in industry and community assistance grants were available for individuals, businesses and companies that had been affected by the impacts of the buy-back and/or by the new management measures. Five hundred and fifty licences were voluntarily surrendered and those fishers either consolidated their existing business or left the industry altogether. The programme ceased in 2010.

In 2018 the Australian Institute of Marine Science, the University of Tasmania and Reef Life Survey, a citizen science group, published the results of a ten-year study of 531 ocean sites around Australia. It found that in areas open to fishing, exploited fish populations fell by an average of 33 per cent between 2005 and 2015, closely matching a 32 per cent reduction in total Australian fishery catches through the same period. In marine parks, where they could not be fished, the same species had increased by an average of 25 per cent.[46]

In response the Australian government conducted its own survey of 324 fish stocks. Its overall finding was that 'Australia's fish stocks are well-managed and a majority are healthy, with almost 85% classified sustainable or recovering.' Of the 324 stock assessed, 254 were classified as sustainable, 18 stocks were classified as recovering, 29 stocks were classified as depleting and 23 stocks were classified as depleted. 'Importantly,' the survey concluded, 'all have recovery management plans in place that aim to rebuild the stocks.'[47]

The other response to declining wild catches has been to develop aquaculture throughout Australia's climate zones. Over forty different types of seafood are cultivated in Australian aquaculture farms, including barramundi, silver perch, Murray cod, mussels, prawns and oysters. In 2012–13 aquaculture products comprised 43 per cent of Australian seafood production by value and 35 per cent by weight. Since 2002–3 the real gross value of aquaculture production has increased by 12 per cent to over $1 billion. The bulk of the value increase came from farmed salmon and trout (mainly from Tasmania) and oysters.[48] Pilot programmes are underway for snapper and mulloway. Responsibility for regulation of aquaculture is split between the Commonwealth government, which has responsibility for biosecurity, aquatic animal health, food safety and some environmental management, and the states and territories that also have responsibilities in health, food safety and environmental management.

One of the main concerns about fish farming is that many farmed species are carnivores (for example, Atlantic salmon, Murray cod and rainbow trout), and so are fed fishmeal and fish-oil sourced from wild fish. The amount of wild-sourced food often exceeds the quantity of fish farmed. In Australia most fishmeal and -oil comes from industrial-scale Peruvian anchovy fisheries. There have been improvements in the balance between fishmeal and quantity of fish farmed for omnivorous species. Another concern has been that effluents from fish waste products can be discharged into open waters or leached into soil. Both situations are strictly controlled in Australian aquaculture businesses.[49]

Climate Change

The overriding reckoning Australia faces today is climate change. The 2019 drought in the Murray–Darling Basin was declared the worst on record by the Bureau of Meteorology. In June 2018 the Lowy Institute, an independent, non-partisan international policy think tank, published the results of an annual poll into the attitudes of Australians to world and global issues. Fifty-eight per cent of those polled said that climate change was a critical threat to Australia in the next ten years, ranking third behind terrorism and North Korea's nuclear programme. Concern about climate change was the highest it had been in a decade. Respondents said that Australia should begin taking steps to combat climate change even if it involved significant costs.[50]

In September 2019 the Intergovernmental Panel on Climate Change released its Special Report on climate change, desertification, land degradation, sustainable land management, food security and greenhouse gas fluxes in terrestrial ecosystems. The report identified land as a critical resource. 'When land is degraded', the Panel said, 'it becomes less productive, restricting what can be grown and reducing the soil's ability to absorb carbon. This exacerbates climate change, while climate change in turn exacerbates land degradation in many different ways.' The Panel recognized that land had to remain able to meet food-security needs, particularly as populations increase, and this puts a limit on the contribution land can make to addressing climate change. Nonetheless, the Panel said, 'Policies that support sustainable land management, ensure the supply of food for vulnerable populations, and keep carbon in the ground while reducing greenhouse gas emissions are important.' Targeting over-consumption and food waste were also important, as was a shift to balanced diets featuring plant-based foods, such as coarse grains, legumes, fruits and animal products, produced sustainably in low greenhouse gas emission systems.[51]

Drought-devastated farmland, Moree, New South Wales, 2019.

Crops like oilseed rape (canola) are highly profitable but rely on agricultural practices that damage fragile ecosystems.

Trends in Australians eating plant-based diets, the growth of organic farming and farmers' markets have been described in earlier chapters of this book. What of Australia's land management practices? Agriculture was responsible for about 16 per cent of Australia's greenhouse gas emissions in 2013, with 15.5 per cent of that coming from carbon release from soils. The majority, 66.3 per cent, came from enteric fermentation in ruminant livestock.[52] Writing in 2019 the garlic farmer Patrice Newell said:

> Australia's agricultural development has historically taken a broadacre industrial approach. It relies on a diminishing selection of new plant varieties, the manufacture of synthetic fertilisers and pesticides, increased farm sizes and the introduction of large-scale mechanical equipment, an approach deemed innovative, as new technology and allegedly science-based, yet that continues to degrade ecosystems.[53]

The picture is bleak. But there are initiatives being taken by farmers to change their practice and achieve the Panel's call to ensure food supply, while keeping carbon in the ground and reducing greenhouse gases.

In Chapter One of this book, the nutrient-poor nature of most Australian soil was described. Subsequent chapters have described a history of poor land management, particularly extending agriculture into marginal land and the consequent overdependence on phosphate fertilizers. In his 2011 *Climate Change Update* Ross Garnaut wrote, 'Compared to northern hemisphere soils, many Australian soils have naturally low soil carbon levels due to their old, weathered nature and the effects of a warm and dry climate. Large losses of soil carbon have occurred since the conversion of native vegetation to agricultural land started in the 1800s.'[54] A 2018 study of a range of strategies that could lead to reduced carbon emissions found that the most effective land-management practice is soil carbon sequestration – that is, managing soil so that much of the carbon which would naturally be released stays locked in the ground. This could achieve a reduction of 2–5 gigatonnes of CO^2 globally each year; afforestation could achieve a reduction by 0.6–3.6 gigatonnes per year; and biochar (charcoal produced from plant matter and stored in the soil as a means of removing carbon dioxide from the atmosphere) could achieve 0.5–2 gigatonnes per year.[55]

All three strategies are being pursued by Australian farmers. Creating biochar at the individual farm level is not practical: the mechanism for doing it is costly and the amount any one farm may produce would do little in carbon-offset terms. Biochar enterprises have been established to produce material in bulk to sell to farmers. Afforestation is a major strategy under Australia's much criticized climate-change-action centrepiece, the Emissions Reduction Fund – under which farmers can get tradeable carbon credits for planting trees – and the continuation of the National Landcare Program.

Increasing numbers of farmers are practising regenerative and agroecological farming. Regenerative farming uses principles and practices aimed at increasing biodiversity, enriching soil, capturing carbon and improving watersheds. 'The farmers in this movement,' write the authors of *Farming Democracy: Radically Transforming the Food System from the Ground Up*,

> aim to maintain their farms at human scale, not industrial scale ... they fit their production into the ecological umbilical of their land size and type, social structures, and family needs ... All [the farmers featured in the book] have diversified and taken more control of their value chains to make small-scale farming viable.[56]

The impact of regenerative farming is limited by its scale. Holistic management is being adopted by farmers who want to continue to engage at commercial levels of farming while also enriching soil and sequestering carbon. Under this system farmers grow crops that require low to nil fertilizer and are productive without chemical maintenance; use cropping practices that maintain the health of soil and water and are regenerative; and have livestock that are maintenance free.[57]

Another approach is being championed by the Indigenous environmentalist Bruce Pascoe. Pascoe looks to Indigenous knowledge and practices as described in his book *Dark Emu*. Speaking with rural writer Gabrielle Chan in 2018, Pascoe says he would like to see a switch from introduced crops to Australian native crops, primarily grasses, which are adapted to the climate and will grow in most places, as they were growing before 1788: 'They are not as productive as wheat per acre, but the on-costs are nil, they are Australian grasses that grow in drought, tolerate poor nutrition, with no fertilisers or pesticides.' He also mentions being overwhelmed by the interest from farming, permaculture and horticultural industries in growing native species at commercial scale.[58]

What the cumulative impact of these measures is will depend very much on how entrenched they become in individual farming practice and how well they are supported by government and private investment.

References

Introduction

1 Paula Thomas, 'Australia's Fire Crisis and Its Impact on Food', www.slowfood.com, 10 January 2020.

two: Foodways of the First Peoples

1 Tim Flannery, *The Future Eaters* (Chatswood, 1994), p. 272.
2 Chris Clarkson, Ben Marwick, Zenobia Jacobs and Richard Fullagar, 'Human Occupation of Northern Australia by 65,000 years', *Nature*, DXLVII/7663 (2017), pp. 306–10.
3 Jim Allen and James F. O'Connell, 'From Sunda to Sahul', in *Islands of Inquiry: Colonisation, Seafaring and the Archaeology of Maritime Landscapes*, ed. Geoffrey Clark, Foss Leach and Sue O'Connor, *Terra Australis*, XXLX (2008), pp. 38–9.
4 Irina Pugach, Frederick Delfin, Ellen Gunnarsdóttir and Manfred Kayser, 'Genome-wide Data Substantiate Holocene Gene Flow from India to Australia', in *Proceedings of the National Academy of Sciences of the United States of America*, www.pnas.org, 29 January 2013, pp. 1–6.
5 Bill Gammage, *The Biggest Estate on Earth: How Aborigines Made Australia* (Sydney, 2011), pp. 123–54.
6 Thomas Mitchell, *Three Expeditions into the Interior of Eastern Australia* (London, 1839), vol. I, p. 90.
7 J. Peter White and James F. O'Connell, *A Prehistory of Australia, New Guinea and Sahul* (North Ryde, 1982), p. 15.
8 Gammage, *Biggest Estate*, p. 162.
9 Andrew Taylor, 'Fighting Fire with Fire: Cultural Burning at Bundanon Brings Life Back to the Land', www.smh.com.au, 22 April 2018.
10 R. J. Rowlands and J. M. Rowlands, 'An Aboriginal Dam in Northwestern New South Wales', *Mankind*, VII/2 (1969), pp. 132–6.
11 Rupert Gerritsen, *Australia and the Origins of Agriculture* (Oxford, 2008), p. 24.
12 Watkin Tench, *A Narrative of the Expedition to Botany Bay* (London, 1789), p. 53.

13 Bruce Pascoe, *Dark Emu, Black Seeds: Agriculture or Accident?* (Broome, 2014), pp. 11–12.
14 Beth Gott, 'Aboriginal Plant Use', www.anbg.gov.au, accessed 21 March 2019.
15 Beth Gott, 'Ecology of Root Use by the Aborigines of South Australia', *Archaeology in Oceania*, XVII/1 (1982), pp. 59–67.
16 Gerritsen, *Agriculture*, pp. 19–20.
17 George Grey, cited in Gerritsen, *Agriculture*, p. 33.
18 Beth Gott, 'Aboriginal Fire Management in SE Australia: Aims and Frequency', *Journal of Biogeography*, XXXII/7 (2005), p. 1205.
19 Mitchell, *Three Expeditions*, pp. 237–8.
20 Gott, 'Fire Management', p. 1204.
21 Mary Gilmore, *Old Days, Old Ways: A Book of Recollections* (Sydney, 1986), p. 188.
22 Keith Farrer, *To Feed a Nation: A History of Australian Food Science and Technology* (Collingwood, 2005), p. 5.
23 R.M.W. Dixon, *Australia's Original Languages: An Introduction* (Crows Nest, 2019), pp. 20–21.
24 S. Anna Florin, Andrew Fairbairn and Chris Clarkson, '65,000-year-old Plant Remains Show the Earliest Australians Spent Plenty of Time Cooking', theconversation.com, 10 February 2020.
25 Mitchell, *Three Expeditions*, p. 100.
26 Gilmore, *Old Days*, p. 64.
27 Ian J. McNiven, 'The Detective Work Behind the Budj Bim Eel Traps World Heritage Bid', www.theconversation.com, 8 February 2017.
28 Peter Dargin, *Aboriginal Fisheries of the Darling–Barwon Rivers* (Dubbo, 1976), pp. 32–49.
29 'Mandjabu (Fish Trap)', www.babbarra.com, accessed 22 March 2019.
30 Peter Beveridge, *The Aborigines of Victoria* (Melbourne, 1889), p. 99.
31 Ronald M. Berndt, Catherine H. Berndt and John E. Stanton, *A World That Was: The Yaraldi of the Murray River and the Lakes, South Australia* (Vancouver, 1993), p. 98.
32 Dargin, *Aboriginal Fisheries*, p. 28.
33 Kate Morse, 'Mandu Mandu Creek Rockshelter: Pleistocene Human Coastal Occupation of North West Cape, Western Australia', *Archaeology in Oceania*, XXIII/3 (1998), pp. 81–8.
34 Pascoe, *Dark Emu*, p. 68.
35 'A Fisherwoman of Warrane', www.sydneylivingmuseums.com.au, accessed 2 November 2018.
36 J. G. Steele, *Aboriginal Pathways in Southeast Queensland and the Richmond River* (St Lucia, 1983), p. 63.
37 Watkin Tench, *A Complete Account of the Settlement of Port Jackson* (London, 1793), p. 136.
38 Michael Westaway, Jon Olley and Rainer Grun, 'Aboriginal Australians Co-existed with the Megafauna for at Least 17,000 Years', www.theconversation.com, 12 January 2017.
39 Flannery, *Future Eaters*, p. 114.
40 Dixon, *Original Languages*, p. 22.
41 Berndt, *World That Was*, p. 89.

42 Loukas Koungoulosa and Melanie Fillios 'Hunting Dogs Down Under? On the Aboriginal Use of Tame Dingoes in Dietary Game Acquisition and Its Relevance to Australian Prehistory', *Journal of Anthropological Archaeology*, LVIII (2020), pp. 1–14.
43 Gilmore, *Old Days*, p. 140.
44 Berndt, *World that Was*, pp. 103–4.
45 Pascoe, *Dark Emu*, p. 106.
46 Gerritsen, *Agriculture*, p. 57.
47 Mitchell, *Three Expeditions*, p. 31.
48 Goddard and Kalotas, *Punu*, pp. 54–5.
49 Cliff Goddard and Arpad Kalotas, ed., *Punu: Yankunytjatjara Plant Use* (Alice Springs, 1985), p. 67.
50 Maggie Brady, *First Taste: How Indigenous Australians Learned about Grog*, book 2: *The First Taste of Alcohol* (Canberra, 2008), pp. 4–8.
51 Anthony J. Barham, 'Late Holocene Maritime Societies in the Torres Strait Islands, Northern Australia: Cultural Arrival or Cultural Emergence?', in *East of Wallace's Line: Studies of Past and Present Maritime Cultures of the Indo-Pacific*, ed. Sue O'Connor and Peter Veth (Rotterdam, 2000), p. 225.
52 David Harris, 'Early Agriculture in New Guinea and the Torres Strait Divide', *Antiquity*, LXIX/265 (1995), pp. 848–54.
53 James A. Baldwin, 'Pre-Cookian Pigs in Australia?', *Journal of Cultural Geography*, IV/1 (1983), pp. 17–27.

THREE: Settlers to Squatters, 1788–1850

1 R.M.W. Dixon, *Australia's Original Languages: An Introduction* (Crows Nest, 2019), pp. 32–3.
2 James Maria Matra, 'A Proposal for Establishing a Colony in New South Wales [1783]', in *Historical Records of New South Wales*, vol. I, part 2: *Phillip 1788–1792*, ed. F. W. Bladen (Sydney, 1892), www.archive.org, accessed 3 April 2019.
3 Watkin Tench, *A Narrative of the Expedition to Botany Bay* (London, 1789), p. 34.
4 Ibid.
5 'List of Livestock, Provisions, Plants and Seeds', www.firstfleetfellowship.org.au, accessed 1 April 2019.
6 Tench, *A Narrative*, p. 71.
7 'Rations in the First Two Years', www.firstfleet.uow.edu.au, accessed 1 April 2019.
8 Tench, *A Narrative*, p. 71.
9 Ibid.
10 Ibid., p. 54.
11 Ibid., p. 55.
12 Ibid., p. 102.
13 Jacqui Newling, 'Sweet Tea, Drunk Universally? A Gastronomic Study of the First Fleeters' Native Tea Alternative', in *Eat History: Food and Drink in Australia and Beyond*, ed. Sofia Eriksson, Madeleine Hastie and Tom Roberts (Newcastle upon Tyne, 2013), p. 89.
15 Ibid., p. 93.

15 Tench, *A Narrative*, p. 106.
16 Ibid., pp. 153–5.
17 'Governor King to Earl Camden [Extracts]', in *Historical Records of New South Wales*, vol. VI: *King and Bligh 1806, 1807, 1808*, ed. F. W. Bladen (Sydney, 1898), www.archive.org, accessed 3 April 2019.
18 Jacqui Newling, *Eat Your History* (Sydney, 2015), p. 70.
19 Heather Hunwick, *The Food and Drink of Sydney: A History* (London, 2018), p. 92.
20 Beverley Kingston, *Basket, Bag and Trolley: A History of Shopping in Australia* (Melbourne, 1994), p. 10.
21 Tench, *A Narrative*, p. 214.
22 Keith Farrer, *To Feed a Nation: A History of Australian Food Science and Technology* (Collingwood, 2005), pp. 24–9.
23 Ibid., pp. 33–4.
24 Tench, *A Narrative*, p. 124.
25 Ibid., p. 158.
26 C. C. Macknight, 'Macassans and Aborigines', *Oceania*, XLII/4 (June 1972), pp. 283–319.
27 Michael Symons, *One Continuous Picnic: A History of Eating in Australia* (Adelaide, 1982), p. 113.
28 'Water Supply Historical Timeline', www.waternsw.com.au., accessed 8 April 2019.
29 Farrer, *To Feed*, p. 23.
30 Ross Fitzgerald and Trevor L. Jordan, *Under the Influence: A History of Alcohol in Australia* (Sydney, 2009), p. 62.
31 Farrer, *To Feed*, p. 23.
32 Geoffrey Blainey, *The Tyranny of Distance* (Melbourne, 1966), p. 156.
33 George Megalogenis, *Australia's Second Chance* (Sydney, 2015), p. 18.
34 Grace Karskens, 'The Appin Massacre', www.dictionaryofsydney.org, accessed 23 September 2019.
35 Samia Khatun, *Australianama: The South Asian Odyssey in Australia* (St Lucia, 2019), p. 94.
36 Boyd H. Hunter and John Carmody, 'Estimating the Aboriginal Population in Early Colonial Australia: The Role of Chickenpox Reconsidered', *Australian Economic History Review*, LV/2 (2015), pp. 112–38.

FOUR: Golden Soil and Wealth for Toil, 1851–99

1 Geoffrey Blainey, *The Tyranny of Distance* (Melbourne, 1966).
2 Michael Symons, *One Continuous Picnic: A History of Eating in Australia* (Adelaide, 1982), p. 60.
3 'Food and Provisions', *Gold: Electronic Encyclopedia of Gold in Australia*, www.egold.net.au, accessed 16 April 2019.
4 Charmaine O'Brien, *Flavours of Melbourne* (Kent Town, 2008), p. 74.
5 Ibid., pp. 78–9.
6 Blainey, *Tyranny*, p. 233.
7 Ibid., p. 234.

8 Samia Khatun, *Australianama: The South Asian Odyssey in Australia* (St Lucia, 2019), pp. 35–6.
9 Joëlle Gergis, *Sunburnt Country: A History and Future of Climate Change in Australia* (Carlton, 2018), p. 86.
10 O'Brien, *Flavours*, p. 83
11 Phillip Muskett, *The Art of Living in Australia* (Sydney, 1893), p. 47.
12 Ibid., p. 77.
13 Richard Twopeny, *Town Life in Australia* (Melbourne, 1973), pp. 63–4.
14 Ibid., p. 63.
15 Ibid., p. 64.
16 Symons, *Continuous Picnic*, p. 90.
17 Keith Farrer, *To Feed a Nation: A History of Australian Food Science and Technology* (Collingwood, 2005), p. 36.
18 Graham Pont, Barbara Santich and Paul Wilkins, *Landmarks of Australian Gastronomy: Catalogue of an Exhibition at the Senior Common Room Club, the University of New South Wales, October 14–November 9, 1988* (Kensington, 1988), p. 30.
19 Mrs Lance Rawson, *The Antipodean Cookery Book and Kitchen Companion* (Kenthurst, 1895), p. 55.
20 Mary Durack, *Kings in Grass Castles* (Sydney, 1997), p. 101.
21 Muskett, *Living in Australia*, p. 78.
22 Hannah Maclurcan, *Mrs Maclurcan's Cookery Book* (Townsville, 1898), recipe number 373.
23 Muskett, *Living in Australia*, p. 82.
24 Ibid., pp. 225–54.
25 Twopeny, *Town Life*, p. 51.
26 Colin Bannerman, *A Friend in the Kitchen* (Kenthurst, 1996), p. 40.
27 Ibid.
28 Mary Gilmore, *Old Days, Old Ways: A Book of Recollections* (Sydney, 1986), pp. 1–2.
29 Farrer, *To Feed*, p. 61.
30 Twopeny, *Town Life*, pp. 64–5.
31 O'Brien, *Flavours*, p. 115.
32 Jacqui Newling, *Eat Your History* (Sydney, 2015), p. 210.
33 'A Keen Curry History', www.mccormick.com.au, accessed 27 September 2019.
34 David Dale, 'New Restaurant of the Year 1831', smh.com.au., accessed 23 April 2019.
35 Henry Lawson, 'The Blindness of One-eyed Bogan', in *The Bush Undertaker and Other Stories* (Sydney, 1982), p. 67.
36 Symons, *Continuous Picnic*, p. 115.
37 Ross Fitzgerald and Trevor L. Jordan, *Under the Influence: A History of Alcohol in Australia* (Sydney, 2009), p. 117.
38 Henry Lawson, 'Water Them Geraniums', in *The Bush Undertaker and Other Stories*, p. 174.
39 David Dunstan, 'The Wine Press', *Meanjin*, LXI/4 (2002), p. 35.
40 'Echuca Coffee Palace', *Riverine Herald*, 16 September 1895, p. 2, www.trove.nla.gov.au, accessed 25 April 2019.
41 George Megalogenis, *Australia's Second Chance* (Sydney, 2015), p. 121.

42 Manning Clark, *A Short History of Australia* (Ringwood, 1986), p. 152.
43 Edward Abbott, *The English and Australian Cookery Book. Cookery for The Many, As Well As for the 'Upper Ten Thousand'* (London, 1864), p. 175.

FIVE: Federation, 1900–1913

1 Manning Clark, *A Short History of Australia* (Ringwood, 1986), p. 163.
2 Ibid.
3 'The Chinese in Australia: Their Vices and Their Victims', *The Bulletin*, IV/171 (1886), p. 24.
4 Clark, *Short History*, p. 165.
5 'The Chinese in Australia', p. 24.
6 Henry Reynolds, *North of Capricorn* (Crows Nest, 2003), p. 41.
7 Ibid., p. 43.
8 'Australia for the Australians!', *The Bulletin*, VIII/387 (1887), p. 4.
9 Clark, *Short History*, p. 177.
10 Henry Lawson, 'Water Them Geraniums', in *The Bush Undertaker and Other Stories* (Sydney, 1982), p. 169.
11 Clark, *Short History*, pp. 17–18.
12 A. B. Facey, *A Fortunate Life* (Ringwood, 1981), p. 26.
13 Marilyn Lake, *The Limits of Hope: Soldier Settlement in Victoria, 1915–38* (Melbourne, 1987), p. 14.
14 Ibid., p. 21.
15 Watkin Tench, *A Complete Account of the Settlement of Port Jackson* (London, 1793), p. 230.
16 Facey, *A Fortunate Life*, p. 87.
17 'Murrumbidgee Irrigation Trust', www.records.nsw.gov.au, accessed 1 May 2019.
18 Sally Morgan, *My Place* (Fremantle, 1987), p. 231.
19 Ibid., p. 412.
20 Ibid., p. 228.
21 'Yiwarra Kuju: The Canning Stock Route', www.nma.gov.au, accessed 6 May 2019.
22 Ibid., p. 419.
23 Reynolds, *Capricorn*, p. 20.
24 'Dairy Products', *Technology in Australia, 1788–1988*, pp. 109–112, www.austehc.unimelb.edu.au, accessed 2 May 2019.
25 Anna Clark, *The Catch: The Story of Fishing in Australia* (Canberra, 2017), p. 54.
26 Ibid., p. 57.
27 Mary Durack, *Kings in Grass Castles* (Sydney, 1997), p. 126.
28 Presbyterian Church of NSW Women's Missionary Association, *Cookery Book of Good and Tried Receipts* (Sydney, 1902).
29 Mrs Theo Winning, *Housekeeping for Two or More: Casserole and General Cookery* (Melbourne, 1915).
30 Barbara Santich, *What the Doctors Ordered: 150 Years of Dietary Advice in Australia* (London, 1995), p. 20.
31 Barbara Santich, *Bold Palates: Australia's Gastronomic Heritage* (Kent Town, 2012), pp. 204–5.

SIX: Between World Wars, 1914–45

1 Judith Smart, 'Food and Nutrition (Australia)', *International Encyclopedia of the First World War*, encyclopedia.1914-1918-online.net, accessed 5 September 2019.
2 Ibid.
3 George Megalogenis, *Australia's Second Chance* (Sydney, 2015), p. 180.
4 Marilyn Lake, *The Limits of Hope: Soldier Settlement in Victoria, 1915–38* (Melbourne, 1987), p. 143.
5 A. B. Facey, *A Fortunate Life* (Ringwood, 1981), pp. 294–5.
6 Ibid., p. 296.
7 Ibid., p. 303.
8 Ibid., p. 304.
9 Megalogenis, *Second Chance*, p. 181.
10 Sarah Sargent, *The Foodmakers* (Ringwood, 1985), p. 30.
11 Noris Ioannou, *Barossa Journeys: Into a Valley of Tradition* (Sydney, 2000), p. 19.
12 Angela Heuzenroeder, *Barossa Food* (Kent Town, 1999), pp. 13–14.
13 Ioannou, *Barossa Journeys*, p. 113.
14 Heuzenroeder, *Barossa Food*, p. 16.
15 Ibid., p. 18.
16 Hal Porter, *The Watcher on the Cast-iron Balcony* (London, 1963), p. 21.
17 Ibid., p. 21.
18 Ibid., p. 59.
19 Beverley Kingston, *Basket, Bag and Trolley: A History of Shopping in Australia* (Melbourne, 1994), p. 62.
20 Myrtle Rose White, *No Roads Go By* (Adelaide, 1932), p. 60.
21 Ibid., pp. 166–7.
22 Ibid., p. 64.
23 Ibid., pp. 76–7.
24 'Proved Recipes', *Australian Woman's Mirror*, vol. I, 23 October 1924, p. 22, www.trove.nla.gov.au, accessed 24 May 2019.
25 'Best Recipes', *Australian Women's Weekly*, 1 July 1933, p. 35, www.trove.nla.gov.au, accessed 24 May 2019.
26 The New South Wales Society for Crippled Children, *Household Book* (Sydney, 1940).
27 Dr Frances McKay in *The Electrical Association for Women (Australia) Sydney Cookery Book* (Sydney, 1938), p. 3.
28 Kingston, *Basket*, p. 105.
29 *Lousy Little Sixpence* (1983, dir. Alec Morgan).
30 Ibid.
31 Ibid.
32 Porter, *The Watcher*, p. 216.
33 Charmaine O'Brien, *Flavours of Melbourne* (Kent Town, 2008), p. 164.
34 Emery Barcs, *Backyard of Mars: Memoirs of the 'Reffo' Period in Australia* (Sydney, 1980), p. 31.
35 Ibid., p. 28.
36 Margaret Fulton, *I Sang for My Supper* (Sydney, 1999), p. 32.
37 Fulton, *I Sang*, p. 27.

38 Effy Alexakis and Leonard Janiszewski, *Selling an American Dream: Australia's Greek Café* (Sydney, 2013); Andrew Farrington, trans., *Life in Australia* (Sydney, 2009); Hugh Gilchrist, *Australians and Greeks*, vol. I: *The Early Years* (Rushcutters Bay, 1991); O'Brien, *Flavours of Melbourne*.
39 Ross Fitzgerald and Trevor L. Jordan, *Under the Influence: A History of Alcohol in Australia* (Sydney, 2009), p. 195.
40 Fulton, *I Sang*, p. 13.
41 Wendy Lowenstein, *Weevils in The Flour: An Oral Record of the 1930s Depression in Australia* (Melbourne, 1978), p. 213.
42 Ibid., pp. 385–6.
43 Ibid., pp. 419–20.
44 Ibid., p. 10.
45 'Winning Recipes', *Australian Women's Weekly*, 23 May 1942, p. 21, www. trove. nla.gov.au, accessed 28 May 2019.
46 'Prize Recipes', *Australian Women's Weekly*, 2 January 1934, p. 23 www.trove.nla. gov.au, accessed 28 May 2019.
47 Keith Farrer, *To Feed a Nation: A History of Australian Food Science and Technology* (Collingwood, 2005), p. 130.
48 Ibid., p. 129.
49 Ibid., p. 130.
50 Ibid.
51 Fulton, *I Sang*, p. 2.

SEVEN: Boundless Plains to Share, 1946–65

1 Eric Richards, *Destination Australia* (Sydney, 2008), p. 185.
2 Ibid., p. 186.
3 Donald Horne, *The Lucky Country* (Melbourne, 1964), p. 84.
4 NSW Board of Jewish Education, 'Australian Jewish History', www.bje.org.au, accessed 6 June 2019.
5 Tom Kelemen, *A Sour Sweet Life: A Memoir* (Sydney, 2014), pp. 267–8.
6 Stephanie Alexander, *A Cook's Life* (Melbourne, 2012), p. 66.
7 Kelemen, *Sour Sweet Life*, p. 283.
8 Tania Cammarano, 'Food, Fascism and Forward Thinking: Australia's First Italo-Australian Cookbook', in *Eat History: Food and Drink in Australia and Beyond*, ed. Sofia Eriksson, Madeleine Hastie and Tom Roberts (Newcastle upon Tyne, 2013), p. 42.
9 Mia Spizzica, 'When Ethnicity Counts: Civilian Internment in Australia during WW2', www.theconversation.com, accessed 8 June 2019.
10 Gianfranco Cresciani, *The Italians in Australia* (Cambridge, 2003), p. 65.
11 Francesco Ricatti, *Italians in Australia: History, Memory, Identity* (Clayton, 2018), p. 29.
12 Matt Grudnoff and Rod Campbell, 'Dam the Expense: The Ord River Irrigation Scheme and the Development of Northern Australia', *The Australia Institute* (Canberra, 2017), www.tai.org.au, accessed 13 September 2019.
13 Stephanie Alexander, *A Cook's Life* (Melbourne, 2012), p. 66.
14 John Newton, *Wogfood: An Oral History with Recipes* (Sydney, 1996), p. 204.

15 Ibid., p. 205.
16 Steve Manfredi, 'A Public Dialogue between Steve Manfredi and John Newton at the Bonegilla Dinner', in *Fourteenth Symposium of Australian Gastronomy: Preservation or Change – Proceedings*, ed. Lois Butt, Robert Ford and Jeanette Fry (Beechworth, 2005), p. 49.
17 Manfredi, 'A Public Dialogue', pp. 49–52.
18 Margaret Fulton, *I Sang for My Supper* (Sydney, 1999), pp. 80–81.
19 Stefano Manfredi and John Newton, *Fresh from Italy: Italian Cooking for the Australian Kitchen* (Rydalmere, 1993), p. 6.
20 Horne, *Lucky Country,* p. 83
21 'Supper's Served', *Australian Women's Weekly*, 9 July 1952, p. 32.
22 Marion Halligan, 'From Castor to Olive in One Generation; or, A Gastronomic Education', in *The Pleasures of the Table Proceedings of the Fifth Symposium of Australian Gastronomy,* ed. Barbara Santich and Michael Symons (Adelaide, 1990), p. 15.
23 Ibid., p. 16.
24 'Prize Recipes', *Australian Women's Weekly*, 16 June 1951, p. 50.
25 'Continental Flavours', *Australian Women's Weekly*, 11 March 1953, p. 67.
26 'Prize Recipes', *Australian Women's Weekly*, 9 March 1955, pp. 5–8.
27 Maria Kozslik Donovan, *Continental Cookery in Australia* (Melbourne, 1955).
28 Charmaine O'Brien, *Flavours of Melbourne* (Kent Town, 2008), p. 223.
29 Harriet Goodwin, *How to Cook with Wine* (London, 1954), p. 7.
31 David Dunstan, 'The Wine Press', *Meanjin*, XI/4 (2002), p. 36.
32 Ross Fitzgerald and Trevor L. Jordan, *Under the Influence: A History of Alcohol in Australia* (Sydney, 2009), p. 119.
32 Fulton, *I Sang*, p. 155.
33 Ibid., p. 120.
34 'Special Feature – Barbecues', *Australian Women's Weekly*, 7 March 1956, pp. 30–33.
35 Heather Hunwick, *The Food and Drink of Sydney: A History* (London, 2018), p. 160; 'The Women Were Chained to the Brass Rail', 'Queensland This Week', *Canberra Times*, 8 April 1965, p. 2.
36 Barbara Santich, *Bold Palates: Australia's Gastronomic Heritage* (Kent Town, 2012), p. 116.
37 Ibid., p. 117.
38 Ibid., p. 131.
39 Sian Supski, *It Was Another Skin: The Kitchen in 1950s Western Australia* (Bern, 2007), p. 167.
40 'Christmas time is Sunbeam Gift Time' (advt), *Australian Women's Weekly*, 28 November 1956, pp. 68–9.
41 Sunbeam Controlled Heat Automatic Frypan (product brochure, undated, *c.* 1950s).
42 'Tops in Colour' (advt) *Australian Women's Weekly,* 28 November 1956, p. 58.
43 Ibid., p. 34.
44 Supski, *Another Skin*, p. 177.

EIGHT: Transformations, 1966–79

1 A. J. Grassby, *A Multi-cultural Society for the Future* (Canberra, 1973), pp. 4–7.
2 Cherry Ripe, *Goodbye Culinary Cringe* (Sydney, 1993), pp. 9–10.
3 Roy Geechoun, *Cooking the Chinese Way* (Melbourne, 1948), pp. 5, 10.
4 Yep Yung Hee, *Chinese Recipes for Home Cooking* (Sydney, 1951).
5 Margaret Fulton, *I Sang for My Supper* (Sydney, 1999), pp. 140–41.
6 The Australian Gourmet Magazine, *Australian Gourmet Cook Book* (Melbourne, 1967), pp. 101, 125.
7 Melbourne Church of England Girls Grammar School, *Cookery Book* (Melbourne, 1967), n.p.
8 Maria Kozslik Donovan, *The Far Eastern Epicure* (Melbourne, 1951).
9 Festival of Asia Committee, *Cook Book* (Sydney, 1963), pp. 6, 7.
10 Doris Ady, *Curries from the Sultan's Kitchen* (Sydney, 1968).
11 Fulton, *I Sang*, p. 155.
12 Charmaine Solomon, *The Complete Asian Cookbook* (Sydney, 1976), p. 13.
13 John Newton, *The Getting of Garlic* (Sydney 2018), p. 248.
14 Fulton, *I Sang*, pp. 140–41.
15 George Megalogenis, *Australia's Second Chance* (Sydney, 2015), p. 249.
16 Stephanie Alexander, *A Cook's Life* (Melbourne, 2012), p. 161.
17 Jan O'Connell, '1901 Federation Banquet', www.australianfoodtimeline.com.au, accessed 20 June 2019.
18 Barbara Knox, *Something Different for Dinner* (Sydney, 1936), pp. 18, 40.
19 John D. Porter, *The Chef Suggests* (Melbourne, 1949), pp. 97, 112, 149.
20 Fulton, *I Sang*, p. 100.
21 Ted Maloney and Deke Coleman, *Oh, for a French Wife!* (Sydney, 1952).
22 Gay Bilson, *Plenty: Digressions on Food* (Melbourne, 2004), pp. 11, 13.
23 Ibid., p. 16.
24 Margaret Jones, 'The Dining-out Boom', *Sydney Morning Herald*, 5 September 1970, p. 2.
25 Stephen Downes, *Advanced Australia Fare* (Sydney, 2003), p. 47.
26 Helen Frizell, 'In Clubland, Everyman has a Palace', *Sydney Morning Herald*, 12 May 1969, p. 6.
27 Ross Fitzgerald and Trevor L. Jordan, *Under the Influence: A History of Alcohol in Australia* (Sydney, 2009), p. 122.
28 Ibid., pp. 138–9.
29 Ibid., p. 137.
30 A. E. Dingle, '"The Truly Magnificent Thirst": An Historical Survey of Australian Drinking Habits', *Australian Historical Studies*, XIX/75 (1980), p. 246, accessed at www.doi.org, 26 June 2019.
31 'How to Glamorise Quick Frozen Vegetables', *Australian Women's Weekly*, 13 August 1975, pp. 119–21.
32 Keith Farrer, *To Feed a Nation: A History of Australian Food Science and Technology* (Collingwood, 2005), p. 142.
33 Richard Glover, *The Land Before Avocado: Journeys in a Lost Australia* (Sydney, 2018), p. 90.
34 'Break the Monotony of Meat Meat Meat' (advt), *Australian Women's Weekly*, 18 February 1970, p. 25.

35 Edgar Crook, *Vegetarianism in Australia: A History*, ivu.org, accessed 23 September 2018, p. 119.
36 Ibid., pp. 122–3.
37 Silas Snell, 'The Accursed Meat', *The Bulletin*, 21 November 1912, p. 14, www.nla.gov.au, accessed 28 June 2019.
38 'Cooking the Vegetarian Way', *Australian Women's Weekly*, 3 September 1975, pp. 93–4.
39 'Mabo Case', Australian Institute of Aboriginal and Islander Studies, www.aiatsis.gov.au, accessed 13 March 2019; '3 June: The Mabo Decision', Reconciliation Australia, www.reconciliation.org.au, accessed 13 March 2019.

NINE: Foodie Nation, 1980–99

1 Ann Barr and Paul Levy, *The Official Foodie Handbook* (London, 1985), pp. 6–7.
2 Ibid., p. 25.
3 Alison Vincent, 'Sydney Eats, Melbourne Dines: Shaping Australian Tastes, 1970–1995', PhD thesis, Central Queensland University (2019), pp. 115–19, http://dx.doi.org, accessed 16 July 2019.
4 Ibid., p. 123.
5 Graham Kerr, *Guide to Good Eating in Sydney* (Sydney, 1968) and *Guide to Good Eating in Melbourne* (Sydney, 1969).
6 John Newton, *The Getting of Garlic* (Sydney, 2018), pp. 261–3.
7 Australian Bureau of Statistics, 'Apparent Consumption of Foodstuffs 1997–98 and 1998–99', cat. no. 4306.0, www.abs.gov.au, accessed 8 July 2019.
8 Barbara Santich, *What the Doctors Ordered: 150 Years of Dietary Advice in Australia* (London, 1995), p. 150.
9 Ibid., p. 159.
10 Nathalie Havenstein, ed., *Polyunsaturated Cookery* (Clayton, 1974), pp. 10–11.
11 Santich, *Doctors*, p. 176.
12 'Heart Foundation Tick', www.heartfoundation.org.au, accessed 10 July 2019.
13 *The Family Cookbook* (Sydney, 1971).
14 'When you're having fast food, isn't it nice to know your family is eating well' (advt), *Australian Women's Weekly*, 3 January 1979, pp. 23–4.
15 Anna Clark, *The Catch: The Story of Fishing in Australia* (Canberra, 2017), p. 97.
16 Ibid., pp. 110–15.
17 William Fraser and Helen Greenwood, eds, *Good Food Guide to Eating Well In and Around Sydney* (Sydney, 1994), p. 5.
18 Cherry Ripe, *Goodbye Culinary Cringe* (Sydney, 1993), p. 6.
19 Graham Pont, Barbara Santich and Paul Wilkins, *Landmarks of Australian Gastronomy: Catalogue of an Exhibition at the Senior Common Room Club, University of New South Wales, October 14–November 9, 1988* (Kensington, 1988), p. 3.
20 Barbara Santich, *Looking for Flavour* (Kent Town, 1996), p. 92.
21 Terry Durack and Jill Dupleix, *Good Food Guide* (Sydney, 1997), p. iv.
22 Charmaine O'Brien, *Flavours of Melbourne* (Kent Town, 2008), p. 266.
23 Patricia Cook, ed., *Is Emu on the Menu? Historical Homesteads and Recipes of Gippsland* (Bairnsdale, 1965).

24 John Newton, *The Oldest Foods on Earth: A History of Australian Native Foods* (Sydney, 2016), p. 199.
25 Ibid., pp. 192–9.
26 Vic Cherikoff, 'Bushfoods and the True Australian Cuisine', in *Festivity Food Proceedings of the Fourth Symposium of Australian Gastronomy*, ed. Anthony Corones, Graham Pont and Barbara Santich (Sydney, 1990), p. 37.
27 Newton, *Oldest Foods*, pp. 200–201.
28 Ross Fitzgerald and Trevor L. Jordan, *Under the Influence: A History of Alcohol in Australia* (Sydney, 2009), p. 127.
29 Max Lake, 'The Culture of Wine in Australia: State of the Art, 1988', in *Festivity Food Proceedings of the Fourth Symposium of Australian Gastronomy,* ed. Anthony Corones, Graham Pont and Barbara Santich (Sydney, 1990), p. 69.
30 Fitzgerald and Jordan, *Influence*, p. 127.
31 Michael Symons, *One Continuous Picnic: A History of Eating in Australia* (Adelaide, 1982), pp. 1–2.
32 Ibid., p. 12.
33 John Pollard, 'A Hundred Years of Agriculture', *Year Book of Australia 2000*, Australian Bureau of Statistics, no. 83, cat. no, 1301.0, www.abs.gov.au, accessed 21 July 2019.
34 Geoffrey Lawrence, *Capitalism and the Countryside: The Rural Crisis in Australia* (Marrickville, 1987), pp. 139–41.

TEN: Millennium Reckonings, 2000–2020

1 David Alexander, 'How Australia Weathered the Global Financial Crisis while Europe Failed' (2013), www.theguardian.com, accessed 3 October 2019.
2 Department of Agriculture, Fisheries and Forestry, 'Submission to House of Representatives Standing Committee on Infrastructure, Transport, Regional Development and Local Government Inquiry into the Impact of the Global Financial Crisis on Regional Australia' (2009), p. 3, www.aph.gov.au, accessed 3 October 2019.
3 'The Slow but Steady Rise of Vegetarianism in Australia' (2016), www.roymorgan.com, accessed 8 October 2019.
4 Nick Kilvert, 'Veganism is Growing in Australia, But We're Still Some of the World's Biggest Meat Eaters' (2019), www.abc.net.au, accessed 8 October 2019.
5 'CSIRO and Jack Cowin partner to launch Australia's newest plant-based meat startup, v2 food', csiro.au/en/News accessed October 2019
6 'How Much of the Grocery Market Share does each Supermarket Have?', Roy Morgan Single Source Australia, www.roymorgan.com, accessed 3 September 2018.
7 'Layer Hen FAQ', www.rspca.org.au, accessed 16 August 2019.
8 Nancy Cushing, 'Australia's History of Live Exports Is More Than Two Centuries Old', www.theconversation.com, accessed 7 March 2019.
9 Senate Select Committee on Animal Welfare, *The Export of Live Sheep from Australia* (Canberra, 2019), pp. xiii–xvi, www.aph.gov.au, accessed 18 August.
10 Nancy Cushing, 'Live Export Is a Centuries-old Australian Industry, But the Cameras are New', abc.net.au/news, accessed 11 April 2018.

11 Liz Little and Lane Calcutt, '60 Minutes Uncovers Disturbing Video from Live Sheep Export Vessel', www.9news.com.au, accessed 9 April 2018.
12 Australian Bureau of Statistics, 'Internet Activity, Australia, June 2018', cat. no. 8153.0.
13 Shaun Adams, Richard Martin, Susan Phillips, Colin Macgregor and Michael Westaway, 'Truth-telling in the Wake of European Contact: Historical Investigation of Aboriginal Skeletal Remains from Normanton', *Archaeologies*, XIV/3 (2018), pp. 412–42.
14 'Review of Nutrition among Aboriginal and Torres Strait Islander People', *Australian Indigenous Health Bulletin*, XVIII/1 (2018), www.healthbulletin.org.au, accessed 9 August 2019.
15 Aboriginal and Torres Strait Islander Social, Justice Commissioner, Human Rights and Equal Opportunity Commission, *Close the Gap: National Indigenous Health Equality Targets* (Canberra, 2008), p. 24.
16 Department of Prime Minister and the Cabinet, *Closing the Gap: Report 2019* (Canberra, 2019), pp. 118–36.
17 'Eating Healthy', www.diabetesaustralia.com.au, accessed 27 July 2019.
18 John Newton, *The Oldest Foods on Earth: A History of Australian Native Foods* (Sydney, 2016), p. 117.
19 Mark Olive, *Mark Olive's Outback Café: A Taste of Australia* (Milsons Point, 2015), p. 31.
20 'Overweight and Obesity', Australian Institute of Health and Welfare, www.aihw.gov.au, accessed 10 August 2019.
21 'Free Milk for Children', *Sydney Morning Herald*, 1 July 1950, p. 7.
22 Barbara Santich, *What the Doctors Ordered: 150 Years of Dietary Advice in Australia* (London, 1995), p. 115.
23 Robert A. Gardner, *The Value of the Vitamin: The Story of the Oslo Health Lunch Experiment* (Melbourne, 1941), p. 10, repository.monash.edu, accessed 10 August 2020.
24 Ibid., p. 13.
25 Santich, *Doctors*, pp. 116–17.
26 Ibid., p. 116.
27 Department of Health, *Guidelines for Healthy Foods and Drinks supplied in School Canteens* (Canberra, 2014), pp. 2–4.
28 'Household Expenditure Survey, Australia: Summary of Results, 2015–16', Australian Bureau of Statistics, cat. no. 6530.0, www.abs.gov.au, accessed 14 August 2019.
29 Adrian Cameron, Christina Zorbas, Devorah Riesenberg, Gary Sacks and Kathryn Backholer, 'Supermarkets Put Junk Food on Special Twice as Often as Healthy Food, and That's a Problem', www.theconversation.com, accessed 16 August 2019.
30 Michael Clarke, *Australian Native Food Industry Stocktake* (Canberra, 2012), Rural Industries Research and Development Corporation, pub. no. 12/066.
31 Obesity Policy Coalition, 'PC calls for Removal of Unhealthy Food Marketing on Public Transport to Protect Kids', www.opc.org.au, accessed 23 August 2019.
32 Emma Felton, *Filtered: Coffee, the Café and the 21st-century City* (New York, 2019), p. 67.
33 'Cafes and Coffee Shops – Australia Market Research Report', www.ibisworld.com.au, accessed 19 September 2019.

34 'Australian Health Survey: Nutrition First Results – Foods and Nutrients, 2011–12', Australian Bureau of Statistics, www.abs.gov.au accessed 19 September 2019.
35 Andrea Hagan, 'Australian Wine Industry Strongest in More Than a Decade', www.ausfoodnews.com.au, accessed 31 January 2018.
36 'Impact of Investment', www.wineaustralia.com, accessed 22 August 2019.
37 'Supermarkets Continue to take Alcohol Market Share from Hotel Bottle-shops', www.roymorgan.com, accessed 22 August 2019.
38 Patricia Menéndez, Don Weatherburn, Kypros Kypri and Jacqueline Fitzgerald, 'Lockouts and Last Drinks: The Impact of the January 2014 Liquor Licence reforms on Assaults in NSW', Australian Bureau of Crime Statistics and Research (Canberra, 2015).
39 Michaela Whitbourn, 'Sydney Lockouts: Assaults "Displaced" to Suburbs around CBD and Kings Cross', *Sydney Morning Herald*, 6 March 2017, smh.com.au, accessed 3 September 2018.
40 Foundation for Alcohol Research and Education, *Annual Alcohol Poll* (2019), p. 6.
41 Ibid., p. 39.
42 Anthony Morgan and Amanda McAtamney, 'Key Issues in Alcohol-related Violence' (2009), www.aic.gov.au, accessed 5 June 2018.
43 M. Livingstone, 'The Association between State of Origin and Assaults in Two Australian States', Centre for Alcohol Policy Research (2018), pp. 5–6, www.fare.org.au, accessed 4 June 2019.
44 'Fisheries Inquiry Commission', *Sydney Mail*, 15 May 1880, p. 928, trove.nla.gov.au, accessed 21 August 2019.
45 'Fish Stocks: Measures of Australia's Progress', Australian Bureau of Statistics (2010), cat. no. 1370.0, www.abs.gov.au, accessed 21 August 2019.
46 Graham Edgar and Trevor J. Ward, 'Australian Fish Population Decreasing', www.utas.edu.au, accessed 21 August 2019.
47 'Status of Australian Fish Stocks Report: Key Results', www.fish.gov.au, accessed 21 August 2019.
48 'Aquaculture Industry in Australia', Department of Agriculture, www.agriculture.gov.au, accessed 21 August 2019.
49 'Australia's Sustainable Seafood Guide', Australian Marine Conservation Society, www.sustainableseafood.org.au, accessed 22 August 2019.
50 '2018 Lowy Institute Poll', www.lowyinstitute.org, accessed 23 August 2019.
51 Intergovernmental Panel on Climate Change, *Special Report on Climate Change, Desertification, Land Degradation, Sustainable Land Management, Food Security, and Greenhouse Gas Fluxes in Terrestrial Ecosystems*, www.ipcc.ch, accessed 23 August 2019.
52 Department of Primary Industries and Regional Development, 'How Australia Accounts for Agricultural Greenhouse Gas Emissions', www.agric.wa.gov.au, accessed 23 August 2019.
53 Patrice Newell, *Who's Minding the Farm?* (Sydney, 2019), p. 164.
54 Ross Garnaut, 'Transforming the Land Sector', *Climate Change Review Update 2011*, www.garnautreview.org.au, accessed 23 August 2019.
55 Sabine Fuss, William F. Lamb, Max W. Callaghan et al, 'Negative Emissions – Part 2: Costs, Potentials and Side Effects', *Environmental Research Letters*, XIII/6 (2018), www.iopscience.iop.org, accessed 23 August 2019.

56 Paula Fernandez Arias, Tammi Jonas and Katarina Munksgaard, *Farming Democracy: Radically Transforming the Food System from the Ground Up* (Sydney, 2019).
57 'The RCS Vision for Agriculture', www.rcsaustralia.com.au, accessed 24 August 2019.
58 Gabrielle Chan, 'All About the Land: Drought Shakes Farming to its Indigenous Roots', www.theguardian.com, accessed 23 August 2019.

Bibliography

Abbott, Edward, *The English and Australian Cookery Book: Cookery for the Many, as well as for the 'Upper Ten Thousand'* (London, 1864)

Alexander, Stephanie, *A Cook's Life* (Melbourne, 2012)

Bannerman, Colin, *A Friend in the Kitchen* (Kenthurst, 1996)

—, *Seed Cake and Honey Prawns: Fashion and Fad in Australian Food* (Canberra, 2008)

Barcs, Emery, *Backyard of Mars: Memoirs of the 'Reffo' Period in Australia* (Sydney, 1980)

Barker, H. M., *Camels and the Outback* (Carlisle, 1964)

Berndt, Ronald M., Catherine H. Berndt and John E. Stanton, *A World That Was: The Yaraldi of the Murray River and the Lakes, South Australia* (Vancouver, 1993)

Beveridge, Peter, *The Aborigines of Victoria and the Riverina* (Melbourne, 1889)

Bilson, Gay, *Plenty: Digressions on Food* (Melbourne, 2004)

Bingle, A. S., *This Is Our Country* (Turramurra, 1986)

Blainey, Geoffrey, *The Tyranny of Distance* (Melbourne, 1966)

Choi, C. Y., *Chinese Migration and Settlement in Australia* (Sydney, 1975)

Clark, Anna, *The Catch: The Story of Fishing in Australia* (Canberra, 2017)

Clark, Manning, *A Short History of Australia* (Ringwood, 1986)

Cresciani, Gianfranco, *The Italians in Australia* (Cambridge, 2003)

Dargin, Peter, *Aboriginal Fisheries of the Darling–Barwon Rivers* (Dubbo, 1976)

Downes, Stephen, *Advanced Australia Fare: How Australian Cooking Became the World's Best* (Sydney, 2003)

Durack, Mary, *Kings in Grass Castles* (Sydney, 1997)

Facey, A. B., *A Fortunate Life* (Ringwood, 1981)

Farrer, Keith, *To Feed a Nation: A History of Australian Food Science and Technology* (Collingwood, 2005)

Fitzgerald, Ross, and Trevor L. Jordan, *Under the Influence: A History of Alcohol in Australia* (Sydney, 2009)

Flannery, Tim, *The Future Eaters* (Chatswood, 1994)

Fulton, Margaret, *I Sang for My Supper* (Sydney, 1999)

Gammage, Bill, *The Biggest Estate on Earth: How Aborigines Made Australia* (Sydney, 2011)

Gergis, Joëlle, *Sunburnt Country: A History and Future of Climate Change in Australia* (Carlton, 2018)
Gerritsen, Rupert, *Australia and the Origins of Agriculture* (Oxford, 2008)
Gilmore, Mary, *Old Days, Old Ways: A Book of Recollections* (Sydney, 1986)
Glover, Richard, *The Land Before Avocado: Journeys in a Lost Australia* (Sydney, 2018)
Gould, Nat, *Town and Bush* (Blackburn, 1974)
Grassby, A. J., *A Multi-cultural Society for the Future* (Canberra, 1973)
Griffiths, Billy, *Deep Time Dreaming: Uncovering Ancient Australia* (Carlton, 2018)
Heuzenroeder, Angela, *Barossa Food* (Kent Town, 1999)
Hunwick, Heather, *The Food and Drink of Sydney: A History* (London, 2018)
Ioannou, Noris, *Barossa Journeys: Into a Valley of Tradition* (Sydney, 2000)
Kelemen, Tom, *A Sour Sweet Life: A Memoir* (Sydney, 2014)
Khatun, Samia, *Australianama: The South Asian Odyssey in Australia* (St Lucia, 2019)
Kingston, Beverley, *Basket, Bag and Trolley: A History of Shopping in Australia* (Melbourne, 1994)
Knox, Malcolm, *Supermarket Monsters: The Price of Coles' and Woolworths' Dominance* (Collingwood, 2015)
Lawson, Henry, *The Bush Undertaker and Other Stories* (Sydney, 1982)
Lowenstein, Wendy, *Weevils in The Flour: An Oral Record of the 1930s Depression in Australia* (Melbourne, 1978)
Manfredi, Stefano, and John Newton, *Fresh from Italy: Italian Cooking for the Australian Kitchen* (Rydalmere, 1993)
Megalogenis, George, *The Australian Moment* (Sydney, 2012)
—, *Australia's Second Chance* (Sydney, 2015)
Mitchell, Thomas, *Three Expeditions into the Interior of Eastern Australia*, vol. I (London, 1839)
Morgan, Sally, *My Place* (Fremantle, 1987)
Muskett, Philip, *The Art of Living in Australia* (Sydney, 1893)
Newell, Patrice, *Who's Minding the Farm?* (Sydney, 2019)
Newling, Jacqui, *Eat Your History* (Sydney, 2015)
Newton, John, *Wogfood: An Oral History with Recipes* (Sydney, 1996)
—, *The Oldest Foods on Earth: A History of Australian Native Foods* (Sydney, 2016)
—, *The Getting of Garlic: Australian Food from Bland to Brilliant, with Recipes Old and New* (Sydney, 2018)
Nunn, Patrick, *The Edge of Memory: Ancient Stories, Oral Tradition and the Post-glacial World* (London 2018)
O'Brien, Charmaine, *Flavours of Melbourne* (Kent Town, 2008)
Pascoe, Bruce, *Dark Emu, Black Seeds: Agriculture or Accident?* (Broome, 2014)
Polese, Beppi, and John Newton, *A Life in Three Courses* (Millers Point, 2007)
Porter, Hal, *The Watcher on the Cast-iron Balcony* (London, 1963)
Reynolds, Henry, *North of Capricorn: The Untold Story of Australia's North* (Sydney, 2003)
Richards, Eric, *Destination Australia* (Sydney, 2008)
Ripe, Cherry, *Goodbye Culinary Cringe* (Sydney, 1993)
Santich, Barbara, *What the Doctors Ordered: 150 Years of Dietary Advice in Australia* (London, 1995)
—, *Looking for Flavour* (Kent Town, 1996)
—, *Bold Palate: Australia's Gastronomic Heritage* (Kent Town, 2012)

Supski, Sian, *It Was Another Skin: The Kitchen in 1950s Western Australia* (Bern, 2007)
Symons, Michael, *One Continuous Picnic: A History of Eating in Australia* (Adelaide, 1982)
Tench, Watkin, *A Narrative of the Expedition to Botany Bay* (London, 1789)
—, *A Complete Account of the Settlement of Port Jackson* (London, 1793)
Twopeny, Richard, *Town Life in Australia* (Melbourne, 1973)
Walsh, Amanda, *Globalisation, the State and Regional Australia* (Sydney, 2018)
Wood, Beverley, ed., *Tucker in Australia* (Melbourne, 1971)

Acknowledgements

Thank you to Craig Johnston, Maria Kelly, Ross Kelly, Jacqui Newling, John Newton, Dianne Nixon, Charmaine O'Brien, Barbara Sweeney and Alison Vincent.

Acknowledgement of Country

This book was written on the land of the Gadigal of the Eora nation. I pay my respects to their Elders, past, present and emerging. I pay my respects to their knowledge, upon which I have drawn throughout this book. Australia always was, and always will be, Aboriginal land.

Photo Acknowledgements

The author and publishers wish to thank the organizations and individuals listed below for authorizing reproduction of their work:

Alamy: pp. 77 (Pictorial Press Ltd), 78 (World History Archive), 82 (Album), 93 (Inconographic Archive), 122 (Lordprice Collection); Australian Botanic Gardens: p. 23; Australian Bureau of Meteorology: p. 13; Australian Capital Territory Heritage Library: p. 174; Australian War Memorial: p. 150; Australscope: p. 255 top (Mike Bowers/Eyevine); Brewarrina Historical Society: p. 29; The British Library, London: p. 17; Robert Brookes: p. 255 bottom; Chinese-Australian Historical Images, Chinese Museum: p. 69; William Collins (Australia): p. 202; Flickr: p. 24 (Nardoo); Gavin Gatenby: p. 34; Horwitz Publications: p. 182; Mary Evans Picture Library: p. 173 (Bill Angove); Museum of Applied Arts and Sciences: p. 204 (Mervyn Bishop); National Archives of Australia: pp. 109, 137, 154, 188; National Gallery of Australia: p. 51; National Library of Australia: pp. 31, 49, 80, 94 bottom, 103, 112, 116, 129, 177, 215; National Museum of Australia: p. 114; Northern Territory State Library: p. 57; NSW Government Printer: p. 63; Orbost Historical Society: p. 27; Paul van Reyk: pp. 16, 25, 38, 46, 47 (left and right), 81, 84, 91, 110, 118, 121, 123, 127, 136, 139, 143, 157, 163, 184, 189, 199, 200, 222, 227, 231, 235, 246, 251; Shutterstock: pp. 12 (Ashley Whitworth), 218 (Danny Ye), 226 (The Art Archive); Soldiers' Memorial Institute (Tanunda, South Australia): p. 132; Sphere Books: p. 210; State Library of New South Wales: pp. 8 (from *Australian Aborigines*, attributed to George Charles Jenner and William Waterhouse, pre-1806), 43, 44, 63 (Mitchell Library); State Library of Queensland: pp. 147, 159 (John Oxley Library); State Library of South Australia: pp. 72, 131; State Library of Tasmania: p. 61; State Library of Victoria: pp. 15, 60, 67 (Richard Daintree), 76, 94 top, 95 top and bottom; State Library of Western Australia: pp. 73, 75, 161; Sun Books: p. 214; Sunshine Coast Council: p. 196; Sydney Living Museums: p. 48; Ure Smith: p. 169; Victorian Department of Public Instruction: p. 87; Wikipedia/David Edwards (CC 3.0 Unported): p. 201.

Index

Page numbers in *italics* indicate illustrations

Abbott, Edward 97
Aboriginal Australians' foodways
 animal sanctuaries 33–4
 aquaculture 28, *29*, 35
 archaeological evidence of canoes 29
 'Closing the Gap' (2008) 237–8
 cooking methods 34–5
 cultural burning 20, 24
 diet-related health diseases 237
 domestic service 140–42
 drinking water 36
 earthworks 21
 fermented drinks 36–8, *38*
 fish and fishing techniques 28–31
 food insecurity 237–8
 fruit and nuts 22, *23*, *25*
 hunting weapons 32–3
 Northern Territory Emergency Response (2007) 242–3
 occupation of Australia 18–19
 plant propagation 24
 rations 112–14
 reptiles and insects 33
 seeds 23–4, *24*
 station workers 111–15, *112*, 142
 storage 35–6
 the Dreaming 19
 toxin removal 27
 trade among Aboriginal groups 36
 trade with Makassans 56
 utensils 25, 27
 water 36
 yams and tubers 22
Aboriginal Land Rights (Northern Territory) Act (1976) 204–5, *204*
Aboriginal Protection Boards 141–2
Acclimatization Societies 80
Adam's Café 92
advertising regulation 249–50
 coffee palaces 94–6, *95*
 drink driving offences and breath testing 194–5
 licensing laws 96, 145, 172, 192, 248
 temperance movement 93–4, 145, 198
 violence, alcohol-related 248–52
Ady, Doris 183
Aeroplane Jelly 142–3
African foods 230
agricultural colleges 54
agricultural sector 224–7, *255*
agricultural shows 90
agroecological farming 257
 biochar 256
 chemical pesticides 227
 export and trade 77, 79, 125, *129*, 225, 233
 gold, 1850s, impact of 67
 greenhouse gases 255
 holistic management 255
 regenerative farming 257
 see also selection Acts
alcohol 56, 59–62, 93–6, 172, 192–3, 221–2, 248–52
Aldi 232

Alexakis, Effy 147
Alexander, Stephanie 162, 188–9
 school kitchen gardens 245
American food influences, Second World War 151
animal cruelty
 egg production 232–3
 live export of cattle 233–4
 Senate Select Committee on Animal Welfare (1985) 233
Anzac biscuits 123, *123*
Arnott, William 118–20
assisted immigration schemes 140, 153–4, *154*
Athenaeum Club 82, 90
Australia
 geology 11–12
 location 11, 12
 megafauna 32
 population 16
 rainfall 14
 rivers 14
 size 12
Australian Broadcasting Corporation 211, 235
Australian Bureau of Statistics, consumption trends 1938–1999 211–16
Australian City Farms and Community Gardens Network 228
Australian Dietary Guidelines (2014) 244
Australian Gourmet Magazine 208
Australian Women's Weekly 137, 150, 166, 167, 171, 174, 176, 196, 197, 213

Balfour, William Irvine, *British Possessions and Colonies* (1899) *17*
Barossa Pearl 170
Barossa Valley *see* wine
Barren Jack and Murrumbidgee Canals Construction Act (1906) 110
beer and breweries 59–60, *61*, 191, 194, 221
 men's attitude to women drinking beer 193
 microbreweries 248
Beer, Maggie 228
Bilson, Gay 223
Bilson, Tony and Gay, Tony's Bon Gout, Berowra Waters Inn 191
Birds Eye 119, 196
blackberry 80
Bleasdale, Joseph 93
Bligh, William, governor of New South Wales (1806–10) 62
Bogner, Rosalie 172
Bradley, William, *Sydney Cove, Port Jackson 44*
Bruneteau, Jean-Paul, Rowntress & Riberries 220, 221
Bulletin, The 98, 99, 198
Busby, James 61
Bush Food Buffet, Fourth Symposium of Australian Gastronomy 225
bush tucker *see* native foods
Bush Tucker Man *see* Hiddens, Major Les
bushfire 9, 15

Cahills restaurants 144, 195
Caire, N. J., *Selector's Hut, Gippsland 103*
Calwell, Arthur, Minister for Immigration (1945–9) 153–4, 179
cameleers, Afghan 73, *73*, 135
Canning Stock Route 113
cattle 45, 51, 203
 Aboriginal Australian enterprises 241–2
 diseases 79, 101, 227
 live cattle export 234–5
celebrity chefs 209–11
Chaffey, George and William 108–9, *109*
Cheap Eats 208
Cherrikof, Vic 220–21
Chiko Roll 184, *184*
Chinese
 anti-Chinese migration legislation 70, 100
 anti-Chinese sentiment 68–70, 98–99
 cuisine 181–3, *182*, 211
 food businesses on the goldfields 68–71
 market gardening 71, 149

MSG (monosodium glutamate) in food 230
Tiananmen Square, impact in Australia on cuisines 218
violence against on goldfields 71
wok, popularity of 185
see also Chiko Roll
see also Quong Tart
Chong, Elizabeth 211
Clark, Anna 215
Clark, Manning 98
climate change 9, 254–57
Climate Change Update 256
Emissions Reduction Fund 256
Intergovernmental Panel on Climate Change 254
coffee *94*, *95*, 144, 250, *251*
consumption (2011–12) 251
see also coffee palaces
Coleman, Deke 190
Coles 221, 227, 232, 248
Colombo Plan 181
Commonwealth of Australia
colonies, founding of 53–8
Federation 97–8
inter-colony tariffs 97
states and territories 17
'continental' dining 144–5, 156, 167
Cook, Lieutenant James 39
cookers and stoves
electric 117, 139
gas 82, 117, *118*, 140
wood 117
cookery books 9, 82, *82*, 90, 97, 132, 138–40, 158, 168, 181, 182, 183, 190, 212, 213
cookery classes 86–8, *87*
cookery instruction online 235–6
Coolgardie safe 74, *75*
Country Women's Association 140
Cundall, Peter 211
curry 91, 183
Curtin, John, prime minister of Australia (1941–5) 150
Cushing, Nancy 231
Customs Tariff (Agricultural Machinery) Act (1906) 105
Daintree, Richard, *Mineshaft at the Victorian Goldfields 67*
dairies and dairy products 9, 115, 149
pasteurization 115, *116*
Dale, Dr John 244
Dampier, William 41
Deakin, Alfred, prime minister of Australia (1903–10) 105, 108
delicatessen 156–7, 196
Depression
(1893) 108, 96–7
(1929–30) 147–9
beef riot 1931 148
Happy Valley unemployed people's camp 149
rationing 148
diets 117–18
'Mediterranean diet' 217–18
dingo 33
Divine (magazine) 209
Dodd, Henry Edward 48
Downes, Stephen 192
dried fruits 109, 130, 135
drought 7, 150, *255*
Federation Drought 107
millennium drought 229
Dupleix, Jill 217
Durack, Mary 83, 111, 117
Durack, Terry 217

Early Kooka 140
El Niño *13*, 14, 45, 107, 229
Edgell, Robert 119
Epicurean (magazine) 208
Esbensen, Mogens Bay 191–2, 212
Esky, portable icebox 174–5
European food and dining 156
Evans, Len 171
Evans, Matthew 236
Excise Tariff (Agricultural Machinery) Act (1906) 105

Facey, A. B. 104, 107, 126–8
Farrer, Keith 151
Farrer, William 89
fast food 195, 214–15, 231, 246
fats, consumption of, trends 1938–99 212–15

First Peoples *see* Aboriginal Australians
First World War 120–21
    food shortages and price rises 121
fish, fisheries, seafood 116, 215–16, *218*
    aquaculture 253–4
    marine parks 253
    overfishing 252–3
    oyster saloons 146
    see also Aboriginal Australians' foodways
Flannery, Tim 18, 32
food
    consumption trends 1938–99 211–16
    festivals 208, 239
    foodie 206
    food magazines 208
    television programmes 209–11
Fowler's Vacola *114*, 115
French influences on food 60, 68, 90
    Federation banquet 189–90
    nouvelle cuisine 190–91
French onion dip 197
Fraser, William
Frontier Wars 64–5
Fulton, Margaret 144, 148, 152, 165, 170–72, 183, 185, 186–7, 190

Galluzzo, Salvatore *163*, 165
Gammage, Bill 19
Garnaut, Ross 256
gastronomy, study of 223, 224
Geechoun, Roy
Gelato Bar 158
Germans, Barossa Valley
    anti-German sentiment, First World War 132
    Prussian food 130–31, 133
    settlement of Barossa Valley 130
    viticulture 130–31
gig economy 237
Gill, S. T., *Sly Grog Shop, Victorian Goldfields 94*
Gilmore, Mary 24–5, 28, 33–4, 88
Gilmore, Peter, Quay 239
Glick's bakery 157
gluten intolerance and coeliac disease 230, 231
Golden Circle 196, *196*
goldfields
    food 67
    locations 66
Gondwana, southern super-continent 11
Good Food Guides 207–8
Goodwin, Harriet 168, *169*
Gott, Beth 23
Goyder Line 74
Granny Smith apple 84, *84*
Grassby, Al, Australian minister for Immigration (1972–4) 179–80
Great Barrier Reef 13, 39, 108
Great Dividing Range 11, *12*, 33
Greek cafés and restaurants 146–7, *147*
Greenwood, Helen 216

Haddad, George 218
Haffner, Dorinda 211
halal food and Islamophobia 234–5, *235*
Halliday, James 209
Halligan, Marion 165–7
Hanson, Pauline, senator 234
Harry's Café de Wheels 201, *201*
Hawke, Bob, prime minister of Australia (1983–91) 218, 228
hawkers 51, 116, 134
health foods 140, 202, *202*
    see also vegetarianism
Hee, Yep Yung 182
Heuzenroeder, Angela 130, 132
Hewett, Dorothy 147
Hiddens, Major Les 219–10
Holt, Harold, prime minister of Australia (1966–7) 179

Immigration Restriction Act (1901) 100–101, 179
Indigenous Australians 7–8
Irish female domestic staff 86
Italians 158–165
    Bonegilla riot 164–5
    internment, Second World War 158
    market gardens 161

Murrumbidgee Irrigation Area 159
Snowy Mountains Scheme 159
sugar cane industry 158, 159

Jenner, George Charles, and William Waterhouse, *Aboriginal woman in canoe fishing with a line 8*
Jewish refugees 155–8
Jones, Margaret 192
Juillet, Patric, Le Café Nouvea 191
'junk food' advertising 246–8

kangaroo 12, 17, 18, 20, 33, *34*, 45, 112, 219, *222*
Keen's Curry Powder 91, *91*
Keleman, Tom 155–6
Kelly, William 67
Kerr, Graham 207, 208, 209, *210*
Kersh, Raymond and Jennice, Edna's Table 220, 221
King, Bernard 210
King, Francis William, the Flying Pieman 200
Koeppen, Will 209
Kominos, Ioannis 146
Kozslik Donovan, Maria 168, 183

La Niña 14
Lake, Marilyn 106, 126
Lake, Max 222
Lamington 120, *121*
Larra, James 60
Lavine, Pearl, *Monaco Café* 157
Lawson, Henry 92, 93, 102–3
Le Cordon Bleu 224
Lederer, Andrew, Primo smallgoods 157, *157*
Liardet, W.F.E., *The Melbourne Brewery and Distillery 60*
licensed clubs 192–3
Liew, Cheong 212
Lingiari, Vincent 203, *204*
Lousy Little Sixpence (film) 141
Lowenstein, Wendy 149
Lycett, Joseph
Aborigines cooking and eating beached whales, Newcastle, New South Wales 31
The residence of John Macarthur Esquire near Parramatta, New South Wales 49

Mabo, Eddie Koiki, 205
Macarthur, Elizabeth 49–50
Macarthur, John 49, 62, 63
McCaughey, Samuel 110
McEnroe, Frank 184
McKay, Hugh
Harvester Case, minimum wage 104–55
Sunshine harvester 88–9
Mackellar, Dorothea 13
Maclurcan, Hannah *83*, 86
Maloney, Ted 190
Malouf, Greg 218
Makassan trepang trade 56, *57*
Manfield, Christine 219
Manfredi, Stefano 163, 164–5
Mann's Rooms 58
margarine 213
Martin, Lyn 224
Matra, James Maria 42
Matorikos, Grigorios, Athanaeum 146
Mayi Harvests 241
meat (beef, lamb) 77–9, *78*, 112, 133, *213*, 224
barbecues 174–5, *174*
canned 79
chop picnic 173–4
consumption trends 1938–99 210–11
extract 79
plant-based alternatives 231–2, *231*
meat pie 200–201, *200*
pie floater 200
Sargent pies 201
Megalogenis, George 96, 126, 128
Melbourne Olympic Games 191
Menzies, Robert, prime minister of Australia (1939–4, 1949–66) 179, 187
Middle Eastern food 218–19, 230
migrant labour, exploitation of 240
Migration Act (1966) 179
Milk Arrowroot biscuit 120, 135
Mitchell, Major Thomas 20, 23, 28
'Modern Australian' 192, 216–17

Mora, Georges and Mirka, Café Balzac 156
Morgan, Sally 111
multicultural, multiculturalism 8, 180
Murphy, Dan 169, 221
Murray-Darling system 14, *15*, 71, 108, 109, 161
Murrumbidgee Irrigation Area 110–11, *110*, 158, 160, 180, *188*, 185
Murrumbidgee Irrigation Trust 110
Muskett, Philip 75, 77, 83, 217

National Heart Foundation 212, 213
native foods *46*, *47*, 83, 81, 219–22, *246*, 257
  economic value of 239
  first settlers use of 45–7
  industry 238–42
  nutritional values of 26
  see also Aboriginal Australians' foodways
Native Title Act (Cwlth) 205
Network TEN 209, 210, 211
Newell, Patrice 255–6
Newling, Jacqui 47
Newton, John 185, 208, 221

obesity 243–8
  'junk food' 246–8
  school canteens 245
  sugar in drinks 245–6
  sugar tax 246
O'Brien, Charmaine 68, 146, 217–18
Olive, Mark 247
olive oil 213
O'Meara, Maeve 208, 219
Ord River Irrigation Scheme 160–61, *161*
Oslo Lunch 244

Pacific Island Labourers Act (1901) 101
Pacific Islanders 86
  'blackbirding' 99–100
paddle steamers 71, *72*
Parmenter, Ian 210
Pascoe, Bruce 21, 257
Pellegrini's Espresso Bar 162
Perry, Neil 217
Phillip, Admiral Governor Arthur 42, 47
Polese, Beppi and Norma 162–3
Pont, Graham 217, 223
Porter, Hal 133, 144
Porter, John D. 190
preserving food 115, 117, 134
prickly pear 80, *80*
public houses 60, 92, 193
  ladies' lounge 172–3, *173*
  'six o'clock swill' 145
  sly grog shanties 70, 92

Quamby, Mike and Gayle 240
Quarantine Act (1908) 101
Quong Tart, Mei 68–9, *69*

rabbits 81, 128
  Calicivirus (rabbit haemorrhagic disease) 81
  rabbit-proof fence 81
railways 73
Rawson, Mina 82–3
Redzepi, René 239
refrigeration
  drip safes 74
  electric refrigerators 140, 176–7
  frozen food 196
  frozen water trade 75
  quick freezing 119
  shipping *76*, 77, *77*
Reiby, Thomas 59
Repin, Ivan, Coffee Inn 144
restaurant guides and reviewers 207–9
  social media 236
Reynolds, Henry 100, 115
rice 185–7, *188*
  Australian Rice Marketing Board 186
  Sunwhite rice 185
Ripe, Cherry 180, 191, 216
Ripper, Anne 218
Rum Rrebellion 62–3
Ruse, James 54–5, 107
Russell-Clarke, Peter 209
Ryan, Denis and Marilyn 238
Sahul landmass 11, 19

Sanitarium 197
Santich, Barbara 123, 173–4, 212, 213, 217, 223, 224
Saville, Joanna 208, 219
scabby mouth disease in sheep 233
Schaffer, Phillip 60–61
Schneider, Hermann, Two Faces 191
Schofield, Leo 207
school canteens 245
school milk programmes 243–4
sclerophyll trees (eucalyptus) 15, *16*, 20
Second World War 149–152
  Australian Women's Land Army 151
  displaced persons migration to Australia 154
  rationing 149
  refugees 155–8, 179
  Victory Gardens 150
selectors 102–6
shipping 73
shopping
  arcades 135, *137*
  chain stores 135, 221
  farmers' markets *227*, 228
  malls 177–8, *177*
Slow Food 228
Smith, Robert Boyer 88
Snowy Mountains Hydro-electric Scheme 111, 159–61
soil 12
  degradation 227, 228, 254
  Landcare 228, 256
  manure 106
  salinity 109, 227
  superphosphate 107
soldier settlements 126–30
Solomon, Charmaine 185–7
South Asian cuisines 183, 230
  'hippie trail', influence on 185
  see also curry
Southeast Asian cuisines 180–88, 216
  'hippie trail', influence on 185
  modern Australian, influence on 216–17
  Thai 180, 191–2
  Vietnamese 188, *189*
spaghetti Bolognese 156, 166, 218
Special Broadcasting Service 208, 211, 219, 236
  Eating Guide 208
Splayd 152
squatters 64–5, 102, 126
Squire, James 60
Stabler, Rosetta 58
Stolen Generation, the 140–42
Story, Annie Fawcett 87
sugar 89
  cane farming 99–100, 158, *159*
  Colonial Sugar Refinery 89
  consumption trends 1938–99 216
  tax 246
  see also Italians, Pacific Islanders
Supski, Sian 176
sweets and chocolate snack bars 134, *136*
Sydney colony 1788–1800
  bakeries 53
  cattle 45, 51
  cooking 58
  dairies and dairy products 52
  dining out 58
  expansion to Parramatta and Hawkesbury 48, *48*
  farming 44–5
  First Fleet provisions 42–4
  government farms 44, 48
  imported goods 50
  markets and shops 50–51, *51*
  milling 52–3
  native food consumed 45–7, *46*, *47*
  rations 45
  relations with Aboriginal peoples 46
  salt 52
  water 59
Symons, Michael 223
Symposium of Australian Gastronomy 220, 223

Takasuka, Jō 185
tea 89–90
  sweet tea (native sarsaparilla) 46
  Sunday tea 133
tearooms 90
  see also Quong Tart
television cooking shows 236

Tench, Lieutenant Watkin, 21, 31, 42, *43*, 45, 47, 48, 51, 52, 106
terra nullius, Australia defined as 39–40, 64, 205
Terry, William Henry 199
Thompson, David, Darley Street Thai 218
Thornton, Merle 171
Tip Top Bakeries 157
Torres Strait Islander foodways 38–9
trepang 56, 57
Twopeny, Richard 78, 86, 89

vegan food 231
Vegemite 143
vegetables 42, 50, 85, 135
  canned 119, 151, 152, 196
  dehydrated and dried 135, 151
  quick-frozen 119
vegetarian 197–203, 231
  counter-culture 203
  Hare Krishnas 202–3
  Seventh Day Adventist church 199
  temperance movement 198–9
  Theosophical Society 199
Vegetarian Society of Australia 197–8
Vietnam War 181, 187–8
Vincent, Alison 207

Wakada, Tetsuya 217
Wave Hill walk-off 203–5, *204*
Weet-Bix 199, *198*, *199*
wheat 52, 72–3, 88, 150
  black stem rust 89
  Federation wheat 89
  native grasses as alternatives 257
  Ridley Stripper 88
  soldier settlements 127–8
  stump jump plough 88
  see also Farrer, William; McKay, Hugh
White Australia Policy 101, 140, 153, 154, 178, 179
Whiteland, Josh, Koomal Dreaming 239
White, Myrtle Rose 135
Whitlam, Gough prime minister of Australia (1972–5) 179, 187, *204*, 234
Wicken, Mrs Harriett 85–6
Wilkinson, Alfred J. 82, 90
William Angliss Institute
wine 60–61, 92–6, *93*, 168–71, 192, *226*, 248
  Australian Wine Research Institute 170
  Barossa Valley 61, 131
  Beefsteak and Burgundy Clubs 169
  boutique wine producers 248
  Canberra 194
  change in preferences 191, 222
  fortified wines 130
  Grange Hermitage 132
  Hunter Valley 61, 92
  Margaret River 194, 239
  Parramatta 60–61
  phylloxera, root louse 92, 131
  Rutherglen 92
wine bar 194
wine cask 175, 222
Wine and Food Society (Sydney) 207
  Yarra Valley 61
Wine Society 169
women as consumer 175–8
Women's Christian Temperance Union 94, 198
women's magazines 9, 136, 137
  see also Australian Women's Weekly
Wood, Andrew 209
Woolworths 221, 227, 232, 248

Zelenznikov, Avram and Masha, Café Scheherazade 157
Zonfrillo, Jock, Orana 239